RTI IN THE CLASSROOM

RTI in the Classroom

Guidelines and Recipes for Success

Rachel Brown-Chidsey
Louise Bronaugh
Kelly McGraw

THE GUILFORD PRESS
New York   London

To the honor and memory of Dr. Todd Risley (1937–2007)
with the hope that this book brings meaningful differences
to the everyday lives of American children

—R. B.-C.

To all the classroom teachers who work tirelessly to improve
the state of our children and our nation

—L. B.

To the people at Heartland Area Education Agency
whose innovation and leadership improve the field of education

—K. M.

© 2009 The Guilford Press
A Division of Guilford Publications, Inc.
72 Spring Street, New York, NY 10012
www.guilford.com

Printed in the United States of America

This book is printed on acid-free paper.

Last digit is print number: 9 8 7 6 5 4 3 2 1

Library of Congress Cataloging-in-Publication Data

Brown-Chidsey, Rachel.
   RTI in the classroom : guidelines and recipes for success / Rachel Brown-Chidsey, Louise Bronaugh, Kelly McGraw.
     p. cm.
   Includes bibliographical references and index.
   ISBN 978-1-60623-297-2 (pbk. : alk. paper)
   1. Remedial teaching. 2. Slow learning children—Education. 3. Education, Elementary. I. Bronaugh, Louise. II. McGraw, Kelly. III. Title.
   LB1029.R4B77 2009
   371.9′043—dc22

2009010730

About the Authors

Rachel Brown-Chidsey, PhD, NCSP, is Associate Professor and Program Coordinator of School Psychology Programs at the University of Southern Maine. Prior to obtaining her doctorate from the University of Massachusetts Amherst, Dr. Brown-Chidsey taught middle and high school history and special education for 10 years. Her research areas include curriculum-based measurement, response to intervention, and scientifically based reading instruction methods. She has authored many articles and book chapters on these topics. In 2002, Dr. Brown-Chidsey participated in the Future of School Psychology Conference and subsequently edited *Assessment for Intervention: A Problem-Solving Approach*. With Mark W. Steege, she wrote *Response to Intervention: Principles and Strategies for Effective Practice*. Dr. Brown-Chidsey is a native Alaskan and splits her time between Maine and her hometown of Palmer, Alaska. She is a nationally certified school psychologist and is both certified and licensed for psychology practice in Alaska and Maine.

Louise Bronaugh, PhD, is a licensed school psychologist. She received her doctorate in school psychology from the University of Oregon. As a district-level literacy support specialist, she worked on the development and implementation of a schoolwide response-to-intervention model. Since 2004, Dr. Bronaugh has been conducting district-level trainings on Dynamic Indicators of Basic Early Literacy Skills (DIBELS) administration and scoring, customized districtwide DIBELS data interpretation, small-group literacy instruction, positive behavior support, and response to intervention. She has also taught in special education classes.

Kelly McGraw, PhD, is Assistant Professor at the Chicago School of Professional Psychology. She received her doctorate in school psychology from the University of Oregon. Previously, she worked as a school psychologist and professional learning and leadership consultant at Heartland Area Education Agency in Johnston, Iowa. There she was responsible for using response to intervention to identify student needs and training teachers on district- and agencywide initiatives. Dr. McGraw has presented nationally in the areas of data-based decision making, curriculum-based measurement, and effective instruction. She has also consulted with schools implementing response to intervention and worked with teachers to improve the link between assessment and instruction. Her current efforts involve training students in educational foundations and systems change and consulting with school districts around the Midwest.

Acknowledgments

This book has benefited from many teachers and students with whom I have worked over the years. In particular, I want to acknowledge Dr. Michelle Shinn, who sparked my interest in preventing learning problems. In addition, the students who have responded to my interventions and helped me recognize that all children can learn have contributed to this book. Special thanks go to Ellie Chidsey, my best student ever.

—RACHEL BROWN-CHIDSEY

The idea for this book was inspired by Dr. Mark Shinn during a seminar he gave on response to intervention and the vital need to communicate the three tiers of interventions to the classroom teacher. I thought that the best way to provide teachers with this information was with a simple graphing tool and a color-coded set of intervention recipes. I am also very grateful to my mentors, Drs. Kenneth W. Merrell, Hill M. Walker, and Robert H. Horner. Their collective enthusiasm and letters of support for this project helped push me forward and opened doors to Guilford Publications. I'd like to thank my coauthors for their hard work and their commitment to making this book a reality. In addition to their writing efforts, Rachel Brown-Chidsey led the way with the management of the project, and Kelly McGraw was instrumental in securing a publisher. Finally, and most important, I'd like to thank my husband, Whit, and son, Gavin, for their encouragement, love, and support.

—LOUISE BRONAUGH

I am grateful to Roland Good for his vision and innovation in using data to drive instruction. I am also grateful to Randy Allison for his perspective and insight on being effective in the schools. I would like to thank my sister, a kindergarten teacher, for the hard work she does every day. She consistently demonstrates that effective instruction does make a difference for all kids. Finally, I am grateful to Tom, whose unending support and encouragement cannot be stated enough.

—KELLY MCGRAW

Contents

What Is RTI, and Why Are They Telling Me to Do It?

If you are reading this, chances are you've been told that your school or district will be moving toward a new way of doing things. They may refer to it as *response to intervention* or, in some districts, *response to instruction*. You've probably been told that the goal of this shift will be to keep *all* of your students chugging along successfully in your general education classroom so they won't need to be pulled out for help or, in some cases, special education. If you think that this sounds like a plot to undermine teaching as you know it, you are not alone. Here's how *we* see it. Response to intervention (RTI) is a roadmap for student success in the general education classroom. We hope this book will provide you with enough practical information to show you that RTI is actually a wonderful tool you can use to help all of your students, especially those who keep you awake at night. You know who they are ... the student who is way behind in reading, or the other one who just can't seem to understand the math concepts, or the third student who never remembers her homework, has a hard time following your directions, and doesn't complete seat work without five reminders and three warnings! Wouldn't it be great to know how to help these students? Many of you work in systems that don't really provide much assistance for those students until they are approved for resource or special education (often referred to as a "wait-to-fail" model). By moving your classroom into an RTI model, you will be adding your voice to the growing number of educators who have affirmed that the current model of waiting for students to fail before they receive help is no longer acceptable.

Why do RTI? We now know that providing rigorous intervention when students are younger and before they have "failed" can actually turn them around and make them proficient on grade level with their peers. Also, when we keep our eye on them as they progress through the grades, we can make sure they stay on track for their entire school career.

So what exactly is response to intervention/instruction? First we want you to know what it is not. It is not rocket science. You should not fear it as something that will be difficult to learn and require lots of professional development and outside reading. We have written this book with you and your busy schedule in mind. This book is not an exhaustive descriptive study of RTI (there are many other excellent books out there to choose from if that is what you want). This book is designed to be *practical* and user friendly for any general education teacher, principal, or school psychologist working in a system that is moving into an RTI model. Keep in mind that as you learn RTI, you will *not* be learning and working in isolation. RTI requires teamwork and collaboration with your peers. It is our goal with this book to walk you and your colleagues through the process so clearly and systematically that you may actually find this change enjoyable. OK, that might be a bit strong, but let's check in again at the end of the book and see how close you got to "enjoyable."

To illustrate this process, let's start with a road trip. You will be driving your car from point *A* to point *B*. What would you need to know first? You need to know where points *A* and *B* are before you can plan your route. So, you ask around (pretend you're really lost), you get out a map, and you ask a few people on the street, "Where am I?" You find out that you are actually in San Francisco. (How you missed the landmarks is anyone's guess!) You have also just been informed by your teenage daughter that she needs you to drive her to Denver so that she can visit a college that she is applying to. She has to be there in 5 days. Now you know point *A*, point *B*, and how much time you have to get from one to the other. Now, what would you do? You'd probably get out a map and start to plan your route, keeping in mind that there are many ways to get there, but only a few of them will get you there in 5 days. So you draw a straight line on the map from San Francisco to Denver. Then you look for highways that are closest to your line. You know you need to stick to that line as closely as possible in order to get to Denver (your daughter might be a little upset if you end up in Chicago). You choose your roads and plan your trip. Tomorrow you'll be off. The next day, as the Golden Gate Bridge recedes in your rear-view mirror, you begin your drive to Denver. It all goes smoothly until day 2 of your journey, when you encounter a sign that says "Construction, Road Closed." Now what? Well, you obviously have to get the map out and plan another way to proceed without losing time (your daughter is starting to show early signs of stress and has turned up her iPod). You can see on your map that there is a rural route that will take you around the construction and get you back on the highway within 5 hours. It's your best option given the information that you have at the time. What you don't know (but soon find out) is that your new route is full of potholes and stop signs. After being on it for 2 hours, you decide you've had enough, and you know that your progress is not fast enough to get you to Denver on time. You decide to get the map out and look for another way to rejoin the highway. You find another way and you replot your course. This route goes more smoothly and has you back on the highway in 5 hours. The problem is that you are now 3 hours behind schedule. You decide to drive 10 miles per hour faster in order to make up the time and get to Denver before your daughter has a meltdown. This new plan works, and you arrive safely and on time at the college in Denver. Everyone's happy.

Possibly without realizing it you've just experienced something similar to RTI in your car. Point *A* is your student's academic skill at the beginning of the year and point

B is where his or her skill needs to be at the end of the year. You begin the year with a plan for getting the student from *A* to *B* on time, but find out along the way that some unexpected snags slow down his or her progress. You will need to keep track of progress, change course probably several times, and speed up the student in order to reach the goal at the end of the year.

Here's a "real-life" example of how RTI is working in one elementary school:

Jenna is a first grader in a school that has recently begun using an RTI system. It is September, and as part of the district screening, Jenna and all the other students in her school have just had their reading skills assessed (that's point *A*—San Francisco). The results of the assessment indicate that Jenna and three of her classmates are seriously below where they need to be in order to be readers by the end of third grade (point *B*—Denver). Jenna's teacher meets with the other first-grade teachers to discuss all of their students who have similar reading scores. They review the scores and determine that among all three first-grade classes, there are a total of 10 students who are at the same low instructional level in the same reading skills. They decide to place those 10 students into two groups of five and provide them with an appropriate research-based intensive reading intervention for 30 minutes a day, 5 days a week (your original route to Denver). The first-grade teaching team also decides to monitor the progress of those 10 students every week and to meet every 2 weeks to discuss these results. The team wants to make sure that the intervention selected for those 10 students is working before too many weeks go by.

After 6 weeks and three team meetings, the data on the 10 students are starting to tell a story. The team notices that in each group, three students are making very good progress, and the other two students seem to be moving up, but very slowly. The team recognizes that the slow rate of growth for those four students (two from each group), although positive, is not sufficient for them to catch up with their grade-level peers. The team decides to rearrange the groups (replot your course to Denver). The three students in each group who are making sufficient progress toward the goal are going to be moved together to make a new group of six. The two struggling students from each group will be regrouped into an intervention for just those four. The six will continue to get the same 30-minute intervention that they have been successful with. The other four will now be getting an additional 30-minute block of intensive instruction each day. This arrangement has not only doubled their amount of time in the group instruction, but provided the added benefit of reducing the group size from five to four (speed up 10 miles per hour to get to Denver on time).

Progress monitoring data are still collected weekly, and the first-grade teachers continue to meet every other week to make adjustments as needed. By keeping an eye on incremental, weekly change, the teachers will be able to have all students on track for year-end success (Denver—and on time!).

It is important to note that although this example highlights reading acquisition as the target skill, RTI pertains to all of the major academic subjects as well as student behavior. Therefore, you will be very happy to know that this book contains chapters on and specific intervention "recipes" for reading, writing, math, and behavior.

HOW TO USE THIS BOOK

We have written this book to be practical and user friendly. We have tried to keep the chapter content flowing, and in order to do this, we have intentionally left out most research citations. This does not mean that we have just made all of this up, nor does it mean that the information is not research based. On the contrary, we have gone to great lengths to make sure that the statements made in this book are supported by high-quality education research that has been published in peer-reviewed journals. We have included resources at the end of each chapter that tell you where to go for more information on specific topics.

Here is a brief overview of each chapter:

1. "It Takes a Village" systematically lists and describes the ways in which RTI requires a team effort and will only succeed if you and your colleagues work together to learn this new approach to helping your students. The changing roles of certain school personnel (such as the school psychologist) are discussed.

2. "How to Use the Tiered Framework" provides a thorough examination of the terms *instruction, intervention, accommodation,* and *differentiation.* From there the chapter moves into specifics about what makes an intervention Tier 1, 2, or 3. These are all terms used in any RTI model, so you will want to read this chapter carefully in order to become "fluent" in RTI.

3. "Evaluating the Core Curriculum" makes the case that a school system must have a solid foundation (such as a research-based core reading program) before any RTI system can be attempted. Examples of how to determine the effectiveness of your core program are given, and you are encouraged to examine your own system through the 80–15–5 lens.

4. "How Are the Kids Doing?" lays out both the "why" and the "how" of progress monitoring. If there is no progress monitoring, then there is no RTI. *Period.* This is a critical chapter for any teacher who is attempting to operate in an RTI system.

5. "Yikes! I Have 'Kids at Risk'" is the chapter that will teach you how to use the forms in Appendix B. In order for an RTI system to function, you will need a way to track your students' progress after you've identified that (a) they are not keeping up and (b) you've implemented an intervention. You must use a system to record the changes in your students' behavior or academic pattern. This is a legal requirement of any RTI system. We've also tried to make the forms useful when brainstorming with your team about what has been tried and how well it did or didn't work.

6. "Reading Interventions" provides a detailed and thorough recitation of what we know about teaching young students to read. If you aspire to becoming a building (or district) reading coach working in an RTI system, then understanding this chapter will be an excellent place to start. The actual reading intervention recipes can be found in Appendix C at the end of the book.

7. "Written Language Interventions" gives a concise overview of what is currently known about teaching children to write. Interventions within a three-tiered RTI model are discussed. The actual writing intervention recipes can be found in Appendix C.

8. "Math Interventions" provides a thorough overview of how children learn math and the various tools that teachers can use to encourage this learning. Math intervention recipes can be found in Appendix C.

9. "Behavior Interventions" makes the case that even the best academic interventions will flop if the students are out of control. Therefore, having some techniques for managing student behavior will be essential in your RTI system. Behavior intervention recipes can be found in Appendix C.

10. "RTI with English Language Learners" points out the difficulties that English language learners (ELLs) face in our current system. This chapter also makes a convincing argument in favor of RTI for ELL students. You won't want to skip this chapter if you have any students who are learning English as a second language.

11. "If You're Working in a DIBELS System …" is a chapter for teachers who currently work in an elementary school system in which benchmark data are collected on their students using the Dynamic Indicators of Basic Early Literacy Skills (DIBELS). DIBELS®[1] data and the DIBELS progress monitoring measures are tailor-made for any RTI system, so having this program in place puts you ahead of the game. This chapter will walk you through the steps of using the DIBELS data in an RTI model. If you don't use DIBELS in your school, then you might skip this chapter. Don't worry, there are other ways to collect and manage student academic data, and Chapter 5 covers some of them.

12. "This All Sounds Great, but …" is the "reality check" chapter. This is where we acknowledge that even though we can all agree that RTI is good for kids, you may be wondering how to fit it all in and make the necessary changes to your teaching routine. This chapter is a "must read" for everyone. It will give you lots of good ideas for pacing yourself and scheduling the changes that you are about to make.

Toward the back of the book, Appendix C contains practical, easy to use, research-based interventions written up in a recipe format. You will see that they are divided first by subject—reading, writing, math, and behavior. They are then further divided into colored sections of green, yellow, and red. This is in keeping with the color coding of RTI, where green interventions are something that will be in place for all students, yellow interventions will be used for students who need a little more help than the majority, and red interventions are for those students who really struggle and have not been successful with the green and yellow interventions that you've already put in place. You could think of it as turning up the intensity as you go from green to yellow to red. Appendix A provides an RTI Readiness Checklist, and Appendix B offers a system for tracking student progress, including several forms that you can fill out and bring to your team meetings. These forms will help keep your team informed about what has been tried, what's working, what's not—and what you should do next.

For up-to-the-minute information on helpful RTI tools, books, and links, check out our companion website: *www.rticlassroom.org*. It should be fully up and running by Fall 2009.

This is the roadmap for your RTI journey. Hold on, and enjoy the ride.

---

[1]DIBELS is a registered trademark of Dynamic Measurement Group, Inc.

CHAPTER 1

It Takes a Village

Building Consensus in School and at Home

RTI has brought some interesting changes to schools. For example instead of assuming that what's being done with a student is working, RTI requires that we collect ongoing information about student improvement. RTI can seem very overwhelming because it has many steps, but it is not designed to be done alone. To work, RTI needs all teachers and others in a school to work together; no one teacher can do all the parts alone. This chapter talks about how teachers must work together to make RTI effective for students. There is an African proverb that says, "It takes a village to raise a child." This saying points out how parents cannot raise their children all by themselves; instead, all the grown-ups in a child's life play a role in helping the child grow. If the grown-ups have very different ways of doing things, the child will be confused, but if they work together and share common values, childhood is much easier.

RTI is all about helping children. If teachers work together as a "village," children will benefit. There are four parts to village-style teamwork: (1) distributed leadership, (2) new roles and responsibilities, (3) collaboration, and (4) communication. Each of these four parts is necessary for RTI to be successful.

DISTRIBUTED LEADERSHIP

In a village or town, all citizens work together to help make the community successful. In smaller communities such as villages, there is often shared leadership. For example in villages and small towns, the "mayor" and other leaders may not hold these positions as full-time work, but a number of people might divide the roles to ensure the community needs are met. There are often volunteer police, fire, safety, and emergency personnel. All of these roles must be filled for the community to function.

In a similar way RTI requires "village"-style leadership. This means that all the grown-ups in a school must work together in order for RTI to happen. RTI's three tiers offer a way to make sure that all students in a school get the instruction they need—but no one teacher can do this by him- or herself. For this reason, all the teachers must work together collaboratively so that the needs of all students are addressed. This approach to school leadership can be called "distributed," because no one person is in charge of making RTI happen, but everyone helps to make sure it happens. Consider the following example:

> Lisa is a new teacher in a rural elementary school. At her job interview, the principal explained to Lisa that the school is using a Response to Intervention system of addressing all students' learning needs. Over the summer Lisa attended district-sponsored training in the core reading program. When school opened in the fall, Lisa's new students participated in benchmark screening assessment. Lisa used these data alongside classroom performance to group her students into smaller groups for daily lessons. Some of Lisa's students scored very low on the fall benchmarks, and these students needed additional instruction. In addition to the daily classroom instruction, these at-risk students worked with the reading specialist every day for 30 minutes. In order to monitor student progress, the school psychologist administered weekly brief assessments to the students receiving additional assistance.
>
> In order to support teachers in meeting the needs of all students, a schoolwide problem-solving team meets every week to discuss the students receiving additional instruction. Every student who is receiving Tier 2 support is discussed every 3 weeks. The problem-solving team includes the principal, all specialists, the nurse, and one general and special educator who rotate onto the team each quarter. At the team meetings, the classroom teacher presents the progress data for her student and asks the team for suggestions to enhance the intervention. If a student is making progress, the intervention is maintained. If the student is not making progress, the intervention is changed. If two interventions have been tried and the student has not made progress, then the team considers whether the student needs to be referred for an evaluation.
>
> The RTI activities at Lisa's school require that all the participating staff members each do their part. Lisa needs the fall benchmark data to assist with instructional grouping. She also depends on the reading specialist to provide additional instruction for the students who are most at risk. All the teachers depend on the problem-solving team to help them interpret data and develop new intervention ideas. The principal depends on the staff to implement instruction accurately so that money spent on resources benefits the students as much as possible. In these ways, making RTI happen is very much like living in a village where each person depends on everyone else.

NEW JOB ROLES

As shown in the previous example, some aspects of RTI require changes in job roles. As a classroom teacher, you will probably have the fewest role changes, but other staff might have very different roles because of the collaborative nature of the work. Instead of there being one RTI leader who takes charge, every staff member has a distinct role to play. When leadership is distributed in this way, each person has a set of duties to complete and no other person will do them in quite the same way, and each person's role is unique and important. If you do not provide the planned Tier 1 lessons, the Tier 2 teacher will be unable to build on that foundation. If the weekly progress data are not collected as planned, the teachers on the problem-solving team will not be able to review student progress. If data reviews are not held, it won't be possible to know whether a student is responding to intervention or whether a referral for an evaluation is needed.

At every level, RTI calls upon educators to think differently about their work. Traditionally, U.S. teachers have been very isolated in their classrooms (Spring, 2007). Some historians have suggested that this is because of the tradition of the "one-room school-house" in U.S. history. In recent years schools have focused more on having teachers work in collaborative ways. RTI involves teachers, specialists, and administrators working together to address students' learning needs. In order to work together, we have to get away from thinking of working with students in isolation and focus on working with students as a team. A classic example of this is when one of us refers to our students as "my kids." Although it's good for teachers to have a strong sense of caring for their students, if we are reluctant to share teaching duties, students may suffer.

In order for us to get away from a mind-set of students being linked exclusively with one teacher, it's a good idea for all teachers to become accustomed to sharing students and instruction. In the previous example, some of Lisa's students participated in additional instruction with another teacher, a specialist. The school psychologist supported instruction by administering weekly progress measures. By adding these two people into the classroom, Lisa shared the instruction and assessment work with other adults in the school. This sharing is the kind of role shift that RTI requires.

In the past, when a student has worked with a specialist, the student would often leave the room. Such support has often been called a "pull-out" model, because the student is "pulled" from the classroom. In Lisa's case the specialists came into the room to work with the students. This model is sometimes known as "push-in," because the services come to the students in the classroom. Both "pull" and "push" are terms that suggest a tension between the classroom teacher and the specialists. In RTI, neither pulling nor pushing is needed. Instead, all the people who work with a student should feel equally comfortable working with the student and share in that student's success.

A number of role shifts may accompany RTI activities. The following are some of the possible shifts that can occur for different school staff.

Classroom Teacher

With RTI you are likely to work side by side with other teachers and specialists or paraprofessionals to help your most struggling students. In the past, your struggling students would have worked outside the classroom with a paraprofessional. RTI methods suggest that teachers themselves work with their struggling students directly as part of a team that supports these students.

Reading or Math Specialist

Specialists become more involved with classroom instruction for students at risk. Ideally, specialists will be able to work with the most struggling students in your classroom or in spaces nearby. Such work is neither "pushed" nor "pulled," but complements the classroom instruction.

Special Education Teacher

Special education teachers have traditionally worked very separately from general educators. This is a result of a time when students with special needs were seen as very different from other students. RTI assumes that all students can learn and that it is the work of all teachers to find solutions for school success. Special education teachers are likely to spend less time on paperwork and more time working with students who might later be referred. In addition, special educators are likely to serve as consultants to other teachers as they work to find the instruction that best meets a student's needs.

School Psychologist

The role of the school psychologist is likely to change a great deal in RTI. In the past, school psychologists have been viewed as "gatekeepers" who did very specific types of assessment, such as IQ tests, and that was it. Over time, it has become clear that IQ tests are not a very good way to determine whether a student has a disability. Instead, information gathered from how a student responds to instruction is much more useful. In order to gather such information, school psychologists need to change how and when they conduct assessments. Instead of waiting until a student is very, very behind and failing, school psychologists can participate in helping students from the first day of school. New roles for school psychologists can include serving on the problem-solving team, helping gather benchmark data on all students three times a year, and conducting the weekly progress-monitoring checks for students who receive extra instruction. Another way to think about it is that school psychologists will go from collecting a large amount of data at one point in time to gathering the same amount of data, but over a longer period of time.

Principal

Principals have a new role as well. Instead of primarily being disciplinarians, when RTI is used principals become data managers. The traditional view of principals is that they are the people who deal with the problems. In the old days, principals dealt mostly with discipline issues. Being sent to the principal's office meant that a student was in serious trouble. More recently, principals have focused on academic problems because of the requirements in No Child Left Behind (NCLB). Principals are the ones who are called when a school does not meet the adequate yearly progress (AYP) requirements of NCLB. The traditional role of the principal is very reactive. She has dealt with behavior and learning problems only after they happen. In RTI principals get to be more proactive and work to prevent problems.

Often, principals serve as RTI data managers, collecting and reviewing data about student progress so they can work with the other school staff to anticipate and meet student needs. Principals serve on the problem-solving team and help ensure that information needed for your students is provided. Instead of waiting for a problem to happen in the classroom, principals using RTI use information available about students to prevent problems from happening.

COLLABORATION

Our new roles as part of RTI all point in the direction of active collaboration. The word *collaborate* literally means "to labor together." This means that RTI requires work, but it is shared work. The collaboration required in RTI means that we all work side by side to help students. As noted earlier, U.S. schools have traditionally been places where you would be in the classroom with students and no interaction—or minimal interaction—with other adults happened (Spring, 2007). A collaborative approach to teaching requires that we work together, side by side, with the students to help them succeed.

Collaborative work requires time, and successful RTI has included dedication of time so that we can collaborate. The scheduling details include looking at the daily school schedule to ensure that your students who need Tier 2 instruction can get it without missing Tier 1 instructional time. In addition, collaboration requires allowing time for teachers and others to meet regularly and review student progress. Ideally, we will meet in grade-level teams every week and look at the progress data for our students. The problem-solving team needs to meet once a week and review overall progress of students to determine whether interventions are working. It's essential that our school schedules be organized so that the time needed for effective collaboration can happen.

Figure 1.1 shows a sample schedule that a school could use to facilitate RTI activities. This sample is based on an actual elementary school that has been implementing RTI for 5 years. The schedule was developed by the teachers at the school so that they could collaborate to make RTI effective for their students. This schedule could be used with any elementary grade class. The key to making the schedule work is to have common times for each subject within each grade. By having students in each grade in the same subject at the same time, we can more easily collaborate and group students together for instruction. More information about scheduling is found in Chapter 12.

Flexible Instructional Groups

In some schools using RTI, students are grouped according to current instructional level for the core academic skills of reading, writing, and math. In such schools, the fall benchmark data are used to identify students' initial performance level in these areas. Students are then placed in groups with peers at the same instructional level. It is important to note that students' instructional levels may change during the school year. For this reason, the instructional groups are reviewed regularly and the groupings are changed about every 6 weeks to reflect students' changing needs. Flexible instructional groups can be used in many different ways. We can create such groups in one class, all the teachers of one

Planning time	8:30–9:00
Class starts	9:00–9:05
Phonics activity	9:05–9:20
Reading: literacy centers	9:20–10:05
Bathroom break and recess	10:05–10:25
Math	10:25–11:10
Spelling	11:10–11:30
Lunch and second recess	11:30–12:10
Specials: art, music, library, guidance	12:10–12:50
Intervention groups	12:50–1:20
Written language	1:20–2:05
P.E.	2:05–2:40
Science/social studies	2:40–3:25
Line up for buses	3:25–3:35

FIGURE 1.1. Sample daily classroom schedule for RTI activities.

grade level can pool their students to create instructional groups within the grade level, or teachers of different grades can pool students to create intergrade groups.

It is important to note that flexible grouping requires collaboration by teachers and students. Because groupings change at regular intervals, we have to learn how to handle changes in group membership. There are many advantages to flexible grouping. For us, it means that we will not necessarily work with the same students in the same way all year. For students, it means they get to interact with different students and teachers over time. It also means that additional adults can be in the classroom during core instruction time to assist with the small groups. In an RTI system, all students[1] participate in Tier 1 activities. This means that no students are removed from this instruction. In order to make this work most effectively, instructional groups work with one adult during the Tier 1 time. Because no students are removed from Tier 1 instruction, the specialists and paraprofessionals are available to help us lead small groups in the Tier 1 classroom.

Assignment of teachers to the instructional groups is based on our expertise. The most expert teachers should work with the neediest students. If paraprofessionals are part of the staff who participate in Tier 1 instruction, they should be assigned to work with the strongest students who need less direct teacher support. Sometimes in the past, the less-skilled staff have been assigned to work with the students who are struggling the most. This does not make sense, because these students need the most support. Many students will make progress as a result of the Tier 1 instructional program, but not all of

---

[1]This really means the vast majority of students. There will be a very small number of students enrolled in a school who have severe and profound disabilities and who may not participate in Tier 1 instruction.

them will. For this reason, Tier 2 instruction is provided on a daily basis for students who need it. In order for such instruction to happen, there should be time in the schedule. In the sample schedule there is a daily "skills block" time, which is when Tier 2 instruction happens. During this time those students who need extra support participate in small-group instruction led by specialists and special educators.

Closing the Gap

In order for students who are struggling in school to catch up to their peers, there must be a way to "close the gap" between grade-level performance expectations and their current skills. The size of a student's gap between current performance and expectations will affect how much effort will be needed to close the gap. Regardless of the size of the gap, only one thing can close the gap: effective instruction (Chall, 2000). Reading instruction has been studied scientifically for about 100 years, and over time, one method for teaching reading has been shown to be the most effective for struggling readers (Chall, 1967; Huey, 1913). This method is direct instruction. Although math and writing instruction have not been studied to the same degree as reading, mounting evidence has shown that direct instruction works very well in these areas, too. One of the keys to RTI success is selection and use of effective instructional methods and programs at all levels (Coyne, Kame'enui, & Carnine, 2007). For more information about the research on reading instruction see the Resources section at the end of this chapter as well as Chapter 6 (Adams, 1990; Haager, Klingner, & Vaughn, 2007).

Effective instruction takes time, and struggling students need the additional time provided from a skills block in order to develop missing skills. An important consideration is how much additional instruction your students will need. This cannot be determined until instructional sessions are held to assess how the student responds. The goal is to get all your students to grade-level performance as quickly as possible. Students who are significantly behind will need more instruction than those who are only a little behind. Only by working together as a team will we have the energy we need to help students catch up. Successful collaboration also requires keeping all team members informed about what's happening.

COMMUNICATION

Because RTI calls upon us to work together, it also requires effective communication. Imagine what happens in a village when some villagers know certain things and others don't. At best, some community members could be offended and feel left out. At worst, key villagers who are not informed about urgent matters cannot participate in community activities or decisions. The same is true in a school. If some staff are "in the know" about RTI activities and others are not included in the information loop, someone is likely to feel left out. Or, as is often the case, valuable information about students will not get shared at a critical juncture. Effective RTI depends on communication so that the right information gets to the people who need it in a timely fashion.

The most basic communication loop for RTI activities is to ensure that the data we collect about an individual student "follows" that student across the tiers of services provided. If your student is struggling in Tier 1 and then gets Tier 2 instruction, the data from Tier 1 should be accessible to those who provide Tier 2 services. If the student makes progress and is ready to transition out of Tier 2 supports, then you need to have access to the Tier 2 data to plan for the transition. In the same way, if your student does not respond to intervention and is referred for an evaluation, it's crucial that the data collected during Tier 2 activities be used as part of that evaluation. Data are like the spinal cord of RTI. Just like a human spinal cord conducts information to and from the brain so that daily functioning can happen, RTI data are essential for the healthy functioning of responsive interventions.

In addition to the communication necessary for student data to be accessible to those who need them, other forms of regular communication are important. The process of determining which students are at risk requires that we all talk with each other about the students' data. These conversations can take the form of weekly meetings among the teachers who all teach one grade, the problem-solving team, and the entire faculty. In addition, parents and other community members need to understand what RTI is all about. The presence of so many communication needs points to the importance of having a communication plan—that is, the set of steps taken to ensure that information is shared with those who need it—as part of RTI activities.

A number of communication tools can assist with ensuring that RTI data are shared as needed. Using a common database is an important part of helping all school staff access student information when they need it. Such data tools can include locally owned software such as Microsoft Excel as well as Internet-based data management services such as AIMSweb. The benefit of Internet-based data tools is that we can access them anywhere there is an Internet connection. There are even ways that parents can access student data from certain services. The purpose of the data is to inform instructional decision making, and having fast access to the data is important so that we can adjust instruction quickly in response to student needs.

Going back to the case of Lisa, here's how she was able to use communication planning and technology to support her students. After organizing her students into flexible instructional groups, Lisa was particularly concerned about one student, Max. Max started the year behind his classmates in math skills, but he was not the lowest-scoring student in the class. Max participated in daily instruction in a group with five other students. In addition, he attended daily skills group sessions with the math specialist. Even though Lisa did not provide Max's daily skills sessions, she could view his progress data by logging in to the Internet-based data service. After 3 weeks, Lisa attended the problem-solving team to discuss Max's math performance. One of the team members brought her laptop to the meeting and was able to show the team Max's data graph. During the meeting, the team member serving as recorder took notes directly onto the computer, and these were saved in Max's intervention file. At the end of the meeting, the team's decision was recorded via computer. Lisa was able to access and review both the data and meeting notes from her computer as she prepared for the fall parent–teacher conferences. The Tier 2 teacher who worked with Max was not able to attend the problem-solving meeting, but could open and view the data and meeting notes at a later time. Additional communication activities that could be supported from a central database are summaries of RTI data across classrooms and grades and data concerning overall student progress.

Lisa was able to keep track of Max's progress by using communication tools and planning to ensure that information about his school work was accessible. Planning ahead for the types of communication necessary to support RTI is important because of the collaborative nature of RTI. We can work as a strong team if effective communication planning is used from the start, but if communication is fragmented, we may feel isolated and left out of RTI activities. When communication is effective, we can work just like a village community to support the needs of all members.

ECOLOGICAL FACTORS

Another way to think about the "village" nature of RTI is to see it as a way of combining "ecological" factors in students' lives. "Ecological" approaches to helping students consider all parts of the child's environment. Basically, this means including not only teachers, but also parents, community members, and anyone else who is involved in the child's life in activities that help the child succeed. All of the people and settings in the child's life are that child's "ecology." A number of things have an effect on an ecosystem. Recent evidence of global warming has led many of us to change our daily habits. In the same way, how teachers, parents, and others work together will affect how helpful they can be for students. Susan Sheridan and Merilee McCurdy at the University of Nebraska have looked at how ecological variables in children's lives affect their school success (Sheridan & McCurdy, 2005). Their findings have shown that when teachers, parents, and others work together with a common goal, student success is better.

As you think about using RTI to help your students, it's important to pay attention to the ecological variables affecting your work. This "big-picture" aspect of RTI is what can connect all the "villages" (i.e., schools) into larger communities (like states) with common goals. While you are thinking about how to get started with RTI, think about the ecological variables that will influence your success. Here are questions to consider:

- How well do you get along with other teachers who might work with your students?
- How informed is your principal about your students' learning and success?
- Who else works with your students each day?
- How often do you talk with parents about school progress?

All of these are ecological factors that will influence the success of RTI practices in your classroom and school. If you already have strong working relationships with the others who can help your students, including parents, then you are ready to get started with some RTI activities. If you don't have strong relationships with your students' parents or other teachers who might work with them, creating such partnerships will be an important first step.

RTI READINESS

We recognize that you may be at a different level of readiness for RTI than some of the other teachers in your building or district. This is okay. Not everyone has the same background, and it's important to recognize that getting ready for RTI is a step unto itself. Several U.S. state departments of education have developed checklists and planning tools that teachers can use to assist them with RTI activities. Colorado, Oregon, Pennsylvania, Tennessee, and Vermont all have RTI readiness checklists or surveys on their department of education websites. These have been developed to help teachers and teams in schools consider how ready they are to use RTI. A review of the currently available checklists showed that many of them were adapted from one that the Colorado Department of Education created. For this reason, the Colorado form is included in Appendix A at the end of this book. If you or your colleagues fill it out, you can learn how ready you are to work as a team to make RTI successful.

The checklist is three pages long and includes five sections. All of the items about RTI are in the middle of the form, and there are two sets of columns where you mark your readiness. The columns on the left side indicate what level of priority each part of RTI is to you. Three priority levels can be indicated: low, medium, and high. On the right side of the checklist are columns where you mark your current level of implementation of each RTI step. The four levels of implementation are:

1. We do not do this in our school.
2. We are starting to move in this direction.
3. We are making good progress here.
4. This condition is well established.

These ratings indicate what RTI steps have already been put into place in your school. The benefit of these ratings is that they can show change over time. Once you have filled out the checklist, you can look and see what steps still need to be implemented and then look at the priority for these steps. Start by adding new steps that are a high priority. If all the teachers in your school fill out the checklist, you will all have a better idea of where you are on RTI work. Sometimes, it will first be necessary to get agreement among the teachers about what steps have the highest priority. Once everyone is in agreement about the most important next step, it will be much easier to get going on it.

CREATING AND SHARING SUCCESS

When all members of a school community work together to implement RTI, it is much more successful. Just like villagers who share the common goal of having a safe and prosperous community, we need to work together to support the needs of all students. Successful communities value all members, distribute leadership, adjust job roles over time, collaborate on common goals, and communicate effectively. In effective schools we do the same things. It takes a village to raise a child, and it takes an entire school to implement RTI effectively. RTI cannot happen if only a few teachers are supporting it. RTI requires time and commitment from all of us. When we work together for the common goal of helping all students succeed, RTI will work.

RESOURCES

Intervention Central

www.interventioncentral.org

This site offers free tools and resources to help school staff and parents to promote positive classroom behaviors and foster effective learning for all children and youth. The site was created by Jim Wright, a school psychologist and school administrator from central New York. Visit to check out newly posted academic and behavioral intervention strategies, download publications on effective teaching practices, and use tools that streamline classroom assessment and intervention.

National Center on Response to Intervention

www.rti4success.org

This center is funded by the U.S. Department of Education Office of Special Education Programs and the American Institutes for Research. The site provides resources for teachers, parents, and state departments of education about how to implement RTI.

RTI Action Network

www.rtinetwork.org

The RTI Action Network is dedicated to the effective implementation of RTI in school districts nationwide. Their goal is to guide educators and families in the large-scale implementation of RTI so that each child has access to quality instruction and that struggling students—including those with learning disabilities—are identified early and receive the necessary support to be successful.

More information about the collaborative work needed to support RTI can be found in a number of works. Joel Spring's (2007) history of U.S. educational practices tells about how teachers have been left to their own devices for many years, until very recently. Huey's earlier work (1913) shows that interest in reading instruction methods is not new and documents that effective practices have not really changed. In the 1960s Jeanne Chall provided evidence of the need for changes in teacher preparation for teaching reading, findings confirmed by Marilyn Adams in her seminal work *Beginning to Read: Thinking and Learning about Print* (1990). In 2000 Chall extended prior findings to show that effective instruction is needed in all subject areas. Chall's work documented that effective instruction works for students from many backgrounds. Similarly, Coyne, Kame'enui, and Carnine's (2007) book *Effective Teaching Strategies That Accommodate Diverse Learners* (3rd ed.) provides concrete descriptions of specific teaching methods supported by scientifically based research. Haager, Klingner, and Vaughn (2007) extended this work to reading and offer specific instructional methods for all five areas of reading. As the chapter points out, implementing multi-tiered effective instruction for all students requires collaboration among all school personnel. In order to make collaboration possible, attention to the ecological variables identified by Sheridan and McCurdy (2005) is needed.

CHAPTER 2

How to Use the Tiered Framework

THE TIERED FRAMEWORK

Everyone doing RTI talks about "tiers" of instruction. When we describe Tiers 1, 2, and 3, we are referring to different types of instruction that is used with students. Tiers are one way that instruction can be described to differentiate among levels of intensity. Many people using RTI use three tiers, but some districts use four. For example the state of Georgia uses a four-tiered model, while Texas uses a three-tiered model. It does not really matter how many tiers there are; what matters is how instruction differs between them. This chapter talks about different types of instruction for each level, or tier, of RTI.

Intervention versus Instruction: What's the Difference?

We are often asked, "What's the difference between intervention and instruction?" The truth is these words can be used to mean the same thing, but (just to make things complicated) not everyone uses them that way. *Intervention* is a general word that means "to come between." This term is used by doctors, teachers, psychologists, and others to describe any circumstance that is put into place to change a situation. By intervening, it is hoped that what comes after the intervention will be different from what came before. Instruction is a more precise term that is really a type of intervention. The word *instruction* means to direct or teach. We can use instruction as a type of intervention to help students. Instruction is the primary type of intervention used in schools, which is probably why so many people use the terms interchangeably.

To help make things clearer, in this book we use the word *instruction* when we are talking about teaching used with *all* students, and we use the word *intervention* when we talk about teaching used with just *a few students* at a time. There are some other words that are sometimes confused when people talk about RTI. We define those before we go on to explain how the different tiers work.

Accommodation versus Intervention

Many teachers are familiar with the term *accommodation*, a word that is often used to describe ways of helping students who are struggling with an assignment. The word *accommodate* means "to make fit." Another word that is often used to mean the same thing as accommodate is *adaptation*. These words are often used to describe changes in teaching for students with disabilities. Both accommodation and adaptation are methods of including students in classroom activities. For example for a student in a wheelchair, it would be important to ensure that the door to the room was adapted to fit the wheelchair. If there were steps into the room, it would be important to adapt them so the student could enter. Such accommodations are changes in the environment designed to allow one or more individuals to participate. Accommodations make it possible for students with disabilities to participate in school activities. Interventions are different.

Intervention ("to come between") is very different from *accommodation* ("to make fit"). Intervention includes anything that is designed to change the setting or individual in specific ways. Doctors often use medication for intervention. They know that the presence or absence of a specific substance like aspirin or Tylenol will affect body temperature. For this reason, they use such medicines to intervene with a fever and change the body temperature. Similarly, teachers can intervene to change a student's learning outcomes. If a student has very poor reading skills, specific reading instruction can be used as an intervention to change the student's reading skills. In this case, instruction is a type of intervention for a student who needs it.

Differentiated Instruction

Another term that is often brought up when talking about RTI is differentiated instruction. We have already defined instruction. The word *differentiate* means "to make distinct or different." *Differentiated instruction* is teaching that is different from what was used before or what is used for other students. Differentiated instruction is really another way of saying instruction as intervention and is what RTI is all about. It means using the kind of instruction that a student needs, even if it is different from what other students need. Basically, the different tiers of RTI provide differentiated instruction to students according to what they need. Differentiated instruction is not separate from RTI, but is how RTI happens. Now that we have defined these words, let's look at how differentiated instruction can be used as intervention.

WHAT ARE THE TIERS?

As mentioned earlier, there are different ways of describing RTI tiers. Table 2.1 summarizes a number of the terms that have been used to define what happens at each tier. At the end of the day, it does not matter what you call the type of instruction at each tier. What matters is that it's different from what came before and it is based on what the student needs. For example, the three tiers can be referred to as core, supplemental, and

TABLE 2.1. Terms Used to Describe Multiple Tiers of Intervention

Tier	Terms		
1	Primary	Universal	Core
2	Secondary	Strategic	Supplemental
3	Tertiary	Intensive	Intensive

intensive instruction that students receive. Alternatively they can be known as primary, secondary, and tertiary, or as universal, strategic, and intensive. All of these are terms that help *differentiate* how instruction is different at each tier. It is important to know that there are aspects of the instruction at each tier that are similar to what's happening at other tiers. Each level is similar in some ways and different in others. These distinctions are described and instructional examples are provided for each tier of support.

Changing Tiers = Changing Intensity

The main way that instruction differs across the tiers is the intensity. *Intensity* means "degree of strength." A less intensive intervention is not as "strong" as a more intensive one. The strength, or intensity, of instruction is the main way we can provide intervention for students. When we think about increasing the intensity of instruction (for low- or high-performing students), we consider the following main characteristics: grouping, time, assessment, and format. Grouping refers to how students are grouped for instruction. Time refers to how long instruction will occur each day. Assessment refers to how often student progress is measured. Format refers to how skills are taught that are matched to student needs. Table 2.2 shows what instructional features are used at each tier.

Each of these characteristics is distinct. While important on their own, they are more powerful when used together in the right amounts. Think of baking, for example. Unlike some other types of cooking, where there is freedom for tasteful expression, baking requires specific amounts of ingredients to produce the right result. Too much flour and the batter is not moist enough. Too little baking powder and the cake does not rise. It is important to follow the recipe in order to learn the right amounts and combine the ingredients together so we can hope for a good result.

The same is true for increasing the intensity of instruction for students. A teacher can put her students in small groups according to need, but if she doesn't have enough time, she won't be able to get them to where they need to be. Another teacher might target the skills her students need to learn, but if she doesn't monitor their progress, it will be difficult to tell accurately who is improving. To increase intensity, it is important to consider the right mix of ingredients to make it work for the students. With the right balance, teachers can propel kids to make great gains in performance and end up with the best results. We want you to review your school year in June, look back on the year, and realize how much you did for your students.

TABLE 2.2. Characteristics of the Tiers in Reading

Tier	Who?	Grouping	Time	Assessment	Format
			Instructional features		
1	All students	Whole group and small group	90 minutes per day	Monitoring quarterly or three times per year	Derived from the core curriculum and adapted to meet student needs and address standards and benchmarks
2	Below grade level	Small-group instruction (three to six students)	30 minutes per day plus core group instruction, 2–3 days a week; 120 minutes total, 2–3 days a week	Progress monitoring once per week or twice per month	Targeted toward skill deficits and matched to student area of need
3	Severely below grade level	Small-group instruction (two to three students)	30 minutes per day plus core group instruction, 5 days a week; 120 minutes total, 5 days a week	Progress monitoring once per week	Intensive, targeted instruction with ample opportunities to respond and multiple opportunities for practice

The Triangle

Most people doing RTI use a triangle to represent what RTI is all about. Since one of us had previously published a triangle graphic, we have reproduced it here to show all the parts of RTI in one picture. Figure 2.1 shows all the steps of RTI. We use a triangle in RTI graphics to portray how each tier is used by successively smaller groups of students. The base of the triangle can be thought of as the front door of a school. It is the point of entry for all students. When a student comes to school, instruction starts with the core curriculum, which is Tier 1. This part of the triangle is used for Tier 1 because it is the largest, which reflects how it is something applied with *all* students. About 80% of the students in a school should be successful with Tier 1 alone. The rest of the triangle shows the supports available for the other 20% of students. Tier 2, portrayed in the middle of the triangle, includes additional instruction for those students who have not yet succeeded with Tier 1 alone. About 95% of your students should succeed with Tier 1 plus Tier 2.

There are some students who will not be successful even with Tier 1 plus Tier 2 instruction, however. For these students, Tier 3 is offered. Tier 3 makes up the smallest part of the triangle because it represents only about 5% of your students. If a student is still struggling after getting Tier 1 plus Tier 2, he or she is having a lot of trouble in school. Although specific procedures must be developed in each district, once a student moves from Tier 2 to Tier 3, it can mean that the student may need special education. Tier 3 usually includes more intensive intervention for the student as well as a comprehensive evaluation to see whether the student needs special education. But the good news is that Tier 3 will only be needed by about 5% of your students. One of the main features of Tier 3 is diagnostic teaching.

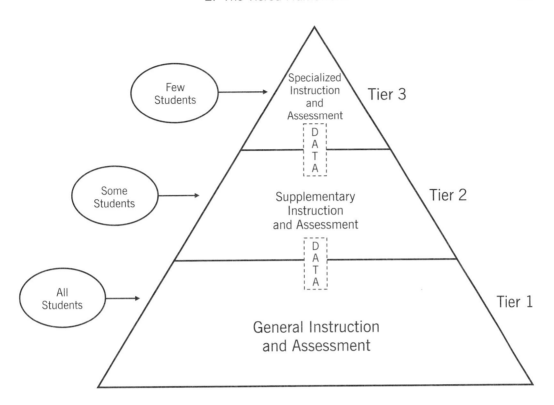

FIGURE 2.1. The three-tiered RTI model. From Brown-Chidsey and Steege (2005). Copyright 2005 by The Guilford Press. Reprinted by permission.

Diagnostic Teaching

Diagnostic teaching is a method of using data from teaching sessions to help identify a student's learning needs. In many ways, all of RTI uses aspects of diagnostic teaching, which includes teaching specific skills to students and monitoring their learning to see whether they "got" it. If the student learns what's taught, more difficult new material is taught. If the student does not "get" it, then the skills need to be retaught.

In RTI, teaching on the basis of what students have or have not learned before is used all the time. The difference between doing this across the three tiers is the intensity of instruction. Some students are not able to succeed with Tier 1 plus Tier 2 instruction, and for them Tier 3 becomes important. For such students, more intensive, specific, diagnostic teaching is helpful because it allows the teachers to learn exactly where learning is breaking down. In addition, diagnostic teaching can show what instructional methods do work for a student.

Diagnostic teaching is more intensive and time-consuming than general instruction, and for this reason it makes sense to use it only when needed. The data gained from diagnostic teaching can be used as part of the comprehensive evaluation. For example diagnostic teaching methods could be used with one or two students at a time to figure out why they have not mastered specific math skills. Such teaching could include asking the student to complete a page of math facts while a teacher or specialist watches. Once the student has completed the page, the teacher can correct the answers and then review them with the student individually. At this point the teacher would point out and describe specific errors.

The next phase of the teaching would be to use direct instruction to teach the student the skill(s) matched to the prior errors; then the student would be tested again to see whether the instruction worked. For students who make gains from the teaching sessions, there would be evidence that very structured instruction is effective for the student. For students who don't make gains from such sessions, there is evidence that even highly prescriptive teaching is not effective. For students who still struggle after Tier 3 instruction, it may be necessary to conduct additional assessments to see whether there are generalized problems with skills such as memory that affect all learning activities.

You probably noticed that there is a box with the word *data* between each of the tiers. The box has a slotted line around it. That box goes across the tiers with the slotted line to remind us that decisions about which tier a student needs are only made according to data. Put another way, data are the pathway by which instructional decisions are made. For example, students who need Tier 2 instruction for a while will eventually not need it anymore, and when the data show this, they will go through the door back to Tier 1. The goal is to find the intervention that helps each student succeed while providing core instruction for all (Coyne, Kame'enui, & Simmons, 2004).

Consider the instructional features shown in Table 2.2. Think about the following two questions:

1. What steps seem easy?
2. What steps seem difficult?

For the steps that seem difficult, what are the reasons for the difficulty? Could you brainstorm ideas to address the potential barriers? We emphasize focusing on the "alterable variables" of instruction like time, grouping, and assessment because they are characteristics that we can control. Unlike a student's background, socioeconomic status, or innate abilities that we cannot change, we can change the factors that influence instruction in the classroom.

Tier 1 Interventions

At Tier 1, or the core curriculum, all students are involved. Notice the word *all*. This means everybody, everyone, the whole class. With the exception of students with severe disabilities, all of your students should receive core instruction. There may even be some students with severe disabilities who benefit at Tier 1. That is a decision for the individualized education plan (IEP) team that works with such students. The question about who participates in the core instruction comes into play when students who receive special education services are pulled out of core reading instruction to receive special education reading instruction instead. Special education reading instruction is important; it is necessary to teach students with reading difficulties using a skills-based format, focusing on the critical skills they need. It is targeted, focused, and essential for growth. The rule for deciding whether a student can be "pulled" from core instruction is if it's written into an

IEP. State and federal rules require that *all* students participate in the general education core instruction *unless* not doing so is explicitly written into the student's IEP. So if you have any students whose IEPs say that they will be pulled from core for instruction in any subject, those are the only ones who should not be in the room for core instruction; every other student should participate during core (Tier 1) instruction time.

Students who require Tier 2 interventions, or supplemental support, need solid core instruction as the foundation for the additional instruction provided in Tiers 2 and 3. This core forms the base of their learning. It allows students to learn from their peers, including high and low performers. The core helps the teacher to see how everyone is doing and note what skills might need to be emphasized more. It is the crux of their instruction, and everyone should have the opportunity to learn from it. For these reasons, it is critical to create a schedule that allows all students to participate in core instruction and has room for the supplementary help provided in Tiers 2 and 3. If the scheduling question is really bugging you, jump ahead to Chapter 12 and read about daily schedules that fit in all tiers of intervention.

Grouping

Grouping at Tier 1 can take many forms. While the core implies all students, it does not mean that instruction is provided to all students in a large-group setting. Core is something everyone receives, but it does not have to only occur with whole-group instruction. Grouping at Tier 1 is a combination of whole-class and small-group instruction.

Whole-group instruction occurs daily and is part of the routine schedule. It is designated by the teacher and used to communicate concepts. Small-group instruction also occurs daily and provides students more opportunities to work on the skills they need. In these small groups, students work closely with the teacher, receiving the instruction that matches their needs. These small groups are flexible in that they change according to how students perform. Students are not locked in, as they were in ability groups of the past. Students are grouped according to need and reorganized based on data showing acquisition of skills and rates of growth.

Time

The time factor is huge for teachers. It is the instructional characteristic that can make such a huge difference, if there is enough of it. And of course, it's the hardest to find. Research in the area of beginning reading indicates that students need at least 90 minutes of daily instruction at Tier 1 (Florida Center for Reading Research, 2008). With this time, students have the opportunity to learn in whole and small groups and use time to practice their newly learned skills.

That's an hour and a half—a lot of time in a day already packed with activities. But it is what is needed. The more time devoted to instruction, the more progress students will make. Many districts feel the pinch when they learn this information, and they slowly try to take it in as they consider their school day. It's true, there's not enough time for everything. It is here that you consider your mission statement, your values, and your goals as a district. What are the priorities? What do you keep? What do you consider minimizing? How do you work in 90 minutes of reading instruction? Every district does it differently, but they make it happen. It takes time, creativity, conversations, and approval, but it is doable and it is necessary to get our students to where they need to be. For examples of daily classroom schedules that include 90 minutes of daily reading instruction, see Chapter 12 on schedules.

Assessment

Assessment at Tier 1 occurs either quarterly or three times a year. All students will be assessed during these times to ensure that they are making progress and acquiring new concepts and skills. If your core curriculum is meeting the needs of most of your students, then they will only need to be assessed a few times a year. As a teacher you are always doing quick informal assessments, though. You're always collecting information, whether it's notes, portfolio products, test results, or quizzes that you give as part of your core instruction. Formal assessments can be saved for the end of the quarter, when everybody is assessed with the same measure to compare students again and note rates of growth. The assessments conducted at Tier 1 are often known as universal benchmark screening. More information about how to do universal screening can be found in the book *Response to Intervention: Principles and Strategies for Effective Practice* (Brown-Chidsey & Steege, 2005).

Instructional Format

There are many curricula from which districts can choose. Refer to Chapter 3 to review the considerations for adopting a new core curriculum. It is important to consider whether the curriculum is research based and whether it will match the needs of your student population. It is also important to review the program's ideas for differentiation and determine whether there is enough time to teach the lessons adequately. Finally, it is crucial to consider the assessments within the curriculum and whether they provide useful information to teachers when administered to students. Even if a district reviews each of these components and considers the implications, there is a dilemma that still may be faced. Consider the following school.

Reconciling "Each" with "All"

There is a common struggle among teachers: Do I address all of the students' needs or try to get through all of the lessons? Covering all of the content in each lesson is a task in itself, let alone trying to balance individual student needs as well. This was the case at Willow Elementary School among the second-grade teachers. A new core curriculum was purchased the previous spring, and the teachers were working together to learn the materials and prioritize the skills. Each lesson was filled with a lot of content, activities, and ideas for generalization. Although the teachers appreciated the options, they were also overwhelmed with prioritizing what to definitively teach and what to use if time allowed. If they weren't going to teach the whole lesson, what should they leave out? What should they emphasize? How should they make these decisions and feel confident that they are heading in the right direction? Clarity was reached on a professional development day when they were given time to work as a team. During this time, the teachers used the district standardized benchmark to guide them in knowing what to include and what to use as needed. With the help of their educational consultant, Amy, they were able to determine what skills should be emphasized when, and identify the strategies in the book that would work best for each skill. The teachers used their student screening data to determine what students needed support and what skills should be explicitly taught. Using that information, they were able to supplement the core with additional activities to support those students in need.

Mrs. Lyons and Mr. Dell were pleased to know that giving the weekly word test was beneficial for some students, but not mandatory for all. This provided everyone more time to work on fluency and comprehension with their students. Ms. Jackson and Mrs. Ray were happy with the decision to make paired partner reading optional, because they were already doing it as part of their introduction activities every day. They decided it was useful for students in need of additional fluency practice, but not all students would benefit from it. Some students were performing too well to simply focus on fluency. Others were still working on phonics and needed lower-level stories to read with a partner. The second-grade teachers reached consensus on both decisions and agreed to implement the ideas as a grade level. Finally, they worked with the third-grade teachers to ensure that they were covering all of the necessary skills before students moved on to the next grade.

Communicating about the key concepts and ensuring that the main components were covered helped the teachers to know that they were teaching what they were supposed to, even if they weren't covering all of the material in each lesson. This discussion helped them to see that while the curriculum should be followed, it also needs to be differentiated to meet student needs in the most effective and efficient ways. It was the beginning of a series of conversations they had throughout the year. Implementing and evaluating the curriculum was an ongoing process, but one that became easier as they learned more about their students and how to prioritize their needs.

You may be looking at your lessons now, wondering, "How do I get it all in?" It is likely that you can't, given the time in each day. Even with 90 minutes of reading instruction, it would be difficult to get it all in, so you don't. You realize as a teacher that your instruction is derived from the district's standards and benchmarks and that the curriculum is a tool to get you there. You realize that getting everything in is not the point. You start to see that when you focus on the standards and benchmarks, you have a destination for your students.

The core curriculum, your Tier 1 instruction, is not the end. It is the means to the end. It is a tool, a set of materials, a package of concepts and skills that you use to help your students meet the standards and benchmarks of your subject and your grade level. With that realization comes freedom—not necessarily freedom to do whatever you want, but freedom to choose the activities and techniques that address what you need to work on, to select the tasks that address the benchmarks, and to pick the skills that your students need to improve. Think of the standards and benchmarks as your destination, and the curriculum as the map that will get you there. You do not have to do it all. Working as a grade-level team with school support staff like an educational consultant or the reading specialist can foster good conversations and make these decisions easier. It is helpful to work together and decide what is most important for your students, given their skills and specific needs.

Tier 2 Interventions

At Tier 2, students have been identified as being in need of additional instruction. They require a combination of supports to help them make progress and succeed. Who are these students? These are the ones who have been identified as performing below where they need to be. They are not severely different from their peers, but they are performing below the norm. These are the students who may just need a little "bump" to get them going, or they may need structured support over time to help them catch up to their peers. They fall somewhere in the middle, between students who are on track and students who are significantly at risk and at least two grade levels below their peers.

Grouping

To provide the supplemental support, students can be placed in groups of three to six students. This size is beneficial for two reasons. First, it allows each student to receive additional individual time with the teacher. Each student receives more attention than he or she would in the larger setting. Second, it allows the students to learn from one another. Being in a small group, they get to hear other students' responses, work together, and practice new skills as a team, rather than on their own.

You may be thinking, "It would be nice if I only had three to six students in my class who needed extra support." And this often can happen. Each class is unique, with their own strengths and areas to improve. You may have seven to ten students who need additional support, or even more. In this situation, it is important to ask the question, "How would my time be spent most efficiently?"

Let's say you are faced with a class in which 10 students are below grade level and in need of supplemental support. Many teachers operating in an RTI model faced with this situation will decide to set up two supplemental groups. Then there are five students per group, and they can be divided by skill level. The teacher will work with one group and his associate will work with the other. On the surface, this is a fine solution. Students are receiving the support they need, and the groups are small enough to teach well. But is this the best way to help 10 students in need?

Thinking back to the 80–15–5 rule, we know that if 80% of the students in our class struggle with the core instruction, then something needs to change within the core. If you have a class of 25 students, and 10 of them need additional instruction, what does that tell you about your core? Sixty percent of your students are successful with the core, while 40% are not. We're hoping for 80% who are successful and 20% who need more support. There are more students who need support within the core, so changing the core instruction would be the most efficient way to meet all of the students' needs.

Instead of setting up two additional groups, teach the skills to the whole class, because a large enough percentage of students need this support. You will reach more students by teaching everyone the necessary skills and you will be more efficient with your time. Adding to the core by reteaching and practicing concepts allows you to teach what is missing to the students who need it. But when more than 20% of students in a class need such instruction, teaching it to everyone is the most efficient solution in situations when progress is not sufficient with the core alone.

Time

The time necessary to help students make progress at the supplemental level is an additional 30 minutes, two to three times a week. This provides students anywhere from 60 to 90 additional minutes of instruction, which they receive along with their regular core instruction. This amount of time is effective for helping students make the jump and catch up to their peers. Alternatively, the time could be organized so that students get 10 to 15 minutes of extra instruction five days a week. The main thing is that the students receive *extra* instruction in addition to the core program.

It may seem like a lot, and it is. It's supposed to be. This is what students need to accelerate their growth. They won't be able to improve their skills without additional time. Think of a situation where you learned something new—in small doses, it is difficult to learn a new skill because there is limited time to practice. The same is true for students learning to read, do math, write, or improve their behavior. They need ample opportunities to learn so they can practice, practice, practice, and begin to generalize their new set of skills.

Assessment

Students participating in Tier 2 should be assessed once a week or once every other week. This provides you with data frequently, so you can make decisions about what is working and what needs to be improved. At first, it sounds like a lot of assessment. By using brief progress monitoring measures, though, the testing is quick and relatively easy over time. With many measures requiring 3 minutes or less, you get a good bang for your buck. For more information on Tier 2 assessment see Chapter 4, on progress monitoring.

Instructional Format

Instruction at Tier 2 comprises a variety of research-based interventions that are targeted in that they are skill specific and matched to student need. There are many available interventions to choose from, and some are highlighted in the following intervention chapters. One of the most important steps in implementing an intervention is that it is matched to student need. Without a match, the student will be practicing skills that are good, but not directly related to what they *need* to make progress. Spending 30 minutes two to three times a week working on skills that are not necessary becomes a waste of time for you and an unfair waste of time for the student. The format for Tier 2 lessons depends on the skills the student needs to learn. Generally, Tier 2 lessons will focus on a specific skill area such as blending or fluency. By focusing the lesson on just the area in which the student needs help, the value of the lesson time is maximized.

Tier 3 Interventions

At Tier 3, students are severely below grade level. They have been identified as having significant needs and require ample additional instruction to help them succeed. These are students who may be receiving Title 1 services or be placed in special education. They typically see a reading specialist or special education teacher in a separate room, where they go to receive support.

It is important to note here that because these students need so much instruction, they should be receiving it with intensity, meaning that they receive very directed instruction for a significant period each day. In some schools, these students have traditionally been pulled from their core instruction in reading, for example, to receive their reading instruction in the special education room. This instruction may occur for 45 to 60 minutes, which is all the student will receive per day. Sadly, this is the opposite of what these students need. Not only do they receive less time than they need, but they miss out on their core instruction with peers, losing the opportunity to learn from them and be exposed to grade-level content.

In school districts using a collaborative model with special education, students may be exposed to the core instruction and receive additional help as needed. They still need to meet the time requirements, though. In school districts using a pull-out model for special education services, these students are unlikely to receive the time that they need to be successful. They are separated from their peers, receive different instruction, and come back to the classroom having missed what other students in their class learned. Regardless of the model your district operates under, it is important to note that these students should be exposed to as much instruction in their area of need as possible. With such a gap to close, they need ample opportunities to practice, so they can begin to learn new skills and make them part of their repertoire. It's important to note that students with severe gaps in learning may or may not have an IEP. This points out that, at the end of the day, it's the instruction that matters. For this reason, some Tier 3 interventions include both general and special education students.

Grouping

Students at Tier 3 still benefit from working in a group and learning from their peers. They do require intense attention as well. Thus, groups of two to three students work well at this level. The teacher can devote time to each student individually as well as work easily with the whole group on specific skills. Keeping the group small is important, because of the intensity of their needs.

Time

Similar to the Tier 2 group, it is recommended that Tier 3 students receive 30 minutes of additional instruction. The difference is that instead of receiving extra instruction two to three times a week, they receive 30 minutes additional every day. This results in 120 minutes of instruction in the area of need per day.

"One hundred twenty minutes of instruction!" you may be saying. With limited time already, how are we supposed to make this work? There is no magic answer. If there is not enough time, then the schedule must be changed. Priorities need to be determined and used to analyze the schedule and make changes as needed. Administrative support is crucial. There must be an understanding that this is necessary to get students where they need to be. Without this time, it will be difficult to help students make the progress they need.

Assessment

Progress monitoring must occur once per week at Tier 3. These students have such gains to make that weekly data are important for determining progress. Without this information, it is hard to determine what is going well and what needs to be fixed. The weekly data help you as a teacher to decide whether your intervention is working. If it isn't, something needs to be changed. If the student is getting help from several people including yourself, the data play a key role in showing whether your coordinated efforts are working.

Instructional Format

Instruction at Tier 3 is composed of a variety of research-based interventions that are intensive, specific, and address student skill deficits. As at Tier 2, there are many available interventions to choose from. Some can be done easily, with little preparation. Others require more preparation time. Some are best used as practice activities, while others provide a new way to teach concepts and skills. Regardless, the match to student need is the priority. Find the need, target the skill, and remediate the deficit. That is the ultimate goal. If done correctly, students who were the lowest in your class at the beginning of the year can make gains to become among the highest performers. This is the case with Julia, a kindergarten teacher who works in a large suburban school district.

Hit the Ground Running

Julia is a kindergarten teacher who is faced with a diverse class each year. About half of her students come from families whose native language is something other than English. Many of them receive free and reduced lunch. At the beginning of the school year, her kindergartners are given the district assessment to determine who is considered at risk, some risk, and low risk. One of her students, Manuel, began in August scoring low on the literacy assessment. He was considered an "at-risk" student because he scored low on letter recognition, letter sounds, concepts of print, rhyming, beginning sounds, and sight words. Manuel and seven other students in Julia's class received low scores and were placed in a literacy intervention group to support their skills. Julia's reading block is 2½ hours each day. Her at-risk students received an additional half-hour intervention on top of the reading block 4 to 5 days a week.

During the intervention, Julia worked with a small group of five to eight students, focusing on early phonemic awareness skills. She used the alphabet chant, played the "Closer to Z" game, used dice with different letters on it, and many other instructional strategies that allowed her students to practice their emerging skills.

During the 2½-hour reading block, her at-risk students also received small-group instruction with Julia where they continued to practice their skills. Their block consisted of small-group instruction for a half-hour, center activities for a half-hour, a reading intervention program for a half-hour, whole-group instruction for a half-hour, and writing instruction for a half-hour. There were many activities to hold the students' interest and many opportunities to learn with a partner or in a small group.

This combination of instruction, along with a solid block of time, contributed to Manuel's reading success. At the end of the year in May, Manuel had made amazing progress. He moved from the "at-risk" category to being one of the top five performing students in Julia's class. He is reading many words, enjoys picking up books, and has greatly improved his spelling when writing. Julia believes it is the instruction that made a difference, but it is also because she had the time.

With a 2½-hour block of time that was protected, Julia was able to work intensely with her students, targeting those performing at all levels. She helped her students make progress because she determined their areas of need and matched her instruction to those needs. She maximized her reading time, understanding that many of her kids did not have books at home, and she left the school year almost forgetting how her students performed in August. She had to look through their files to remind herself that she actually did get many of her lowest kids to do what they need to be doing: reading.

The Instructional Match

Imagine you were skiing, took a hard fall, and broke your ankle. When you went to the doctor, an X-ray was done to confirm that you broke a bone. The doctor decided to give you aspirin, because it is a research-based medicine that has been proven to alleviate pain. While you appreciated the minor relief from pain, you then expected something more: a cast, for example, to set the broken bone, and crutches to make you more mobile, as your ankle healed over the weeks. You expected that the doctor would give you directions on how to take care of your ankle. The doctor, however, did not provide any of these remedies. He insisted that aspirin was enough, as it has been proven to work, and will likely address your pain. You understood that aspirin would be helpful, but knew that without other support, your ankle would take a long time to heal, if ever.

This is an extreme situation that we would never expect to happen. Physicians are trained to know how to most effectively and efficiently help a broken ankle heal, and it does not just include a daily regimen of aspirin, which is not strong enough and not targeted to the real issue: a broken bone.

Consider this situation and compare it to your students in need. Let's say you have a research-based reading intervention that you have used in the past. It has many studies supporting its use, and you have found it to work with your kids in the past. It has become a default option, where you consider it before any other interventions, similar to aspirin.

While this intervention works and does wonders for some, it doesn't always give you the results you want. Over time, some students respond, but others don't. Some make great progress, but others come to a standstill for weeks at a time. What is going on here?

While you have found a research-based intervention, it will not work for everybody. While many interventions are effective, just like aspirin, without a match to specific need, the intervention will not help your students make progress, or make your ankle heal any faster. The critical piece in solving these problems is the match. In both health care and teaching, it is important to match the need to the support. If I need a cast, give me a cast. If I need phonemic awareness instruction, give me phonemic awareness instruction. If I need long division instruction, give me long division instruction. Find the need, match the support, and begin to see the progress.

As you read the interventions in subsequent chapters, it is important to keep the match in mind. Select the strategy based on what you know about the student. If you don't know exactly what he or she needs to work on, find out. Use your classroom assessments. Create tasks for students to complete. Determine what you do and don't know about the student. Figure out what they need to work on, prioritize the skills, and use this information to select the most appropriate intervention.

RESOURCES

Building RTI Capacity

buildingrti.utexas.org

This project is part of the Vaughn Gross Center for Reading and Language Arts (VGC) within the College of Education at the University of Texas–Austin. Major activities include supporting Spotlight Reading and Math RTI, building the knowledge and skills of RTI specialists statewide, conducting statewide RTI conferences, and using technology to promote RTI-related information.

National Center on Response to Intervention

www.rti4success.org

The center's mission is to provide technical assistance to states and districts and building the capacity of states to assist districts in implementing proven models for RTI. There are four areas of service: (1) knowledge production, (2) expert training and follow-up activities, (3) information dissemination, and (4) an evaluation that provides formative assessments to help improve the delivery of their services.

What Works Clearinghouse (WWC)

ies.ed.gov/ncee/wwc

Established in 2002, the What Works Clearinghouse (WWC) is a central and trusted source of scientific evidence for what works in education. An initiative of the U.S. Department of Education's Institute of Education Sciences, the WWC produces user-friendly practice guides for educators that address instructional challenges with research-based recommendations for schools and classrooms. WWC provides reports about a number of specific curricula.

CHAPTER 3

Evaluating the Core Curriculum

How Do We Know If It's Working?

It was the first year that Meadow Elementary collected schoolwide reading data. As part of this process, the principal set aside 2 days to sit down with the teachers and review the data. Each group of grade-level teachers participated in a 2-hour meeting with the principal, school psychologist, and counselor. Each group of teachers reacted differently, but the data were the same. Across all grades, first through sixth, approximately 50% of the students were below benchmark in reading. These numbers struck home and forced the teams to see an accurate picture of what they faced. Simply by doing the math, they saw that in a school of 500 students, approximately 41 students in each grade required supplemental instruction in reading to increase their skills. Even if the students were divided into groups of six, that still meant seven additional instructional groups per grade level. This was not a feasible option, given the finite reality of time, resources, and teachers available. The teams decided to start small by organizing two to three supplemental groups per grade level and addressing the most pressing student needs first. But this begged the question "Why aren't we making the most efficient change to support student performance? Why aren't we changing the core reading curriculum?" By changing the core, not only could they aim to meet the needs of most of their students, but they could do so in a way that was research based, fast, and efficient. And it was clear that the issue of time was imperative. Setting up multiple supplemental groups required vast amounts of time to plan and train teachers in the new materials and monitoring methods. While adopting a new core would also mean more work and training, it would be time devoted to learning a program that was research validated and efficient by design. In the interim, the teams moved forward with the intervention groups, but they were left wondering whether they had done all they could to meet the needs of their kids.

DEFINITION OF CORE CURRICULUM

Historically, many different types of reading, math, and written language curricula have been used in schools. A combination of general education curricula, intervention strategies, and supplemental instruction has frequently resulted in a disjointed instructional plan. Students get a little bit of this, and a little bit of that, and we hope that our concoction will be the right formula for success. If you're in Mrs. Nelson's classroom, you may get one combination. If you're in Mr. Bright's classroom, you may get another. With a lack of cohesion, students are often exposed to pieces from a variety of curricula, which can result in lower student performance and inhibited growth.

By design, a core curriculum is the program intended to meet the needs of most students. It is the main program that is used to guide instruction in each grade level. The core should be systematic in design and comprehensive in content. Core programs contain a variety of materials that help teachers decide what to teach and how to assess student skills. Simply stated, the core is what all children receive.

Multiple core programs are available in the areas of reading, math, and written language. Schools adopt different core curricula based on a variety of factors like philosophy, pragmatics, cost, and instructional design. An important consideration is matching the core program to the student population needs, so the majority of students succeed with what is being taught in each classroom.

USING DATA TO EVALUATE THE CORE CURRICULUM

How Do We Know If It's Working?

It is the year after the adoption of a new curriculum. Last year the reading adoption team used a set of criteria to select a new core program. The team reviewed the content and examined the evidence of efficacy that was provided in the materials. They also found other sources of information to ensure that there was research to support its effectiveness. The team also discussed their thoughts on following the program with fidelity. Given the issues of time and structure of the school day, they wanted to ensure that every teacher would be able to follow the program as designed. In addition, they reviewed the instructional methods provided and found that there were ideas for differentiation. They looked at the number and type of opportunities for practice, so different students could receive different levels of support. Finally, they talked about the assessments included in the curriculum and how they could use these to evaluate student performance and guide future instruction.

Now that the program is being implemented in the school, the adoption team is confident that the process was a successful one. They reviewed each of the essential components and ensured that the curriculum would meet the needs of their students. Teachers now are using it in their classrooms and have commented that they like the layout of the program, appreciate the ideas for differentiating the lessons, and overall, find it to be fairly manageable in terms of time. The adoption team, teachers, and principal are satisfied with the process and think that the new curriculum is going well. Yet the question remains: How well are the students performing?

On the end-of-unit tests, most students are doing well, but some still struggle. On the weekly quizzes, most students do well, but again, some students experience difficulty. On the state standardized test, students achieve scores that follow a range of performance, from below proficient to highly proficient. This is similar to last year, and somewhat expected, since students will always perform at different levels. But what does it all mean? How should the principal and teachers interpret this information to determine if the new core curriculum is actually working? How will they know if it's meeting the needs of enough of their students?

This is where screening assessments come in. Screening assessments can be thought of as quick measures that flag students who may need additional instruction. They are brief, economical tests that provide a snapshot of how each student is doing in the target area. Some examples include the Dynamic Indicators of Basic Early Literacy Skills (DIBELS; *www.dibels.org*) and AIMSweb (*aimsweb.com*). DIBELS provides a series of screening assessments in reading, and AIMSweb includes a series of screening assessments in reading, written language, and math. Both systems offer measures for assessment and ways to analyze the information.

Typically requiring a few minutes per student, screening measures act as a first catch for students who may need additional support. These measures provide critical pieces of information that, when combined with other sources of data like state assessments and end-of-unit tests, provide a detailed picture of which students require support. This combination of data indicates who needs assistance and validates which students are doing well.

When coupled with a framework for decision making, universal screening assessments place schools in a position for success. A decision-making framework is important for several reasons. First it details clear guidelines of how to interpret the data. Second it provides guiding questions that help school teams decide what steps to take next. Finally it prompts educators to continuously review the data and determine what worked, what didn't, and how further educational needs should be addressed.

One way of thinking about data comes from Brown-Chidsey and Steege (2005). This framework emphasizes prevention, rather than just intervention, and systems, rather than just individual students. It provides a way for schools to look at data, determine whether their core curriculum is working, and assess how many students require additional support. Their model of the three-tiered RTI triangle is shown in Figure 2.1 on p. 21.

The base of the triangle is the largest part and refers to the universal systems in place that are proactive and address the needs of *all* students. In academics this refers to the core curriculum in target areas like reading, math, or written language. In behavior this refers to the core curriculum or core expectations that you teach your students regarding how to behave in school.

Approximately 80% of students should be successful with the core curriculum. This means that 80% of students are at benchmark with the screening assessments and performing well on the end-of-unit tests. This also means that 80% of students are successful with the core behavioral program. This should be a goal for schools to work toward.

The middle part of the triangle represents those students who need additional support. There will always be students who require more instruction than the core curriculum offers to be successful. Between 10 and 15% of students require support at this level.

In academics, this may look like small-group instruction that is provided in addition to the core curriculum. In the area of behavior, this may look like additional social-skills instruction in addition to the schoolwide behavioral expectations.

The top part of the triangle represents those students who have the most intense needs. These are individual students who require extensive instruction and assessment of higher intensity and greater duration. Between 5 and 10% of students will require support at this level—it should be a small group of students.

If the data from your school indicate that the students requiring core, supplemental, and intensive instruction fall within the guidelines set above, then we know the core curriculum is working. It is meeting the needs of most of the students, and fewer students require supplemental and intensive support. If the data from your school indicate that larger percentages of students require supplemental and intensive instruction, this may indicate that the core curriculum is not working for your students.

If your school data indicate that 20% or more of students need additional support, then it becomes time to ask and answer some serious questions. If it's not working, why is it not working? What are we missing? Should we change the core curriculum? If so, what components do we look for in a new core program? How do we know if the new core we select will work for our students? Consider the following elementary school.

George Washington Elementary uses a collection of screening assessments in reading to gather data on their students three times during the year. It is September, and the teachers have just received the printouts of their students' fall data. Individually, teachers review the data to determine (1) whether it validates what they are seeing in the classroom and (2) what percentage of students in their class require additional support to remediate low skills or support advanced skills.

The principal looks at the data from a larger view. She reviews the data for each grade level and is able to determine for what grade levels the core curriculum is working. She knows that if around 80% of kids are successful in that grade, the core is doing its "job" by meeting the needs of most of the students. At this benchmark period in September, at least 80% of students in grades 1, 2, and 4 are meeting the criteria in reading. In grade 3 and 5, however, a larger percentage of students require supplemental and intensive support to be successful with the core curriculum.

The principal sets meetings with each grade level to review the data and participate in the decision making to organize the additional instructional groups. Her discussion with grades 1, 2, and 4 revolves around the logistics of grouping, planning and scheduling, and ensuring there is help for progress monitoring. A framework for the discussion may include the questions in Figure 3.1.

Grades 1, 2, and 4 meet as grade-level teams to discuss the student needs and determine who will be running additional groups in target areas like phonemic awareness and the alphabetic principle. The teachers each agree to take a group and provide instruction in addition to the core curriculum each week. For students who fall into the supplemental group, they receive an additional half-hour of instruction 3 days a week on top of their core instruction. For students who require intensive support, teachers meet with them for another hour of instruction 4 days a week.

The discussion with grades 3 and 5 looks different. The principal and grade-level teams have larger questions to consider. Because fewer than 80% of the stu-

- What skill areas do we need to target in the supplemental and intensive groups?
- What students will be placed in the supplemental and intensive groups?
- What teachers will teach what groups?
- When will the groups meet?
- How much time will students spend in the supplemental or intensive groups?
- How often will the groups meet?
- When will planning time for the supplemental and intensive groups occur?
- Who will monitor the students' progress?
- How often will the students' progress be monitored?
- When will grade-level teams meet to review the progress monitoring data?
- What criteria will be used to determine whether a student is making progress?
- What steps will be taken if data indicate that a student is not making progress?
- What steps will be taken if data indicate that a student has made significant progress?
- What additional support do my teachers need to implement the supplemental and intensive groups?

FIGURE 3.1. Questions to guide supplemental and intensive group planning.

dents' needs are being met through the core curriculum, the principal and teachers discuss whether the curriculum is actually working as it should be in addition to setting up supplemental and intensive groups. A framework for this discussion may include the questions in Figure 3.2.

The questions asked of grades 1, 2, and 4 are quite different from the questions asked of grade 3 and 5. For grades 1, 2, and 4, the goal is to organize and implement supplemental and intensive groups that will support low- and high-achieving students. For grade 3 and 5, however, the questions target the core curriculum itself. If our data indicate that it is not working, then why not? Can we change something to make it work better? And if not, then what do we consider in a new core curriculum?

These are not easy questions, but there can be easy answers. Evaluating the core can be simple in that school teams use data to determine whether it's working. The resulting action steps are where the process becomes more complicated, yet still doable. With an instructional vision of where students should be and ideas of how to get there, the process of evaluating the core becomes feasible for school teams.

- What content is covered well in the curriculum?
- What content is missing from the curriculum?
- Does the curriculum follow an organized progression?
- What does your instruction look like with this curriculum?
- Are you able to teach the program the way it was designed to be taught?
- Is there enough time to get through each of the lessons?
- Are you able to differentiate the lessons based on student needs?
- Do the assessments in the curriculum provide useful information to evaluate student performance and guide your instruction?

FIGURE 3.2. Questions to guide an evaluation of the core curriculum.

As we see in our current example, when using the 80–15–5 guidelines, one of three situations will result when a school team reviews the data. The possible outcomes are:

1. The data indicate that all grade levels have at least 80% of their students meeting grade-level benchmarks. The entire school is successful with the core curriculum.
2. The data indicate that all grade levels do not have at least 80% of their students meeting grade-level benchmarks. The entire school is *not* successful with the core curriculum.
3. The data indicate that some grade levels have 80% of their students meeting grade-level criteria and some grade levels do not. Some of the school is successful with the core curriculum, while some of the school is not.

In the first outcome, it is clear that most students are successful with the core across grade levels. While supplemental and intensive groups are still needed, most students perform well in the core curriculum. In the second outcome, it is clear that many students are not successful with the core across grade levels. A school in this situation would benefit most by changing their entire core curriculum, so students can be supported most efficiently. At George Washington Elementary, some grade levels were meeting the 80% criteria, while others were not. This represents the third outcome. Some grade levels are meeting expectations, but some grade levels clearly require more support. This poses more interesting questions than the first two examples.

The principal and school teams have a lot of issues to discuss when this is the case. Because the core curriculum works at some grade levels, the task is to determine what is missing in the other grade levels. Do the teachers need more support to make it work, or is the curriculum faulty at those grade levels? Can the teachers supplement the missing skills, or should the core be changed? A related question to consider is how well will a core program work if it is not consistent across grade levels. There can be some serious gaps in knowledge if the core changes from grade level to grade level. A better option may be to keep the core consistent, but supplement missing skills in the grade levels that need it. All of these questions have major implications for teachers and, more important, for students. These issues should be addressed by an instructional leader like the principal, curriculum coordinator, and content area specialists, and answered with data evaluated by the school team.

By using the data, school teams can identify the impact of the core curriculum and its level of success. And if the data indicate that the core curriculum is not successful, it becomes clear that the most effective and efficient step to take is to change the core curriculum. If this is the path that needs to be taken, school teams can use the following information to guide their decision in selecting a new core curriculum.

COMPONENTS OF CORE CURRICULA

A framework for thinking about how the core curriculum corresponds to instruction is important to consider here. While there are varying definitions and perspectives on these concepts, the remaining sections of this chapter are organized around the ideas of curriculum, instruction, and assessment. These three components form the basis for education.

Curriculum is defined as what we teach. It includes the skills, concepts, and applications that we convey to our students and is the crux of the content and material.

How we convey the information to students is our *instruction*. Instruction is defined as how we teach. Are the skills taught explicitly with repeated practice and review? Or are the skills imparted in a student-directed manner, where students discover the ideas on their own? Considering the goal of the lesson is important when deciding what teaching methods to use.

Finally, *assessment* allows us to answer the question "Is what we are doing working?" Assessment can take many forms, including chapter tests, curriculum-based measurements, standardized state tests, and criterion-referenced tests. Measures like these should be used according to what information is being sought. Matching assessments to instruction is important so that data are used to address student needs and guide further instruction.

SELECTING A NEW CORE

Greenview Elementary was up for a reading adoption. With funds to purchase a new reading program, the adoption team began searching for a curriculum. Based on programs used in nearby districts, and what they had heard was "good," the adoption team invited publisher representatives to speak at a half-day inservice for the teachers. The representatives came to the school, presented on their programs, and were available afterward to talk with the teachers. The teachers appreciated that they could view the programs themselves and ask questions of the representatives. It was also nice to hear directly from the representatives and be assured that their program was "research based" and would work with the population at their school. There were a lot of good materials, and each teacher preferred one program over another for different reasons. Once all the teachers had learned about each of the programs, they were given the opportunity to vote. Each teacher placed a vote for one curriculum. At the end of the day, the principal counted the votes. The curriculum with the most votes was to be the one that they purchased. The vote was close, but one program surpassed the others, and the principal placed an order with the publisher the next day. A new core curriculum would arrive in a few weeks. Overall, this was an easy way of getting teacher input and ensuring that everyone felt like their voices were heard. The principal was satisfied with the outcome and happy that his teachers were content. But this made some people think, "What if this curriculum doesn't help our kids?" and "How do we know if we selected the right one?" These questions circulated throughout the school, causing more people to wonder whether they really had made a good decision. How would they know? They decided to wait and see how their kids were doing once the new curriculum was up and running. Then they might be able to tell whether the new program was effective. But that was something they weren't going to think about until next year.

Buying a new core curriculum is no small task. It takes time, resources, energy, and research to begin the process of reviewing programs and determining which ones best meet the needs of your kids. In a day that is already strapped for time and resources, how do schools decide how to buy a new curriculum without a clear direction? Sometimes a situation like the one described is what happens. Teachers are given the chance to select what they want based on what is made available to them. Other times, the school creates an adoption team that spends a year reviewing curricula, looking at the research. And there are times when curriculum coordinators make the decision based on their knowledge, philosophies, and background.

In each situation, every individual has good intentions. But without a match to student needs, a "research-based program" can be inefficient, or worse, ineffective in teaching students core skills. Because it can take a while to be fully implemented, it can be a few years before the school staff realize that kids are still struggling. And with another adoption year far away, the question becomes, "What do we do now?"

This question guides the following discussion. This chapter details what to look for in a core curriculum and the critical components that should exist in the program. These characteristics are important and necessary and should be reviewed in the selection of a new program. Yet these are not the only factors to consider when adopting a new curriculum. The curriculum should connect to student needs and act as a tool that works for your student population.

Think of the issues above as the initial selection criteria. These components need to exist in the curriculum, so it can pass the first stage of your selection process. Once that is completed, you can move on to looking at student data and finding a program that meets your school's instructional needs. But first, let's start with the essential pieces that should be in a core curriculum.

Effective core curricula provide evidence of efficacy, describe explicit instructional strategies, outline scheduling procedures, explain how to differentiate lessons, include multiple opportunities for practice, and provide assessment tools to measure student performance and growth. Appendix 3.1 (at the end of this chapter) provides a worksheet that can be used to review different curricula.

EVIDENCE OF EFFICACY

Evidence of efficacy addresses the question "Does this program work?" As core curricula are designed, they can be tested with a variety of student populations and their results analyzed in many ways. With the push for scientifically based research, there are stricter standards and higher expectations for the studies that are conducted in piloting new core programs.

It is important to ensure that the curricula are tested using carefully designed experimental studies. Experimental studies should be rigorous in their design and analysis of results. The What Works Clearinghouse, a division of the U.S. Department of Education's Institute of Education Sciences, was developed to provide educators and researchers with a source of scientific evidence of what works in education. They utilize a variety of strategies to assess the research behind curriculum programs.

The first component they assess is the study's design. The ideal design is a randomized control trial study. A randomized controlled trial (RCT) is an experiment in which investigators randomly assign eligible subjects (or other units of study, e.g., classrooms, clinics, playgrounds) into groups to receive or not receive one or more of the curricula that are being compared. The results are analyzed by comparing outcomes in the groups.

Another important component of the research is ensuring that the two groups used in the study were comparable before the curriculum was tested (e.g., the two groups performed similarly on assessments at the beginning of the study). For example, both groups would receive similar scores on a series of reading assessments before the study occurred so that the effects of the reading curriculum can be attributed to the instruction, not previously existing differences in performance in the two groups. There are other characteristics that are analyzed as well; these can be found at *ies.ed.gov/ncee/wwc*.

Once the reviews have been completed, the What Works Clearinghouse categorizes the curriculum and gives it a rating. "Meets Evidence Standards" are RCTs that do not have problems with randomization, attrition (participants leaving the study), or disruption to the study's procedures. "Meets Evidence Standards with Reservations" are studies that have comparison groups and meet other What Works Clearinghouse evidence standards, but may have some randomization, attrition, or disruption problems. "Does Not Meet Evidence Screens" are studies that provide insufficient evidence of causal validity or are not relevant to the topic being reviewed.

In summary, curricula are analyzed and reviewed using a series of criteria. Some programs reveal strong results, indicating sufficient evidence of effectiveness. Other programs have weaker results or inconclusive data. Once the data behind the program are reviewed, district teams can make appropriate decisions about which core program is valid, reliable, and supported by the evidence.

Our intent is not to provide a list of "research-based" programs, but rather direct you to resources to use when considering a new core curriculum. There are many programs available, and what is important is matching your core to your student needs. More of these resources are provided at the end of the chapter.

TEACHING WITH FIDELITY

Once a decision for a new core curriculum has been made, the next step is essential for it to be effective: teaching the program the way it was intended to be taught. What this means is that each component of the program is taught the way it is described in the teacher's manual. Known as intervention fidelity, this refers to teaching with accuracy; that is, content is instructed exactly the way it was designed in the curriculum. This helps to ensure that the positive results from the research studies will also be demonstrated in the student population at your school.

Addressing each component of the core curriculum is important and necessary to achieve the desired outcomes. If your school has gone through the process of selecting a new core program that has sufficient research to support it, you want to ensure that you'll see the same results at your school. That is why it is critical to discuss the importance of teaching the curriculum the way it was designed. This helps to ensure that all kids are exposed to the same research-based curriculum.

Teaching with fidelity is similar to following a recipe for baking a cake. When baking a cake, you use specified amounts of flour, sugar, baking soda, vanilla, eggs, and oil. You follow the recipe closely, knowing that adhering to the directions will help you create a better cake. To ensure that you're following it as outlined, you use measuring cups and spoons, leveling off any excess. You mix the batter so it's consistent throughout. You find the right type of pan so the cake will cook evenly, and you select the right oven temperature and the correct cooking time to help bake the cake correctly. You know that by doing all of these things, you will get the cake you want. If you were to change an ingredient, alter the amount of an ingredient, mistake the cooking temperature or time, or not mix the batter well, the cake will not be as good. The success of your cake depends on following the directions exactly, because that has been proven to work in the past.

The same is true for teaching the core curriculum. There are multiple ingredients, an outline of what to teach first and what to add next, specified amounts of skills, time to practice, and ways to ensure that you are helping the students learn and generalize those skills. Following the core as it's outlined will help ensure that your students are learning. Changing an ingredient of the core may alter the outcome and affect student performance. Therefore, following the core curriculum is important to help you achieve your goals as a teacher: increased student success.

INSTRUCTIONAL METHODS

Explicit instruction is direct, straightforward, and clear. It means fully demonstrating the concepts and providing all of the necessary information so nothing is implied. The teacher instructs each part of the lesson by telling students exactly what the skill is, how to use it, and how to apply it to what they already know.

The key components of explicit instruction are that (1) materials are broken down into small steps and arranged into a prerequisite order, (2) the objectives are clearly stated and related to student performance, (3) students are provided opportunities to connect new knowledge to what they already know, (4) practice activities are embedded in each lesson, (5) students receive additional practice activities that promote independence, and (6) feedback is provided after each practice opportunity. It is a direct approach, one that provides a structure based on a systematic progression of skills.

This teaching method has been found to be effective (Carnine, 1976; Darch & Gersten, 1985; Gersten, Carnine, & Williams, 1982; Bock, Stebbins, & Proper, 1977; Watkins, 1997). Because it is direct and explicit, students are instructed on exactly what they need to know. Students benefit greatly from instruction that clearly provides the goal for each task, informs them exactly what to do, and provides multiple practice opportunities to apply new knowledge and connect it to previously learned skills.

While explicit teaching strategies help many students, it is important to remember that the curriculum should be matched to student needs. Thus higher-performing students may not require the explicit level of instruction that benefits average and lower-performing students. Above-average students can benefit from an inquiry-based approach, where they are guided in their learning and taught to explore skills and ideas. This model encourages discovery and inquiry, rather than simply learning the concepts.

SCHEDULING

Scheduling is an important facet of the core curriculum, as it addresses the main issue that teachers face: time. Time is critical to achieve instructional goals, yet it seems that there is never enough. With that in mind, it is important to consider the correspondence between the time allotted for core instruction and the time designated for each lesson in the core curriculum. For example if the core curriculum designates that 60 minutes per day is required for each lesson and there are only 45 minutes devoted to reading each day, there will not be enough time to teach the curriculum with fidelity. Allotting adequate time to cover all of the content is important to ensure positive outcomes in your students.

In addition, there are issues of time to consider when planning supplemental and intensive interventions. While most students should respond well to core instruction, no matter how great the core curriculum is, there will always be 10–15% of students who require additional support. RTI is organized around the use of effective practices at every tier. In this way, it is a "value-added" model of instruction, but there must be additional time for the interventions, so students requiring extra support can access it on a daily basis.

Time is one of the most important factors in determining positive student outcomes and often is a scarce resource in schools. It is a powerful factor in instruction and can propel students to great lengths or inhibit their progress over the course of the year. With assemblies, early outs, late starts, field trips, and other activities that arise throughout the year, it is apparent that time is not on our side. With a finite number of hours in the school day, it is important to prioritize. This means having conversations with district administrators and school teams that address the needs of the student population and the required time to encourage growth in academic areas.

DIFFERENTIATION

As mentioned earlier, teaching the curriculum as it was designed is very important in achieving strong student outcomes. This is not to say that every student needs to receive the same exact instruction. Differentiating the content, process, and products to meet varying student needs is critical to student success. With different students performing at different levels, it is important to think about how the core curriculum is designed so it can meet a range of needs.

Differentiation is defined by *Webster's* dictionary as a "discrimination between things as different and distinct." It is a way of creating differences in curricular experiences and providing multiple options for learning, that is, a method of taking the core curriculum and making it work for a variety of students. And it provides a framework for giving every student the opportunity to learn at a high rate and progress toward greater skill acquisition.

By matching instruction to student needs, differentiation also does a wonderful thing for the classroom environment: it helps manage classroom behaviors. For those kids who get bored because the task is too easy, or for those kids who act out because the task is too difficult, tailoring content to their level can help keep them interested and engaged. Students will feel competent and able to complete the task at hand, which will increase their motivation to learn. They will feel more supported in the classroom and better able to meet their learning goals.

Although differentiation can do a lot for the classroom, it can also still appear like a lot of work. It takes time, energy, and effort at the outset of each lesson to consider how to differentiate the content, how it will be taught, and how student skills will be assessed. "When do I have the time?" is surely something teachers are thinking. "How will I know how to do this for each different lesson?"

Some of it is obvious. For example, for a third-grade student who is reading at the sixth-grade level, it would be a poor use of his time to read grade-level materials. So the teacher might find sixth-grade-level materials so that student can complete the tasks at a level that is challenging and interesting for him. In contrast, a first-grade student may be struggling with number sense. Instead of asking her to complete one to five addition facts, the teacher will work with her on learning the numbers 1 through 5 first. Yet, not every situation is this easy.

In a solid core curriculum, ideas and strategies for differentiation will exist throughout, providing insight into how exactly to vary the tasks and match the strategies to different levels of need. Ideas for changing the material to match students' abilities will assist with differentiating the content. Strategies to match the complexities of the tasks to students' current levels of understanding and skill will assist with differentiating the process. Methods of varying the complexity and structure required for communicating learning will assist with differentiating the product.

What to look for, then? The first thing to look for in a core curriculum that will help with differentiation is consistent ways to assess students. Inevitably, students will progress at different rates, regardless of the level at which they start. There should be a way to gather that data and use it to form student groups that are flexible and can change over time. Katie and Doug may start out in the same instructional group, but if Doug makes faster progress than Katie, he can easily move up to the next group.

Another important aspect to look for with regard to differentiation is multiple ideas for small-group teaching activities. Small-group activities will allow students to be with similar-performing peers and be able to learn at an appropriate instructional level. At an appropriate instructional level, students know some of the content, but not all of it. It is not difficult to the point of frustration, but it is not so easy that they become bored. You want students to be ready to learn the content because they have enough background, but they should have enough questions to need to learn more.

Finally, there should be a variety of individual alternatives for instruction. For students who are ready to accelerate, there should be an option for them. For students ready for the next lesson, they should move on to it with ease. And for students who need additional practice, there should be review options before they have to move on. In this way, all students' needs are met efficiently, because the core curriculum provides many options and, as the teacher, you are not spending all this time creating these ideas on your own.

OPPORTUNITIES FOR PRACTICE

Each student needs time and opportunities to practice the skills he or she learned in each lesson. During this time students are reintroduced to the skills, as they practice what they just learned. This time, in fact, is critical because this is when students begin the move from the instructional level to the mastery level. Here, they will master their skills and begin to incorporate them into other activities and tasks in the classroom and outside of school. This is the point at which it can all come together, if there is enough time and opportunity allotted for it.

Multiple opportunities for practice are essential to a core curriculum. These opportunities should also vary in their design, format, and length. Practice activities should be included that fall anywhere on the continuum from individual to large group, written response to oral response, and entire class period to a few minutes in length. By providing a variety of practice options, teachers can tailor the type and number to student needs.

An important aspect of practice to consider is that it does not need to occur only in one part of the day. For example practice is not limited to practicing only within the lesson. In fact, distributed practice, or practice that occurs throughout the day in short bursts, can be very effective in helping students acquire and maintain their skills. This method of providing practice opportunities can actually be more effective than longer periods at a time, because students are exposed to more opportunities overall.

This is exciting to think about, considering the time constraints in a typical school day. Often there is not time to practice new skills for half an hour at a time in each subject area. Instead, teachers can find the small moments throughout the day to rehearse a new vocabulary word, review a new math fact, or rehearse the main parts of a story. These reviews are brief but frequent, which gives them their power. They are also very student friendly, because they are quick. Consider using these small moments during the day to review a newly learned skill. Figure 3.3 provides a list of brief times when practice can happen.

- First thing in the morning
- Standing in line
- Transition from desk to small group
- Coming back from lunch or specials
- Out the door as they leave for home
- Study hall
- Other subject areas (i.e., science and social studies)

FIGURE 3.3. Opportunities for practice.

ASSESSMENT

Take a moment and think of the assessments you currently use in your classroom. Which ones do you like? Which ones make you cringe? Do you get useful information? Are you able to use the data to guide your instruction? Are you unsure of why you're giving them? Do you know what you're supposed to be getting out of them? Think about why you like the tests that you do and why you dislike the ones that you don't. What distinguishes your assessments from falling into the "waste of time" category or the "useful" category?

Assessment is often a dirty word in education. While it has its advantages, many teachers feel it takes too much time away from their instruction, thereby moving the focus from teaching to testing. With so many assessments to give, it quickly becomes overwhelming to fit all of the instruction in as well.

Why *are* we giving all of these tests, anyway? Part of the reason is to meet state and federal requirements. Part of the reason is to examine students by state, district, and school to determine who is in need and who is doing well. Part of the reason is to examine growth over time, to see increases or decreases in performance of students as a whole.

Assessments can be divided into four categories. Screening, diagnostic, progress monitoring, and outcome/accountability form the main framework for thinking about assessments. Each has its own purpose, design, and results.

Screening assessments help us answer the question "Is there a problem?" Screening measures are typically administered to all students. They are brief, economical tests that provide a snapshot of how each student is doing in the target area. Typically requiring a few minutes per student, screening measures act as a first catch for students who may need additional support. They also alert teachers to students who may need accelerated support. Screening measures are sensitive to academic skills and serve as indicators of performance. Because screening measures are quick, simple tools, they also provide room for teacher judgment. If the measure itself did not pick up on a student needing additional or accelerated support, teachers provide input, and these students can be further tested to obtain more information. They act as the thermometer of the education world. Screening measures, like thermometers, assess a small part of the whole picture. They provide an indication that something is wrong, but don't tell you what exactly needs to be fixed.

Diagnostic assessments help us answer the question "What is the problem?" Now that a screening has been done, students can be organized into accelerated, benchmark, strategic, and intensive groups. For those students who need additional support, diagnostic measures help us determine what exactly they need to work on to increase their performance in the target area. Diagnostic assessments are detailed, specific, and allow for flexible administration.

Depending on how the student is doing, you can test more here, less there, to refine and pinpoint exactly what skills they need to work on. For example in reading, a diagnostic assessment might tell you that the student needs to work on vowel teams in isolation and consonant digraphs in real words. In math a diagnostic assessment can inform you that the student needs additional help with multiplying a two-digit number by a one-digit number with regrouping. And in written language, a diagnostic assessment can indicate that the student needs support with punctuation, specifically commas.

Once we know what the problem is, we can provide the "treatment" or intervention that he or she needs. As time passes, though, we start to wonder whether what we are doing is working. How will we know? This is where progress monitoring assessments come in. They allow teachers to answer the question "Is the instruction successful?" Progress monitoring measures are brief and economical, like screening measures, because they are quick tools that are used over time to document growth.

In fact, progress monitoring measures can be the same format as used in the screening assessments. This means that the screening and progress monitoring measures often are different forms of the same test. These forms are created to be of similar difficulty level, so teachers can provide students with a different assessment but track progress over time. Because they are brief, they provide teachers with immediate information on how a student is doing.

An important feature of progress monitoring measures is that they are sensitive to small growth over time, so little changes in performance can easily be determined. Typically, teachers give these measures once a week or once every other week to document change in performance. If there is an increase in student skills, then the teacher has evidence that the targeted instruction is working. If there is a decrease in performance, then the teacher has evidence that the instruction needs to be changed. More information about specific progress measures and how to understand student performance is found in Chapter 4, on progress monitoring.

Now that we've evaluated the individual student through diagnostic and progress monitoring assessments, we can get back to the big picture. Outcome assessments help us answer the question "How well are we doing overall?" Outcome measures help schools evaluate general outcomes and accountability requirements. These are "high-stakes" tests that are administered to all students, and results are used to determine performance for state and federal requirements. Because these results are important and have a huge impact on schools, outcome tests are typically strong in their design. What this means is that they have gone through an extensive development process to ensure that the tests measure what they are supposed to and are consistent among test items, administrators, and over time. Thus they have strong reliability and validity, so schools can trust the results and use the information confidently.

These tests reflect a general outcome; that is, they provide a picture of how everybody is doing overall. They have the capacity to inform teachers of how well their class is doing, the principal of how the school is performing, and administrators of how the district is performing overall. This provides a general idea of where you are as a whole, and what steps might be taken to further improve results or remediate difficult areas.

PROFESSIONAL DEVELOPMENT

Now that we've reviewed the essential components of a core curriculum, it is important to address the practical issues of implementation. The importance of structured, systematic professional development to support a new core curriculum cannot be overstated.

To be able to teach a new program well, you have to be taught all the components, be given ample time to practice, and have the opportunity to ask questions and review the materials in depth. This will help to ensure that you know what is expected with the new curriculum and how you can teach it in your classroom.

All too often, a new core curriculum is purchased, and there is one day or less of professional development for teachers. After one day of training in May, for example, teachers are expected to come back in August and be ready to go with the program. Although this is feasible, it is not ideal. Without more time to review the materials and practice over time, it is easy to forget what exactly to do. As we become more familiar with the curriculum it becomes more natural. But until that point, teachers may struggle to determine what exactly to do and how to do it. It is in this interim that student progress can be affected.

Therefore, in an effort to lessen teachers' anxiety and prepare them with the skills they need, there should be multiple opportunities to practice and review the new curriculum. This can occur over a series of afternoons, a few full-day meetings at the end of the school year, or whatever works best with the school schedule. There is no specified length of time that will work with every curriculum within different schools. The more time teachers have to practice, the more knowledgeable they will be, which will result in higher student outcomes.

CONCLUSION

In a school day packed with activities and a school year strapped for time, selecting a core curriculum that is both effective and efficient is important. A program that meets student needs, provides time for practice and opportunities for differentiation, and is based on research is a lot to consider, but it's necessary for student success. It is a combination of components that, when coupled with your instruction, will support student performance and growth.

By design, the core curriculum is provided to all students and should meet most of their needs. If school data indicate that it is not meeting student needs, there are some decisions that need to be made. Do we keep doing what we're doing and hope for success? Or do we make significant changes to our practices to ensure student achievement? The latter question should be easily answered, but often is not because of the extensive process required to select and implement a new core curriculum.

With the guidance of an instructional leader, and a team armed with the knowledge and ability to spend the time, schools can easily take the information from this chapter and begin to carefully and pointedly ask questions, find answers, and make decisions about the core. The core curriculum should be a powerhouse. It needs to be a solid, comprehensive, detailed program that will guide your instruction and create gains in student growth. It will make your life easier. You will have less individual preparation and you won't have to reinvent the wheel for each class. You will know it will work for most of your students, be confident that your time is well spent, and understand that your day-to-day teaching is based on a program that will help your students succeed.

RESOURCES

Access Center: Improving Outcomes for All Students K–8

www.k8accesscenter.org

The mission of the Access Center is to provide technical assistance that increases awareness of research-based programs, practices, and tools; strengthens the ability of educators to be informed consumers of programs, practices, and tools; and helps educators implement and evaluate programs, practices, and tools.

Big Ideas in Beginning Reading

reading.uoregon.edu

This website is designed to provide information, technology, and resources to teachers, administrators, and parents across the country. It includes definitions and descriptions of the research and theories behind each of the big ideas, describes how to assess the big ideas, gives information on how to teach the big ideas including instructional examples, and finally, shows you how to put it all together in your school.

Florida Center for Reading Research

fcrr.org

The mission of this center is to conduct basic research on reading, reading growth, reading assessment, and reading instruction that will contribute to the scientific knowledge of reading and benefit students in Florida and throughout the nation. The website provides excellent resources for teachers, administrators, and parents, including implementation guides and student center lesson activities.

National Association of State Directors of Special Education

www.nasdse.org

NASDSE offers support through a range of activities, including targeted training to address current issues, technical assistance, policy analysis, research, cutting-edge publications, specialized websites, national initiatives, and collaborative partnerships to enhance problem solving at the local, state, and national level.

There are a number of resources for evaluating the core curriculum in reading. The Big Ideas in Beginning Reading website, *reading.uoregon.edu*, offers a consumer's guide for evaluating the core curriculum in reading in grades K–3. The Florida Center for Reading Research provides important considerations for core curriculum in reading. In the areas of math and written language, there are fewer resources available, but the What Works Clearinghouse (*ies.ed.gov/ncee/wwc*) offers data on a variety of programs in reading and math.

Core Curriculum Review

	Exceeds standards	Meets standards	Below standards	Does not provide enough information
Evidence of efficacy				
Instructional procedures				
Fidelity components				
Scheduling and time				
Differentiation strategies				
Practice opportunities				
Assessments				

CHAPTER 4

How Are the Kids Doing?
Progress Monitoring Is Not Optional

This chapter is about how to monitor student progress to see whether a student *responds to intervention*. This chapter will describe what, why, how, and when to conduct progress monitoring as part of RTI activities. You'll need regular progress data to see whether your intervention is working.

PROGRESS MONITORING RESOURCES ON THE INTERNET

As you read this chapter, an excellent resource to be aware of is the National Center on Student Progress Monitoring. This is an Internet-based resource center with many types of information about progress monitoring. The website is *www.studentprogress.org* and resources from this site are referenced in this chapter.

WHAT IS PROGRESS MONITORING?

Progress monitoring includes frequent assessment of the skills you're teaching. The purpose of progress monitoring is to see whether interventions provided to students are effective. It's similar to checking a patient's temperature to see whether she is getting better. It's a quick way to see if we need to keep doing what we're doing or change something. And here's something to think about for later … which patient would the nurse check more frequently? The one with a temperature of 100 degrees or the one with a temperature of 104 degrees?

One of the benefits of progress monitoring is identifying differences within groups. For example when you progress monitor all five students in your reading group you may find that four of the students respond very nicely and one does not. This gives you additional information about that one student because he or she looks significantly different from the others in the group. You will use this information to guide your next decision on reorganizing the group and answering the question: What will you give that one student who clearly needs something different?

Progress monitoring has the advantage of providing useful information early in the course of instruction. You will have plenty of time to make changes and see students' growth when you monitor their skills several times a month. The more traditional model of using end-of-the-year tests leaves us with no time to make changes. For example by the time you find out that the student can't pass the comprehension section of the test, it really is too late to make changes to his instruction. We should probably call this the "too little, too late" model.

Progress monitoring uses *formative assessment* to check on student progress. Formative assessment includes many small "tests" of student performance over time. By measuring student skills on a regular basis over time, formative assessment allows teachers to have a current picture of student progress. Formative assessment is different from *summative assessment*, which is most traditionally used in schools. Summative assessment comes at the end of a period of learning, most often in the spring of a school year or at the end of a program of study (e.g., high school completion). Summative assessments tend to be big tests that include a wide range of information covered over a long period of time. Although summative assessments tell what information your students have mastered for the year, they do not provide teachers with the chance to change instruction for students who fail them. By the time the teacher and student get the results of a summative assessment, the opportunity to change instruction to help the student master the knowledge and skills has passed. By contrast, formative assessment includes many short tests that give the teacher frequent opportunities to adjust instruction to students' needs.

WHY USE PROGRESS MONITORING?

There are three major reasons to use progress monitoring: (1) to see whether a specific intervention is working, (2) to show students the outcomes of their learning and engage them in the intervention, and (3) to provide information about how best to change your instruction if needed.

Is the Intervention Working?

The first reason to use progress monitoring is to see whether your intervention is working. By gathering data weekly or every 2 weeks, you have a quick insight into whether your intervention is working. If the data show that your efforts are paying off, then keep the intervention in place until it's time to gradually remove it. If the data show that the intervention is not working, then you have a reason to do something else (National Center on Student Progress Monitoring, 2008).

Student Engagement in Learning

A second reason to use progress monitoring is to let students see the effects of their learning activities. In addition to the importance of your knowing whether an intervention is working, there is a benefit from having your students see whether it's working. Nancy Safer and Steve Fleischmann have shown that teachers who share progress monitoring information with their students have noticed that, in general, the students will work harder to make gains and improve their skills (Safer & Fleischman, 2005). Showing your students their own data during an intervention is just as important if an intervention is not working. Then the student can see for herself that something needs to change. When students and teachers review progress data together, they have a shared picture of whether an intervention is working. If it's not working, they can share ideas for a different approach.

Data Inform Instruction

A third reason to use progress monitoring is to identify potential instructional changes. Even when the progress data indicate that an intervention is not working as hoped, the data might offer you information about what to try next. For example the data may show that your student made some gains, but they were not high enough to meet the goal. In such a case your student probably needs more intensive instruction. Instructional intensity refers to the strength of lessons. The main ways to intensify instruction are by increasing the time, decreasing the size of the intervention group, or changing the instruction and refocusing on the skills that the student needs to be successful. We will talk more about these later. Some of your students may need much more intensive instruction in order to make the desired gains. When your student shows improvement above the starting point, it's clear that the intervention has helped. But if the student is still a long way from the goal, she may need more frequent or longer intervention sessions.

Intervention data can also show when a student is ready for instruction to be reduced (Powell-Smith & Ball, 2008). Once your student has met a learning goal and demonstrated maintaining the skill over a period of eight data points, she is ready for less instruction. Research has shown that when a student has demonstrated eight data points of sustained improvement above a learning goal, the intervention can be reduced. She has made progress and maintained it, so we can be confident that she is doing well.

Finally, data can suggest whether a student needs a totally different intervention. If your student made absolutely no gains during the intervention (and it was implemented with integrity), then it's a good bet that the student needs an entirely different type of intervention. Eight weeks have gone by, your student's data are still relatively low, and she has barely made any progress with the additional support. In these circumstances, we don't have time to waste. We don't want to continue to do something that's not working. So we make planned, thoughtful decisions based on data to guide our instruction for the next intervention. More information about the research on progress monitoring can be found in the Resources section at the end of this chapter.

HOW DO I USE PROGRESS MONITORING?

The steps for using progress monitoring are really very simple and will be explained in this section. If you are new to progress monitoring you may find yourself saying right now, "No way! They want me to do one more thing? There's no way I have time." If you are thinking this, please take a deep breath and read to the end of this chapter. Progress monitoring does not take much time, and it provides a great deal of information about students who are struggling in school. Indeed, progress monitoring can help you meet the needs of the students who keep you awake at night. Consider the following example.

Holly is a third grader with reading difficulties. On the fall universal benchmark screening, Holly scored 37 on oral reading fluency (ORF). The fall benchmark goal for third graders is 77. Based on her low score, her teacher arranged for her to participate in daily fluency intervention. The intervention was provided by a paraprofessional for 20 minutes each day. Holly's progress was measured with weekly ORF probes. At the end of 4 weeks, Holly's progress was reviewed by the third-grade team. Holly had scored 29, 31, 35, and 33 on the weekly measures. The team decided that the fluency intervention was not working for Holly. In order to know the best option for Holly, the team decided that it would be good to get additional assessment data. A brief survey level assessment was conducted to learn more about Holly's reading skills. The special education teacher administered the second- and first-grade DIBELS benchmark probes. The results showed that Holly had difficulty not only with fluency, but also with nonsense word fluency (NWF) and phonemic segmentation fluency (PSF). Holly's teacher arranged for Holly to participate in a different daily intervention group that focused on mastering sound–symbol correspondence. Holly's progress in her new intervention would be monitored using NWF measures.

Holly's situation shows how progress data are essential for knowing whether an intervention is working. There are five main steps to using progress monitoring (Johnson, Mellard, Fuchs, & McKnight, 2006): (1) selecting the progress measure; (2) choosing the person, time, and place to collect data; (3) collecting data weekly; (4) reviewing the data at regular intervals; and (5) making instructional changes based on the data.

Selecting the Progress Measure

The first step in progress monitoring is to decide what progress measure to use (National Center on Student Progress Monitoring, 2008). To be useful, the progress measure must assess a skill that the student is being taught as part of the intervention. For example if your student is participating in an intervention focused on mastery of multiplication facts to 9, the progress measure should include multiplication problems up to 9 times 9. If the progress measure includes other types of problems (e.g., addition to 10) it would not show the student's growth in the target skill. Sometimes your students will have many instructional needs. It's best to organize instruction so that easier skills are taught first, followed by more complex skills. In such cases, the progress measure will change as the students' skills develop. This is okay. Progress measures can and should change according to your students' instructional needs. When a student has many instructional needs, it's best to start with the most basic skill first and monitor progress in mastering that skill.

There are a number of published progress measures that you can use to monitor student progress. When a published measure is not available for the skill being taught, locally created measures can be used. Whether published or teacher-made, all progress measures need to have certain features to ensure that they are effective. A summary of the technical features needed for all progress measures can be found at the website of the National Center on Student Progress Monitoring (*www.studentprogress.org*). The core features that a progress measure must have are: reliability, validity, availability in alternate forms, sensitivity to student improvement in conjunction with adequate yearly progress (AYP) benchmarks, demonstrated links to improving student learning and teacher planning, and specified rates of improvement. In general, progress measures need to accurately measure the skill being taught. In addition, there must be enough equivalent versions of the measure to be used over time.

This may sound like a lot of requirements. It is. To accurately assess student progress, we must ensure that the measures we are using are technically sound. That way, we can focus solely on the effectiveness of the intervention, not whether the assessments are measuring what they are supposed to. So while making up your own progress monitoring assessments is something that some districts have done, it is much easier to use the forms that already exist. Save yourself the time and use the measures that have already been validated to work and are reliable so you can count on the results.

Generally, you will need about 20 equivalent forms of the measure so it can be used weekly. Published progress measures that meet the above standards are available for monitoring student progress in reading, spelling, writing, and mathematics. Some of these assessments must be administered with one student at a time (e.g, DIBELS), but others can be used with a group of students at one time (e.g., AIMSweb math computation). Some measures are available in a computer-based format.

An important thing to know about progress measures is that they are very short assessments. The published measures require a range of 1 to 3 minutes per student to administer. Progress measures can be very short tests because they are completed by students on a high-frequency basis. The high frequency of measures (e.g., weekly; more on that below), means that there are enough data points to determine the pattern in your student's performance over time.

Choosing the Person, Time, and Place to Collect Data

Once the specific set of progress measures for a student has been selected, you need to decide who will collect the data. You (the classroom teacher) are the best person to administer the progress measures. This is because such regular monitoring allows you to know whether your student is making progress in key areas. Since interventions can be provided by a range of personnel, you may not always be the one doing the intervention, but if you administer the weekly measures, you will always have updated information on your student's progress. This provides you valuable information sooner rather than later.

If for some reason you cannot administer the measures, other staff can administer them. Whoever does the monitoring must learn how to administer the measure accurately so the results will be useful. All of the published progress measures have detailed instructions for administration, and many of the measures have accompanying videos that can be used to learn accurate administration.

As noted, progress monitoring needs to happen weekly, during the intervention. Usually, it is best to collect progress data at that same time every week. This will allow you and your students to become accustomed to progress monitoring as part of school routines. Many teachers collect progress data on Fridays because it is the last day of the school week and represents the end of the week's learning. While Fridays may be convenient for some classes, there is no rule that all progress monitoring must happen on Fridays. The important thing is to keep the progress monitoring sessions at a consistent time in the week so that the time between progress data points will be similar.

Other teachers choose to collect data on different students on different days of the week. Three of your students may be monitored every Wednesday and the other three of your students may be monitored every Thursday. This is beneficial because you don't lose too much instructional time on one day. The monitoring is still consistent on specific days each week, yet you don't have to spend a large amount of time on one day monitoring all of your students. Choose the option that bests works for you, your students, and your schedule.

The best location for progress monitoring is wherever the student who needs to be monitored is located at the selected time. For example if you pick 1:15 P.M. on Tuesdays as the progress monitoring time for the class, it makes sense to conduct the monitoring where the students are. If the students who need monitoring are all in your classroom for reading instruction at that time, then you would set up a weekly routine for monitoring those students who need it. You would select a space in the classroom that is as quiet as possible and away from big distractions such as opening doors or noisy equipment. The space should be set up so that the students can arrive and depart the monitoring session easily and without disrupting other students. The space should allow your students easy access to any materials they need for the monitoring (e.g., progress graph, pencil).

Collecting Data Weekly

In order for progress monitoring data to be effective it needs to be collected at regular intervals. There is a direct relationship between how often data are collected and how quickly an intervention can be changed. In order to establish reliability of data, you need to have at least four data points from progress monitoring before the effect of the intervention is considered. For this reason, it is ideal if progress monitoring is conducted throughout the intervention. With weekly progress monitoring, the effect of an intervention can be reviewed after a 4-week time period.

Collection of weekly progress data is not a time-consuming process because progress measures are all brief assessments. Most published assessments take 3 minutes or less to administer. For measures that must be used with one student at a time (e.g., 1 minute ORF), the time you will need each week is equal to the number of students times the minutes for the test. For measures that can be used in groups (e.g., AIMSweb math computation), the amount of time you will need is the time allotted for the assessment plus scoring time. Ideally, not many students in each class will need progress monitoring (e.g., 15–20%). If your class has 25 students, this would mean that five of your students would be monitored each week. If your students use ORF as a progress measure, it will take you about 5 minutes to gather their progress data. Since you and the students would need to walk to the space for monitoring, it's reasonable to expect that the process can be completed in 8–10 minutes total.

There are two major ways that you can record student progress data. One is on a paper graph. The other is in a computer format. Paper graphs have the benefit of being inexpensive, easily reproducible, and easy for your students to fill out themselves. If you decide to use paper graphs, a reproducible blank graph for student data is included at the end of this chapter (see Appendix 4.1). You can copy it as often as necessary for recording student data. Recent editions of some progress measures can also be recorded on several different computer formats. Some measures include stand-alone data files that you keep on a computer. Other measures include Internet-based data management that you can access with a password. A few measures have the option of recording data directly onto a personal digital assistant (PDA) such as a PalmPilot device. These data are then transferred to a computer file.

As noted at the beginning of this chapter, there is a benefit to your students if they see and record their own scores. For this reason, it is recommended that, even if computerized recording tools are used, your students from grade 1 onward record their scores on a paper graph as well. The paper copy can serve as a helpful backup if the computer version is lost. If a student is absent on the progress monitoring day, you will need to decide whether to administer the measure on another day or mark the session as skipped. The good news is that if a session is missed, it's not going to be a big problem because another progress measure will be given the following week. Collecting weekly progress data ensures that you have continuous information about student performance. If you have a large number of students to monitor, you can collect the data every other week instead. This means that each student would be monitored twice a month. But remember, there's a relationship between how often you gather progress data and how soon you can review it.

Before we review how to make sense of student data, let's take a moment and review the major parts of a graph. Refer to Figure 4.1. You'll notice that there is a label on the X axis (horizontal line). This refers to time. Typically, we label this line by week, so we can plot data for each week that we collect it. If you are only monitoring some students once a month (the borderline students, who may be just below average), then you can label the X axis in months. The Y axis (vertical line) represents what you are measuring. You will label it and give it a scale. For example if you are measuring oral reading fluency, you can label it "words read correct per minute" and use a scale that increases by two points between each mark. If you are measuring math facts completed in 2 minutes, you can label it "num-

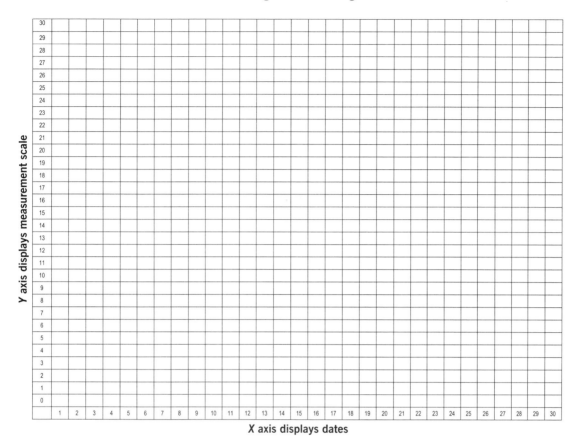

FIGURE 4.1. Sample graph.

ber of digits correct" and use a scale that increases by 1 point between each mark. Refer to Table 4.1 for the common ways that curriculum-based measurements are scored.

There are few hard and fast rules about selecting a scale for the *Y* axis. Most important, you want to ensure that the scale is sensitive enough so you can see change. On most curriculum-based measures, students do not typically increase their scores by very many points each week. This is not to say that it can't happen! Many students have made significant increases in their scores when they were exposed to the intervention that they needed. Large jumps in scores are possible, and we are excited when that occurs.

TABLE 4.1. Common Ways That Curriculum-Based Measurements Are Scored

Skill	How measured
Oral reading fluency	Words correct in 1 minute
Math computation fluency	Digits correct in 2 minutes
Spelling fluency	Correct letter sequences in 1 minute
Writing fluency	Number of letters or words written in 3 minutes
Silent reading (MAZE)	Number of correct word selections in 3 minutes

Yet most students increase their scores little by little each week. So creating a scale that increases by 1 to 3 points is a great way to see change in the data as it is graphed. If your scale on the Y axis instead increased by 5 points each interval, it would be more difficult to see the change visually. If our scale increased by 10 points each interval, it would be even more difficult, because our data points would be more clustered together. If the range of scores on the Y axis changes, the way that the data line looks is not the same. Examples of how data look according to differences in the Y axis scale are shown in Figures 4.2 through 4.4. Notice how the change in value from 40 to 100 in Figure 4.4 makes the student's progress line seem much "flatter."

Let's look at Figure 4.5. This graph is very similar to 4.2, but it includes more student data. We now will be looking at the main part of the graph: the data. We have the baseline or initial data points that indicate how the student was performing before the intervention. This provides a nice comparison when we start to plot the intervention data. Next we have two goal points to mark the goals for the student at the middle and end of the year. In this example there are 20 weeks shown to reflect the amount of school time between January and May. There is a goal line that connects these goals. It is always a diagonal line because students' skills should improve over the school year. Student data for baseline (before intervention) and intervention are shown. There are lines running through the student data; these are known as *trend lines*. Trend lines indicate the general direction (i.e., trend) of the student's scores. We can compare the trend lines with the goal line.

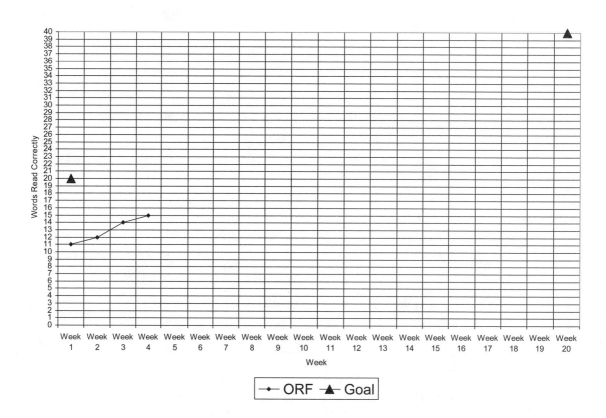

FIGURE 4.2. Sample graph with data plotted by 1's.

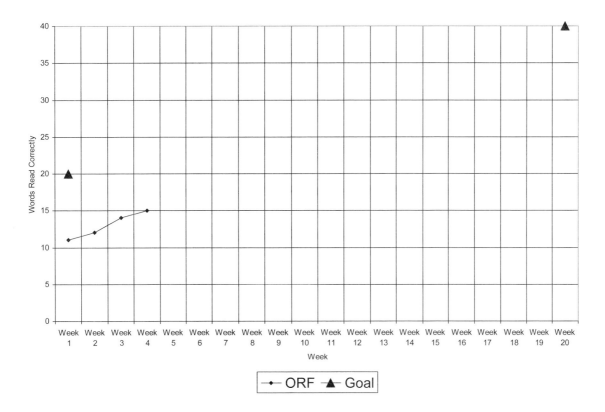

FIGURE 4.3. Sample graph with data plotted by 5's.

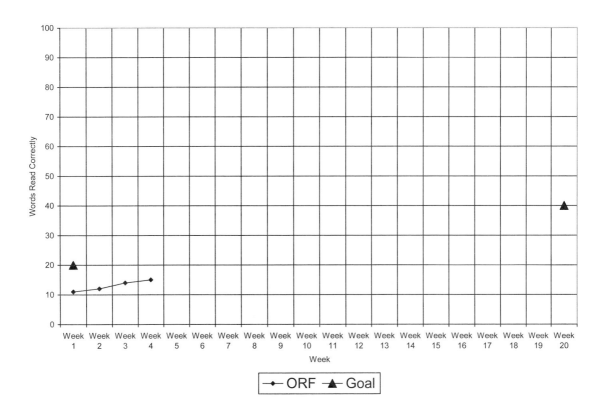

FIGURE 4.4. Sample distorted graph with larger Y axis range.

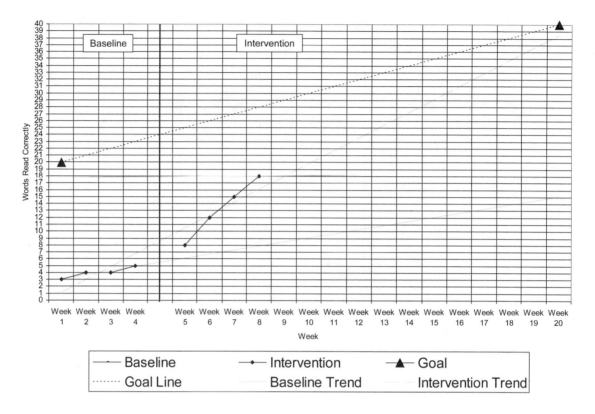

FIGURE 4.5. Sample graph with baseline, phase data, and trend lines.

Goal Lines

When you are progress monitoring in academics, the goal line is increasing, because we want our students to increase their academic skills. When you are monitoring progress in behavior, the goal line typically is increasing as well, as we monitor the development of prosocial skills. This is considered "best practice," because we want to write the goals positively, so we can monitor growth in a way where we see development. There are some situations, however, where school teams have decided to use a decreasing goal line when monitoring severe behaviors. These situations involve serious behaviors that are hurtful to the student or to other students in class. In the case of very severe behaviors, it can help to assess whether the behaviors are decreasing, because they are so dangerous. To complement the graph with the decreasing goal line, it is also a good idea to have a graph with an increasing goal line that monitors the development of prosocial behaviors. That way, two forms of data are collected to assess whether (1) the severe behaviors are decreasing and (2) positive behaviors are increasing in their place.

Next we refer to the vertical line separating the baseline data from the intervention data. This is known as a *phase change line*, which represents when there is a change in instruction. You will always have at least one phase change line to indicate the separation of the baseline data and the intervention data. You likely will have more phase change lines as well as more changes in instruction. For example, if you and the team notice that the intervention is not working, you likely will decide to change the instruction. A vertical phase change line will be included at this point to note that something different is occurring. Throughout the year, you may have a number of phase change lines. At the top of the graph, you can label the name of the intervention or type of instruction that was used. That way, it is easy to see between each phase change line what was done and why it was changed to something else. Multiple phases can be included on the same graph as long as the progress measure stays the same. For example if you try three different interventions for reading fluency, and keep using the same level of ORF measures to monitor progress, the data can go on the same graph. But, if you change the measure to a different grade level or another measure (e.g., NWF), you would need a new graph.

Baseline

The baseline phase shown on the graph includes all the data collected before an intervention was put into place. In research settings, the baseline data must be shown to be stable before the intervention can be started. Stability is shown by having enough baseline data points which are similar to each other. Having multiple similar baseline data points lets you know that the information is reliable. In everyday school practices, we can use smaller numbers of baseline data when we use measures that have been shown to be highly reliable over time. For example the DIBELS measures have been documented to be highly reliable predictors of student reading skills. For this reason, when we use measures such as the DIBELS we can have less baseline data. Many teachers use the student's scores on the fall DIBELS benchmark screening as the baseline. When the DIBELS benchmark scores are used as baseline, you can consider other data sources about the student as well. For example how do the DIBELS scores compare to your students' classroom work? If you are not sure whether the baseline data you have for a student is accurate, then the best thing to do is to collect a few more data points before you start the intervention. Once the data show that the student's scores are similar, it's time to start an intervention.

Goal Setting

In order to understand whether an intervention is working it is important to set specific goals for the student. There are several ways that student goals can be set. In reading, the DIBELS national database includes specific goals for grades kindergarten through 6. These goals are available for three time points in each school year: fall, winter, and spring. There are goals for each of the DIBELS measures matched to all five areas of reading. The DIBELS goals are known as "benchmarks" because they were developed with data from more than a million students in the United States. They offer a clear benchmark of what score a student needs to obtain in order to be on the path for reading success. There are also benchmarks available from AIMSweb for schools that use that system. Local goals can also be set; however, it's important to consider whether attainment of a local goal will be sufficient for the student to meet other learning standards such as passing the state exam.

It is important that the goal be written for the end of the school year. This is critical because it gives you time to make an impact with the instruction, and it gives the student the time she needs to make progress. Unfortunately, we haven't figured out how to work miracles yet and get all students to make huge gains in just a few weeks. The reality is that most students need more time to be exposed to the intervention, learn the new concepts, and take the time to make it part of their skill sets. With a longer-term goal, we give the students more time to receive the instruction that they need to make gains. In the example found in Figure 4.2, the goals show the winter and spring grade 1 ORF DIBELS benchmarks. The time between these goals is 20 weeks.

Being clear about the goal, as well as how to graph it, is important in order for progress data to be helpful. Imagine an end-of-year goal that is written for just 6 weeks out. We gather the data and record it on a graph. What do you think we will see? The goal line is steep because there are only 6 weeks for the intervention. Even though the student has made some progress, the trend line looks flat compared with the very steep goal. Does this mean the intervention was not effective? Possibly. This very well could be the case, and we would need to change the instruction. We don't want to waste any more of the student's time if she is performing so poorly and what we are doing is not working. Does this mean that the goal was set too high in too short an amount of time? Possibly. Our data indicate that the intervention was not effective because our expectations were steep for a shorter time period. So we change the intervention. It may be that the intervention was starting to work, but because the goal was so high, it looked ineffective. In such a case, it may help to identify an interim goal for the shorter time frame.

The point is that you can make data look very different depending on how they are displayed. It is important to consider what you know about the student, her needs, the intervention, and the time needed to see a change. Because we work in education and deal with students, it is not a hard and fast science. We have some rules we can apply based on the research, but we work with humans, not compounds in chemistry. This is something to keep in mind as you are plotting and evaluating the data. Our goal is to write the most accurate and appropriate goals, plot the data consistently, use the decision-making rule we decided on, and make decisions based on all of the information we know about the student. How you set up the graph can greatly influence the data and, ultimately, the decisions that are made about the student. With this in mind, we evaluate the data objectively and consider what we know to make the best and most appropriate decisions.

Reviewing the Data at Regular Intervals

It is helpful if progress data reviews are conducted by a team of teachers as part of school-wide RTI activities. The specific team that reviews the data may vary according to the procedures set up in your school. For instance in some larger schools, a team of all the teachers who teach the same grade will hold a data review meeting and discuss all their students who have received intervention. The grade-level team will consider whether the intervention is working and decide on the next course of action. If your student does not respond to a certain number of interventions, the data are then taken forward to the schoolwide team for review. In small schools, the schoolwide RTI team may be the first level of review and decision making. Your team has three main choices when reviewing progress data: (1) maintain the current program, (2) increase/reduce the current program, or (3) replace the current program with something totally different.

Once the data have been collected, the next step is to review the scores and consider what they mean. There need to be at least four data points before a review of your student's progress can happen. Once four data points are recorded, you can review the data and see whether the intervention is having the desired result. There are two ways to make sense out of student progress data: *counting the data points* and *trend line analysis*, discussed below.

Usually the first step in reviewing data is to compare your student's scores with the goal set for all students in that grade level. For example at the start of the first grade, the goal score on the DIBELS measure NWF is 13. By comparing your student's level to the goal we can learn how far away your student is from the goal. Is your student scoring a 12? If so, it is likely we will not be too concerned. Is your student scoring a 3? In this case, we would be concerned because it is clear she is performing very differently than her peers. She looks discrepant, and now we know we need to do something immediately.

Once we have looked at the student's baseline score(s), we next need to look at the rate of progress being made. The rate of progress is also known as the *slope*. Students who start the year well behind their classmates will never catch up unless they quickly increase their skills. In order to know whether your student's slope is adequate, look at the goal. For example, the first-grade end-of-year goal on NWF is 50. If you have a student who starts the first grade at the fall goal of 13, to meet the end-of-year goal, he or she would need to gain 1.2 points per week on the NWF measure. For a student who starts the year well behind, the rate of gain needs to be higher. For instance, if your student starts the first grade with a score of 0 on NWF, she or he would need to gain 1.7 points per week on the NWF measure. To help you make sense of whether your student's progress is enough you can choose to use one of the two ways of interpreting data: *count the data points* or look at the *trend line*.

Counting Data Points

This method is easy to use and works even if your student's scores are not stored on a computer. This method of checking student progress includes two steps. First you need to count how many of the student's intervention data points are above the baseline number(s). If all the intervention data points are above the baseline, that's a good sign. This means that the intervention led to an improvement in the student's skills. If the data points are all at or below the baseline, that's not so good. This means that the intervention did not have an effect on the student's skills. If more than half of the intervention data points are at or below the baseline, you need to change the intervention. If half or more of the data points are above the baseline, you need to figure out if the student's rate of gain (i.e., slope) is strong enough for him to reach the goal.

To calculate the slope, subtract the last baseline score from the ending intervention score and divide by the number of weeks that have passed. This will show the average number of points gained during each week of the intervention. Then multiply the average gain rate by the number of weeks left until the end of the year. The number you get will be an estimate of what score the student is likely to earn on the same assessment at the end of the school year. If the number you get is at or above the goal, then this intervention is working for the student and should be maintained. If the number is below the goal, then you need to change the intervention and keep monitoring progress. For the data shown in Figure 4.5, here's what the math would look like:

Last baseline data point = 5 words read correctly

Ending intervention data point = 18 words read correctly

Number of weeks of intervention = 4

Number of weeks remaining in the school year = 12

$18 - 5 = 13$

$13 \div 4 = 3.25$ (correct words gained per week)

$3.25 \times 12 = 39$ (estimated score on final ORF benchmark in spring)

For this student, the current slope is estimated to bring him very close to the end-of-year goal of forty words read correctly. It would make sense to maintain this intervention and continue progress monitoring. If the student's slope remains just shy of the goal of forty, a slight increase in intensity would make sense.

Trend Line Analysis

The other method for interpreting student progress is a trend line. The trend line is a prediction of future scores based on the progress data shown so far. It's possible to calculate trend lines by hand, and you can use this method to review student progress. Instructions for calculating a trend line by hand can be found at the National Center on Student Progress Monitoring website. But calculating trend lines is much easier if you use a computer. The DIBELS and AIMSweb data management systems calculate trend lines automatically. The Microsoft Office software Excel, as well as other spreadsheet softwares, will also calculate trend lines automatically for you. The advantage of using trend line analysis for interpreting progress data is that it provides a more precise indicator of whether the student is on track to meet his goal. In addition, a graphed trend line gives you an easy-to-understand visual aid for explaining student progress to parents and others. If the trend line indicates that your student will gain quickly enough to meet the future goal, then the current slope is strong enough. If the trend line indicates that your student will not meet the future goal, then increasing the slope becomes an important part of future intervention.

Figures 4.6 through 4.8 show sample graphs of student data. All three of the sample graphs show data for first-grade students who were identified as being at risk for reading problems using Tier 1 screening assessments. Specifically, all of these students scored

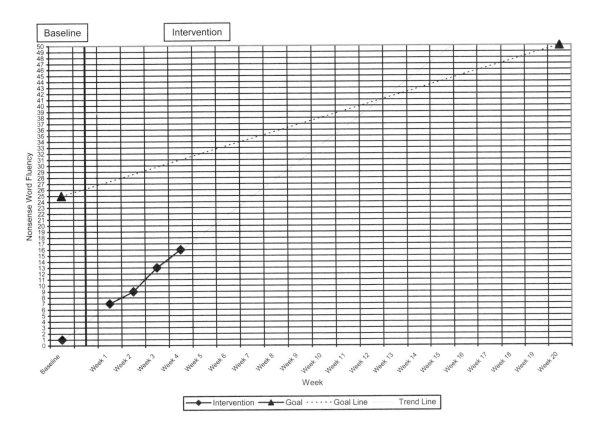

FIGURE 4.6. Example 1: Maintain instruction.

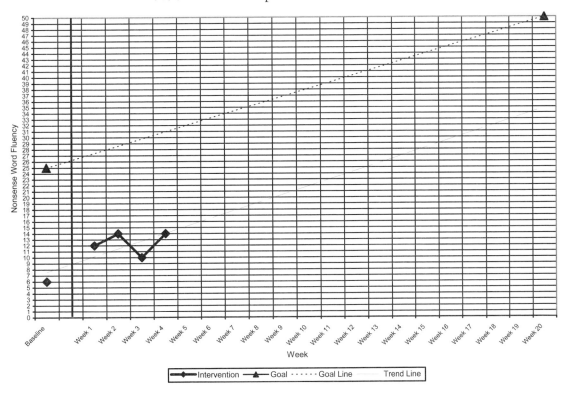

FIGURE 4.7. Example 2: Increase intensity.

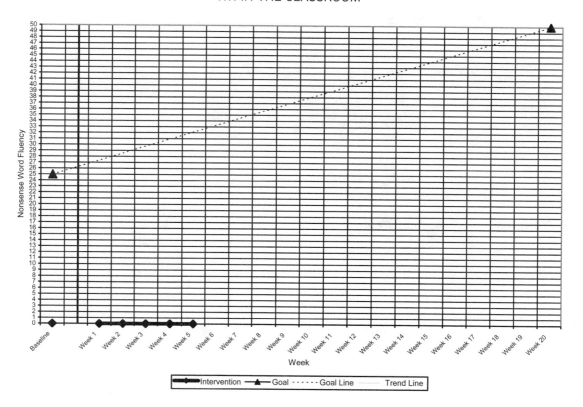

FIGURE 4.8. Example 3: Change intervention.

between 0 and 5 on the fall NWF measure. The students received a specific intervention for increasing their mastery of sound–symbol correspondence between letters and the sounds they make (phonemes).

Example 1 (Figure 4.6) shows a student who made progress with the initial intervention. The data points were all above the starting level and the slope (e.g., rate of progress) was strong enough to indicate that she would meet the year-end goal if this intervention was continued. The decision in this case was to continue the intervention. Eventually, a successful intervention will mean that the student meets the learning goal. If this happens before the end of the school year, the data review team can help the teacher to *reduce* the intervention until it is not needed any more. Once a student has scored at or above the goal for a period of eight consecutive data points (e.g., 8 weeks), it is time to fade the level of support for the student (Johnson et al., 2006). The easiest way to do this is to reduce the intensity of the intervention by decreasing the length of intervention sessions or the number of days each week that your student gets intervention. During the reduced intervention phase, weekly progress monitoring should still continue. If your student maintains scores at or above the goal once the lessons are reduced, the intervention should be removed completely.

Sometimes it is important to *increase* the intensity of an intervention. In the second example (Figure 4.7) the four data points show that the student made some progress during the first 4 weeks of intervention. Her progress data levels were all above the starting score, but the rate of progress (slope) was not high enough to estimate that she would meet the year-end goal if that intervention were continued.

In this case, the best choice for the team is to increase the intensity of the intervention. There are several ways that interventions can be intensified. The most common methods are to lengthen the daily sessions or, if the sessions are not daily, have them become daily so the student will receive intervention more often. If the intervention is already happening daily for a long period of time (e.g., 45 minutes), then it may be best to try a different intervention with the student. But since these data showed that the intervention did improve skills, it would be best to offer a more intense version before changing to another intervention.

The third choice a team has when reviewing intervention data is to change the intervention completely. This is appropriate when the data indicate that the current intervention has had no effect. Example 3 (Figure 4.8) shows data from a student for whom the initial intervention had no noticeable effect on the target skill. The student began the school year with a score of 0 on the NWF measure and continued to show the same score over a 4-week period of progress monitoring. In this case, there is no reason to think that this intervention is going to work for this student. The best choice for the team is to try a totally different intervention. Such a change could also be used if a student has been receiving the maximum "dose" of an intervention such as described above.

Making Instructional Changes Based on the Data

The final step in using progress monitoring is to make the needed instructional changes, if any. When your student's data show that the intervention is working, no change will be needed right away. But once your student has met the learning goal, it will be important to reduce the intensity of the intervention until it is removed completely. For your students who make some progress, but whose slopes are not strong enough to meet the goal, an increase in the intensity of the intervention is needed. Sometimes, the data will indicate that the intervention is just not working and a totally different one will be needed.

Once the progress data are reviewed and interpreted, a plan for implementing the instructional changes should be made. Unless an intervention is removed completely, you should still collect weekly progress data. In order to keep track of these instructional changes, you will want to record them on the paper graph and/or computer record. The same progress measure can be used as long as it still matches the instructional focus of the intervention. If a new progress measure is selected for your student, a new graph is needed. It is important for you to note an intervention change on an existing record with the phase change mark. Make a dark vertical line on the graph at the time point when the intervention changes. Then your student's new progress data can be added to the graph.

WHEN WILL I USE PROGRESS MONITORING?

We hope you have read this far in the chapter! We also hope that you can see the crucial importance of progress monitoring as part of RTI. Teachers who have used weekly progress monitoring as part of their teaching routines have come to view the student data as essential to how they teach and plan instruction. Once progress monitoring routines have been set up in the classroom, both you and your students will benefit greatly from the weekly data. In order to help you get going with progress monitoring, we offer a few other suggestions and steps: knowing which students to monitor, identifying times in your current schedule that would work for progress monitoring, and whether it's possible to replace other assessments.

Which Students Should I Monitor?

The good news is that not all students need weekly progress monitoring. Many (we hope) students in your class will be making fine progress with core instruction and thus will not need monitoring with weekly measures as described above. This leaves the students who participate in supplemental and intensive interventions, and all of these students need to be monitored regularly. Any student participating in supplemental (Tier 2) or intensive (Tier 3) intervention has a higher level of risk for school difficulties. For this reason, weekly progress monitoring is best. Such monitoring is similar to what a physician or nurse does if a patient has a specific condition elevating a health risk. If a patient has high blood pressure, a doctor will monitor that person's blood pressure much more often than patients with normal blood pressure. As we noted at the start of the chapter, a nurse checks the patient with the high fever more often that the one with the low fever. In the same way, weekly progress monitoring of students with school difficulties helps you track their performance. If you have a large number of students in supplemental and intensive interventions, monitor the supplemental students semimonthly (every other week) and the intensive students weekly.

Current Scheduling Options

As a step toward getting progress monitoring going, one suggestion is to look at your current classroom schedule and find a 10-minute block of time that would work well for monitoring. Ideally, this block of time will be when the students are doing quiet activities. If you teach at the K–2 grade levels, it may help to find an assessment "buddy." Your buddy is another teacher in a room near yours. You and your buddy will coordinate your progress monitoring times so that he can work with the rest of your class while you monitor your students. You will do the same for your buddy. An activity that works well for the progress monitoring time block shared with the "buddy" teacher is a story readaloud. For upper grades, your students should be able to do a quiet activity for the 10 minutes of progress monitoring. For grades 3 and above, if your students are monitored in group-based assessments, less time for the monitoring will be needed.

Replacing Other Assessments

When possible, progress monitoring assessments can utilize existing assessments or replace other assessments. A general rule of assessment is never to test any more than is necessary to answer the question. Many other assessments take place in schools. If any of your current assessments meet the criteria for a progress indicator, they can be used for this purpose. For instance, if there are regular assessments embedded in a specific intervention, these could be used as a progress measure. Alternatively, if there are assessments being used now that are not helpful for you to plan instruction, these could be replaced with weekly progress measures that show a student's progress in a specific skill.

FACTORS AFFECTING PROGRESS DATA

A number of factors will influence progress data, and it's important to keep these in mind as you set up a progress monitoring plan and as you implement it. In particular, treatment/assessment integrity and measurement sensitivity are important ingredients in effective progress monitoring.

Treatment and Assessment Integrity

Accuracy in the use of both the intervention and the progress measure are crucial to the usefulness of the data. If your intervention is implemented exactly as planned, and if the progress measures are administered correctly, the data will be very helpful in showing whether the intervention worked. But if either the intervention and/or the measure are used incorrectly, your progress data will not indicate whether the intervention really worked.

A number of factors can affect treatment and assessment integrity. If you have a student who is chronically absent, then it's not possible to know the true effects of the intervention. Or if there are interruptions in the intervention or assessment sessions (e.g., fire drills, announcements) these could affect treatment and assessment integrity. Similarly, if there are variations in your teaching or assessment procedures, these could make the progress data inaccurate. For all of these reasons, it's very important that you work with other teachers to ensure both treatment and assessment integrity so that the progress data will be worth reviewing. In general, it's important for those who will be using specific treatments and assessments to have thorough training in their correct use. In addition, follow-up training in the form of "booster" sessions can be helpful so that everyone using a specific method will be sure to use it in the same way. If you doubt the integrity of an intervention or the progress data, it's important to identify this and address it rather than ignore it. The correct intervention or assessment procedures can be taught and then new data collected. In the long term, this is essential for your students' learning needs.

Measurement Sensitivity

Another factor that can affect progress monitoring data is the sensitivity of the measure to what your student is learning. In order for any progress measure to be useful, it must be matched to the skills taught in the intervention. For example, if I want to know whether my daughter can tie her shoes, but I only give her Velcro shoes to show me, I'll never know whether she can tie her shoes. The best way to ensure measurement sensitivity is to select the progress measure at the same time as the intervention itself is chosen. Here's where having a team of colleagues who evaluate the interventions is a real asset. As a group, your team is likely to have a range of expertise in different interventions and assessments. When these are well matched from the start of the intervention, the data will be very helpful in showing whether the intervention is working. If the wrong assessment is picked to monitor an intervention, the team will end up frustrated because your data do not give them helpful information. As you consider possible interventions and assessments, it is very important to make sure that the measures will be sensitive to the skill being taught.

SUMMARY

This chapter has provided information about how to monitor the progress of your students who participate in supplemental and intensive interventions. We hope you now know what, why, how, and when to use progress monitoring as part of team-based RTI activities. Progress monitoring is an essential part of RTI because it is how you know whether an intervention is working. To be helpful, progress measures need to be matched to the skill your student is learning and need to be administered accurately. There need to be at least four data points in order to review progress. When collected on a weekly basis, your progress data can be reviewed every 4 weeks to see how your student is doing. There are three main options that your team can consider as they review and interpret progress data: maintain, increase/decrease, or remove the intervention. Progress monitoring is an essential ingredient in your students' overall RTI success because it shows whether your students respond to intervention.

RESOURCES

National Center for Student Progress Monitoring

www.studentprogress.org

To meet the challenges of implementing effective progress monitoring, the Office of Special Education Programs (OSEP) funded the National Center on Student Progress Monitoring. OSEP funding for the site has now ended, however, but the website, with all its valuable resources, will continue to be maintained. Please feel free to use the site and share any of the resources provided.

AIMSweb

www.edformation.com

AIMSweb provides both progress monitoring items and data management services. There are progress measures for reading, spelling, writing, and math that cover kindergarten through grade 8. The measures can be used by individual classroom teachers to monitor student progress in specific skills. The data management service can also be used at the classroom level to enter student data and track progress according to specific goals.

DIBELS

https://dibels.uoregon.edu

DIBELS offers reading development progress monitoring measures. There are two ways to get DIBELS progress monitoring items: you can download them for free from the DIBELS website at the University of Oregon, or you can also purchase them in preprinted sets from Sopris West Publishing (*www.sopriswest.com*). The DIBELS website also has a progress monitoring data management service that can be used by classroom teachers to enter data and track student progress in reading.

There are a number of additional resources about progress monitoring. The best source for up-to-date information is the National Center on Student Progress Monitoring (*www.studentprogress.org/chart/chart.asp*). The National Research Center on Learning Disabilities at the University of Kansas has a number of helpful documents, including a handbook entitled *Responsiveness to Intervention (RTI): How to Do It.* Nancy Safer and Steve Fleishman wrote a helpful summary about progress monitoring in *Educational Leadership* (2005). As students make progress, it's important to consider how to transition them to less-intensive services; information about that can be found in a chapter by Kelly Powell-Smith and Patricia Ball in *Best Practices in School Psychology, V* (2008).

APPENDIX 4.1

Graph for Student Data

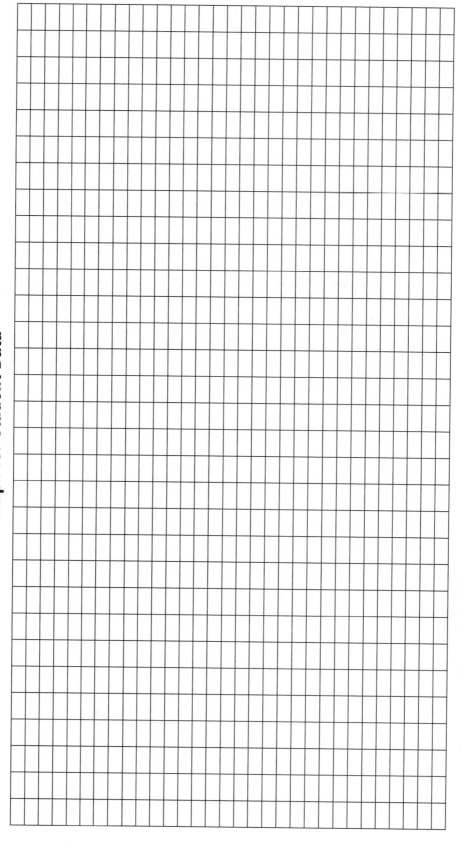

CHAPTER 5

Yikes! I Have "Kids at Risk"

Don't Worry—We've Already Done the Heavy Lifting for You

This chapter assumes that you are now somewhat familiar with progress monitoring. If you skipped the progress monitoring chapter, we urge you to go back and take a look at it before going any farther. To a large extent, this chapter builds upon the progress monitoring chapter (Chapter 4).

Assuming you have read the previous chapter we bet that right about now you are starting to think "How am I going to pull this all together?" What if you are *not* in a DIBELS system that provides progress monitoring in reading? What if you are *not* in a system that is using AIMSweb, which provides progress monitoring in reading and math? What if you are *not* using Wireless Generation products that provide progress monitoring in reading, math, and a full RTI system? Or what if you want to try an intervention for a student who is struggling in a subject other than reading or math? These are all great questions, and many of you will find that they are relevant to your current situation(s). This chapter has been written to guide you in selecting the appropriate intervention recipes within this book, consulting with your colleagues, and keeping track of your students' progress with an easy-to-use paper-and-pencil graph.

Let's start with a brief overview of the additional materials that come with this book. The intervention recipes are the sheets in Appendix C that are color coded in green, yellow, or red. These recipes will guide you as you choose the appropriate intervention(s) for your students' needs. We have carefully hand-picked these interventions based on their proven track records, the research behind them, and ease of implementation.

Documentation of your efforts is very important for you if the student is eventually referred for special education services. At the eligibility meeting you will need to show the team (which includes parents) documentation of precisely what interventions were tried, how long each one lasted, and specific progress monitoring data.

The forms in Appendix B can be used to guide your steps through the process of selecting an intervention, using colleagues as a resource, and documenting your students' progress. Keep in mind that documenting what you do and the progress that your student makes as a result of your efforts is *critical* in any RTI system. Not only has the act of documenting been shown to lead to better results for kids, but it will also be very important for you if the student is eventually referred for special education services (Ardoin, Witt, Connell, & Koenig, 2005; Safer & Fleischman, 2005). At the eligibility meeting you will need to show the team (which includes the student's parents) documentation of precisely what interventions were tried, how long each one lasted, and specific progress monitoring data. Using the forms provided in this book will ensure that you will be prepared if that situation were to arise.

First we will go over the Student Progress and Request for Assistance form. It looks like this at the top and can be found in Appendix B.1 on p. 173.

Student Progress and Request for Assistance

Teacher completes this side and puts in school psychologist's mailbox or brings to next team meeting.

Teacher: _____

Student: _____

Date: _____

Reason for concern: _____

Notice that at the very top it says that you (the teacher) can fill this out on your own, and then ask your school psychologist[1] to meet with you to go over it. Or, if you prefer, you may bring it with you to the next student study team meeting. You may find that just going through the process of filling it out and implementing or revitalizing a green (Tier 1) intervention is sufficient for the student to make progress, and you will not need to request assistance. However, if sufficient progress is not made, then you already have the form filled out, and you can turn it in to the school psychologist or bring it with you to the next student study team meeting.

The *reason for concern* will be important when it comes to choosing an intervention. If the concern is in the area of reading, like oral reading fluency (ORF), then you will be looking at the "Reading Interventions" chapter of this book (Chapter 6). However, if the concern is a behavior issue, such as work refusal, you will be turning to the "Behavior Interventions" chapter (Chapter 9). Keep in mind that each intervention chapter corre-

---

[1]In more and more regions around the country, school psychologists are being trained and hired to be the go-to people for questions relating to RTI. Depending upon your school psychologist's training, you may find that he or she has a wealth of knowledge pertaining to classroom and behavior management, curriculum design and instruction, and academic and behavioral interventions (Deno, 1986). Don't make the all-too-common mistake of assuming that they only know how to give tests for entry into special education. Besides, an effective RTI system will mostly eliminate the need for standardized IQ and achievement tests, so school psychologists will be looking for something else to do! Don't hesitate to ask them for help and tap into their expertise.

sponds to the color-coded recipes in Appendix C, beginning with green (Tier 1), and then yellow (Tier 2), and finally red (Tier 3).

As we turn our attention back to the form you will notice that the next section jumps right into green (Tier 1) interventions. You'll see that we've given you some intervention ideas just to get the juices flowing, but there are also two places for you to write in other Tier 1 interventions that you may have tried. If you are like most of us you will look down that list and realize that there are several things that you haven't tried yet and decide to look up the recipe and see whether it is something that you can do with relative ease and a few extra resources. That really is the point of this section—to help you think about what's already in place and whether there can be more. Here's what it looks like on the form:

Universal interventions already in place—circle Y or N below. See green (Tier 1) intervention recipes for descriptions.	Available?	Used by student?	Comments
Establishing Classroom Expectations	Y / N	Y / N	_____
Managing Transition Time	Y / N	Y / N	_____
Practice, Practice, Practice	Y / N	Y / N	_____
Other _____	Y / N	Y / N	_____
Other _____	Y / N	Y / N	_____

The *comments* section is a good place for you to record when you started using the intervention, if you're finding it useful, and any other things that you think might be important to note.

If, after going through this section, you feel that the green Tier 1 interventions are already in place and are not working, then it is time to go to the next section and fill that out. This part will ask you for some data. This can either be in the form of quiz scores or you can use curriculum-based measurement (CBM) scores if you have them. Examples of CBM would be 1-minute measures of ORF or timed math facts sheets such as the ones that were mentioned in Chapter 4. If you are interested you can find much more detail about CBM in *The ABCs of CBM* by Hosp, Hosp, and Howell (2007). Once you've decided which measures to use, go ahead and finish filling out the section below. You'll be referring to it later.

Most recent scores in area of academic concern (CBM refers to curriculum-based measurement):			
	CBM or Quiz	CBM or Quiz	CBM or Quiz	CBM or Quiz
Date	_____	_____	_____	_____
Student score	_____	_____	_____	_____
Class average	_____	_____	_____	_____

The last half of the form asks for some general information that will be used later, during intervention planning. The items are fairly self-explanatory. Recording the level of urgency just provides a good visual when giving it to the school psychologist or the student support team. Best days and times to meet will be relevant if you are going to ask for help from one of the specialists, like the school psychologist. After you've signed and dated it you can put it into the school psychologist's mailbox and wait for him or her to contact you. That's it. Your part is over until you meet with the school psychologist (or other specialist). It is important to note that we are not suggesting that you no longer meet with your team. You could copy this form and give it out at the team meeting. When it comes time for your meeting, the school psychologist or other specialist will come to the meeting with your Student Progress and Request for Assistance form.

The next form to look over is the Student Planning form (Appendix B.2 on p. 174). In this book the forms are reproduced on two separate pages—Appendices B.1 and B.2—so you'll want to photocopy those two pages back to back, side 1 and side 2, respectively. You will first go over the information that you've written on side 1, then flip over to side 2.

On the Student Planning form (side 2) you will see a graph that you can use to track your student's progress. You will transfer the first four data points that you wrote down on side 1, to the graph on side 2. Time 1 refers to your first CBM, quiz, or behavior measurement, Time 2 the second, and so on. This shouldn't take very long at all because you've already found those scores and written them down on side 1. Together you should determine a reasonable goal for your student by Time 10. Record that goal at Time 10 both on the graph and on the line that is provided just below the graph. Now you will draw a best-fit aimline between the student's current scores and the goal for Time 10. The example in Figure 5.1 illustrates this. Just for reference, we've used oral reading fluency (correct words per minute [CWPM]) for a second grader in the winter. Time 1 to Time 2 is 1 week. This student is considered to be very at risk and needs to improve a lot before the end of the year.

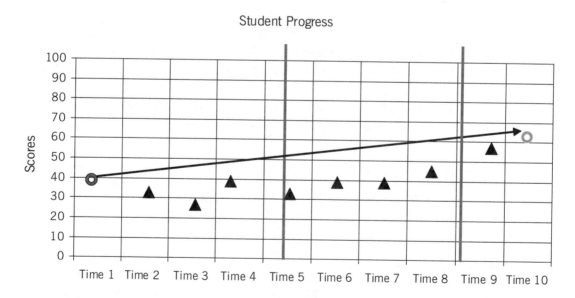

FIGURE 5.1. Graphing student progress. Teacher's goal for student score by Time 10: 60 CWPM; date: second week of February, 2/13.

Intervention/Tier	Date started	Date stopped	Why stopped?
1. Repeated Readings	Time 5 (or date)	Time 9	Not on the aimline
2. Word Sort	Time 9	Not stopped	It's working

FIGURE 5.2. Interventions and outcomes.

Now that you know where you are and where you need to go it is much easier to plan the intervention. This example is fairly ambitious when it comes to gaining number of correct words read per minute (ORF), and knowing this should be considered when choosing an intervention.

There are some general rules when monitoring progress within an RTI system. They are given on the form so that you will be thinking about them as you move into intervention planning. Here's what you need to think about each time you evaluate a new data point from your student's progress:

- If four consecutive data points are below the aimline, *the intervention should be modified or changed.* Contact the school psychologist and/or consult with your school-based team.
- If four consecutive data points are above the aimline, continue with the recommended intervention.
- If four consecutive data points are both above *and* below aimline, continue to collect data to determine intervention effectiveness.

At the bottom of Appendix B.2 there is a section where you can list the interventions you are trying and describe how it all worked out. It is important to keep this updated so that it is easy to see what intervention is currently being used. What if you chose a Tier 2 reading intervention such as Repeated Readings? Let's go through that example in Figure 5.2.

From the graphed example in Figure 5.1 you can see that you don't have enough data from Time 9 to Time 10 to really see what will happen. It would be best for you to finish this graph (with a data point at Time 10) and then attach a second sheet of the same form. Begin the graph where you've left off but keep in mind that you will be readjusting your goal for week 10 because you now have 10 more weeks to intervene with that student. Make sure you know what the year-end goal should be (e.g., in the DIBELS passages, a second grader who is reading 90 CWPM is considered to be at benchmark).

Let's now turn our attention to Appendices B.3 and B.4. It would be helpful to photocopy these two pages back to back, as suggested for Appendices B.1 and B.2. On Appendix B.3, you will see a place to select a Tier 2 (or yellow) intervention—highlighted in gray in the boxed example on the next page. When deciding which Tier 2 recipe to use, you will first want to turn to the appropriate chapter, such as "Reading Interventions," and then turn to the yellow pages in Appendix C that represent the Tier 2 recipes. Use these recipes to guide you in your selection of an intervention. This is something to do with the team or a specialist.

Teacher: _____	Date: _____
Student: _____	
Reason for concern: _____	
See yellow (Tier 2) intervention recipes: Choose one and circle.	
Guess the Word Have You Ever?	
Word Sort Story Mapping	
Repeated Readings Other: _____	

Appendix B.4 has a place for Tier 3 (or red) interventions to be considered and planned. You may not need to use this form if you are able to get a change in the student's progress with the green or yellow interventions. You will most likely find that most of your students who struggle will succeed with just the green and yellow interventions in place. In a good RTI system it is expected that only 5–7% of all students will need Tier 3/red interventions. This will result in less work for you and more success for your students once you become fluent in these practices. You may be surprised at what a difference a green intervention can make for the whole class, not just the student who shows the greatest need. In time you will find that the number of students who struggle will decrease dramatically and then you'll only have a few to focus your intensive interventions on. We hope that you'll e-mail us and tell us your success stories!

RESOURCES

A summary of the technical features needed for all progress measures can be found at the website of the National Center on Student Progress Monitoring (*www.studentprogress.org*). You may also find it useful to go directly to sources for the interventions. One good place is *www.interventioncentral.org*, which provides interventions and many other RTI-related ideas. For reading-related intervention ideas check out *www.freereading.net*.

CHAPTER 6

Reading Interventions

Mr. Greene is a second-grade teacher. He has been teaching for 12 years and has seen his share of students who perform really well in reading and those who experience major difficulty. Some of his high-performing students were referred for talented and gifted support. Some of his low-performing students were referred for special education evaluation. Mr. Greene has seen the whole spectrum of reading skills and feels that he has a pretty good handle on who may need additional services at either end. One of his first considerations is simply listening to how the students sound when they read aloud. Mr. Greene listens for students' accuracy and fluency. He notes how many errors there are and classifies them according to type of error. He also listens for their expression when reading, their ability to attempt unknown words, and whether overall their reading is "smooth," meaning they just seem to do it effortlessly. He makes notes about these characteristics and uses this information to make decisions about students. He answers two types of questions with these data. The first is, do students look different from their peers? If so, how different? Are they reading really well or experiencing major difficulty? Once these students have been identified, he attempts to answer the second question: For the students who are outside the norm, what do they need to work on? In answering these questions, he frequently seeks help from the talented and gifted teacher for instructional ideas for high-performing students. He also asks for ideas from the problem-solving team, a group of teachers who offer instructional strategies for students in need of more support. What he has learned most from this process in 12 years is that reading aloud is just the first step in determining what to do next. He uses this test as a great starting point, to group students according to need. But how many words they read aloud is only a number. He makes notes as they read, and it's these notes that help him determine what to do next. He is planning for the second question—what do they need instructionally to make progress? With this information, he can select an intervention that matches the student's needs. It is this match, he believes, that helps him take students where they need to be.

Mr. Greene is a teacher who knows time is limited. Given this reality, he strives to be efficient, and being efficient means maximizing everyone's time. To do this, he tries hard to ensure that the additional instruction is appropriately matched to the students' needs. With this match, he is giving them exactly what they need. Without it, he would be wasting his and the students' time.

According to the U.S. Department of Education, schools average 180 days per school year. During this time students, with instruction from their teachers, are expected to learn how to read well. With early dismissals, late starts, field trips, assemblies, and other activities, the time becomes even shorter. Yet many teachers across the United States succeed in helping their students become accurate, fluent, and proficient readers.

Veteran reading teacher Louisa Moats (2000) points out that several summaries of research agree that all but 2 to 5% of children can learn to read, even in populations where the incidence of poor reading is often far higher. For more information about research on effective reading instruction see the Resources section at the end of this chapter. It's clear that most children can learn to read. Is it always easy? No. Is it ever easy? Not really. Teaching reading is a complex process, one that must be done with intention, guidance, and evaluation. In this chapter, we focus on what we know about effective instruction in reading and how this can be translated for the classroom.

WHAT DO WE KNOW ABOUT EFFECTIVE READING INSTRUCTION?

In 1997 Congress asked the director of the National Institute of Child Health and Human Development (NICHD) and the Secretary of Education to gather a national panel of experts to determine what we know about how children learn to read and the instructional strategies that support this process. The panel was asked to review the current information on reading research and create a report that is easily accessible to administrators, teachers, and parents. Figure 6.1 includes an abbreviated list of the questions that were asked of the panel.

What resulted from over 2 years of reviewing the research was the report, *Teaching Children to Read: An Evidence-Based Assessment of the Scientific Research Literature on Reading and Its Implications for Reading Instruction* (NICHD, 2000). In this report the panel identified the five major components of teaching children to read: phonemic awareness, the alphabetic principle (e.g., phonics), fluency with text, vocabulary, and comprehension. These skills are important because they predict reading acquisition and later reading achievement and are teachable to students. If taught appropriately, they can improve outcomes for children and help them to achieve reading success. Many of you will be quite familiar with the five components already. For you, we hope the following will be a useful "refresher" as we introduce the specific intervention recipes for reading.

- What is known about the basic process by which children learn to read?
- What are the most common instructional approaches in use in the United States to teach children to read?
- What assessments have been used to evaluate each of these methodologies in actual use in helping children develop critical reading skills?
- What does the Panel conclude about the readiness for implementation in the classroom of these research results?
- How are teachers trained to teach children to read, and what do studies show about the effectiveness of this training?
- What practical findings from the Panel can be used immediately by parents and teachers to help children learn how to read?
- What important gaps remain in our knowledge of how children learn to read and in the effectiveness of different instructional methods for teaching reading?

FIGURE 6.1. National Reading Panel questions.

THE ESSENTIALS OF LEARNING TO READ

Phonemic Awareness

Phonemic awareness is a concept that typically raises questions of definition. Common questions include: What's the difference between phonological awareness and phonemic awareness? Is phonemic awareness the same as phonics? What role does phonemic awareness play in learning to read? These questions are important, because in order to teach phonemic awareness systematically, there must be an understanding of what it is and how it affects the process of learning to read.

First let's think about phonological awareness. Phonological awareness is the ability to detect and manipulate the sound structure of words independent of their meaning. It is a broad skill. One way to think about it is as the larger umbrella that encompasses all of the skills related to hearing, comparing, and manipulating sounds. All of these skills are important because they are highly predictive of children's later ability to read. See the Resources section at the end of this chapter for more references on this topic. Because of its role in learning to read, phonological awareness is a skill that must be taught directly, explicitly, and with opportunities for review and practice. When this is accomplished, children have the best chance to "break the code" in early reading (Moats, 2005).

Now let's consider phonemes. The small units of speech that correspond to letters of an alphabetic writing system are called *phonemes*. The awareness that language is composed of these sounds is called *phonemic awareness*. It is the ability to hear and manipulate the sounds in spoken words and the understanding that spoken words and syllables are made up of sequences of speech sounds. In other words, students can hear sounds when words are spoken and manipulate them verbally. This is a more advanced skill in the continuum of phonological awareness, as students are able to delete and manipulate the sounds that they hear.

Phonemic awareness is important in an alphabetic language system like English because letters represent sounds or phonemes. If students can hear and manipulate the sounds in spoken words, they are able to do things like segment sounds, blend sounds, or change sounds in words. Measures of young children's level of phonemic awareness strongly predicts their future success in learning to read.

In summary, phonemic awareness is about hearing and speaking. Our goal is to have children hear, compare, blend, manipulate, and delete the sounds in words. With this skill, there is no print or sight necessary. Students use their ears to listen to sounds and use their speech to say the sounds. These critical skills should be mastered early, so students can move on to the next component of early reading: the alphabetic principle, or phonics.

The Alphabetic Principle

The *alphabetic principle* describes the ability to associate sounds with letters and use these sounds to form words. Also known as phonics, it is a skill that allows students to associate letters with their individual and combined sounds and then blend them together to make words. It is composed of two parts: alphabetic understanding and phonological recoding.

Alphabetic understanding is the knowledge that letters represent sounds in words. For example, the letters *c a t* make the sounds "cuh" "aaa" "tuh." Phonological recoding is the awareness that letter sounds can be blended together, and knowledge of these associations can be used to read words. This letter–sound knowledge is necessary for word identification. When students have this skill, they are able to decode the text. Students can take the sounds "cuh" "aaa" "tuh" and form the word *cat*.

The alphabetic principle is essential to the process of learning to read because it involves the connection between print and speech. Students learn to match the symbols on the page to the specific sounds that they represent. They learn to "decode" the words, as if they were looking at a map and deciphering its meaning. If you think about learning to read, you realize that learning to read is about facing new words every day. With this task at hand, students need a system that is proven to work and that they understand.

The process of using the alphabetic principle to decode words is described in the following steps by Coyne, Kame'enui, and Simmons (2001):

1. The reader must sequentially translate the letters in the word into their phonological counterparts.
2. The reader must remember the correct sequence of sounds.
3. The reader must blend the sounds together.
4. The reader must search his or her memory for a real word that matches the string of sounds.

You'll notice that when encountering a basic consonant–vowel–consonant (CVC) word like *cat*, the reader must know the individual letter sounds, use short-term memory to remember the sounds in order, combine the sounds together, and do so in a way that matches his or her knowledge of real words. All of this to read the word *cat*. Although some students easily acquire this skill, other students face a more tedious process that requires more time, effort, and instruction.

The alphabetic principle is critical to the process of learning to read because with this skill, students can become more fluent, which ultimately leads them to the main purpose for reading: comprehension. Isabel Beck, in her book *Making Sense of Phonics: The Hows and Whys* (2005), asserts that children must gain control of the print-to-speech mapping system early if they are to become successful readers. With this system figured out, the process becomes more automatic and students can begin to focus their attention on the meaning of the text.

The alphabetic principle forms the foundation for deciphering written English. It is the skill students need to acquire to break the code and figure out how to read unknown words on a page. It is a gateway to fluency and a path to comprehension. With explicit instruction in this skill, children are likely to make progress with basic and advanced, regular, and irregular words.

Fluency with Text

Fluency is the effortless, automatic ability to read words in text. LaBerge and Samuels (1974) described the fluent reader as "one whose decoding processes are automatic, requiring no conscious attention." This skill allows students to read effortlessly. Students are able to read the text without having to focus on decoding the words.

Fluency has been described as the bridge between word recognition and comprehension (Osborn, Lehr, & Hiebert, 2003). With fluency, readers can make connections among the ideas in the text and between the text and their background knowledge. In other words, fluent readers can recognize words and comprehend at the same time. Readers who are not fluent, however, are not consistently identifying words. Think of a student you know who is not fluent. What does he or she sound like? Often, students who lack fluency make errors, go back and repeat words, skip over words, or read word by word, without using a relaxed, easy style.

Fluent reading comprises three elements: *accurate* reading of connected text at a *conversational rate* with appropriate *prosody*, or expression (Hudson, Lane, & Pullen, 2005). Fluent readers are accurate; they read passages with few or no errors, are conversational in their reading, are relaxed and consistent, and vary their tone and inflection.

Imagine a reader without one of those three skills. Without accuracy, what does the reader sound like? The student will struggle with certain words and use decoding skills to decipher the words he or she does not know. Without fluency, what does the reader sound like? The reader will be reading, but it is disjointed, slow at times, and does not seem relaxed and conversational. Without prosody and expression, what does the reader sound like? The reader may be monotonous, demonstrating no change in his or her voice in reading the variety of sentences.

When thinking about building fluency, it is important to consider the text, the reader's skill, and the opportunities for practice. The following questions can be helpful in planning additional opportunities for building reading fluency from the Big Ideas in Beginning Reading (*reading.uoregon.edu*):

- Can the student read the passages with 95% accuracy?
- Is there an explicit strategy for teaching students to transition from accuracy to fluency?
- Is there daily opportunity for building fluency?
- Is there overlap in words (i.e., words show up multiple times in different text)?
- Are target rates identified?

An important issue to point out here is that passages used for fluency practice should be in the student's decoding range. This means that the student is close to 95% or higher accuracy with the passages being used to practice (see Table 6.1). With this accuracy, the student is able to decode most of the words and thus can focus on developing rate and prosody rather than stumbling over the unknown words. If the passage is too difficult, the student instead turns attention to decoding rather than fluency.

Fluency has been a hot topic in recent years (*www.shanahanonliteracy.com*). Think of your district and the conversations that have revolved around fluency. Is there debate? What is the consensus? What is your district's perspective on fluency? Many of us have witnessed or been a part of these discussions. The concern often is that with too much focus on fluency, the emphasis on comprehension will be lost. Some teachers are uncomfortable with the idea of teaching fluency for fear that their students will then lack critical comprehension skills.

Practicing oral reading helps children not only sound better, but also become better comprehenders. In fact, teaching fluency supports comprehension, rather than hinders it—fluent students can comprehend. Students who are not fluent struggle with comprehension. Given what we know about the connection between fluency and comprehension, it seems that the critical question has changed. No longer do we ask, "Do we teach reading fluency?" but "How do we teach fluency in a systematic, structured way to support student progress?"

We want to emphasize the importance of fluency for the role it plays in helping students develop comprehension. It is not about reading fast simply to read fast. It is not about racing during a timed ORF task. It is not about developing fluency and ending the reading process there. It is about developing this skill so mental processing can focus more on comprehension and less on decoding the actual words.

TABLE 6.1. Levels of Reading Difficulty with Percentages of Accuracy

Level	Percentage read accurately
Independent reading	97%
Instructional	94–97%
Frustration	93% or lower

Vocabulary

Vocabulary is the ability to understand and use words to acquire and convey meaning. Reading specialists often refer to two types of vocabulary: *receptive vocabulary* and *expressive vocabulary*. Receptive vocabulary is composed of listening vocabulary and reading vocabulary. Listening vocabulary is the words we need to know to understand what we hear. Reading vocabulary is the words we need to know to understand what is presented in the reading passage. Expressive vocabulary is composed of speaking vocabulary and writing vocabulary. Speaking vocabulary is the words we use while we are speaking. Writing vocabulary is the words we use when we are writing. Both of these types of vocabulary are important because, with these skills, students can understand the words presented to them and express themselves using a variety of words. The larger a student's vocabulary, the better prepared he or she is to communicate explicitly and understand what is presented.

What does it mean to know a word? Beck, McKeown, and Omanson (1987) suggested the following continuum:

- No knowledge.
- General sense, such as knowing the word "mendacious" has a negative connotation.
- Narrow, context-bound knowledge, such as knowing a radiant bride is a beautiful, smiling, happy one, but unable to describe an individual in a different context as "radiant."
- Knowing a word but not being able to recall it readily enough to use it in appropriate situations.
- Rich, decontextualized knowledge of a word's meaning, its relationship to other words, and its extension to metaphorical uses, such as understanding what someone is doing when they are "devouring" a book.

Our goal is to get students to the highest level, where they are able to use words in many ways because they have deep understanding.

When you consider how to teach vocabulary, think about three guidelines. First, provide students with opportunities to learn words independently. For younger children, this means reading books to them and discussing the interesting words in the story. For older children, this means teaching them explicit ways to determine the meaning of the word using contextual analysis. Second, teach children the meaning of words. Third, model a love for and interest in words. Use books that are interesting for students. Make word activities exciting and fun. Show students that learning new words opens up new worlds and new ideas to them. Demonstrating a passion for words can make the instruction more captivating for your students.

In *Bringing Words to Life: Robust Vocabulary Instruction*, Beck, McKeown, and Kucan (2002) emphasize the importance of directly explaining the words, but also using thought-provoking, playful, interactive follow-up activities with students. By doing so you challenge yourself to be creative, but, more important, you challenge your students to access the meanings of words in multiple contexts using a variety of strategies. These activities can have a lasting impact because they are interesting and memorable. With this experience, you help your students not only to learn new words, but also to remember them.

Comprehension

Comprehension is the complex cognitive process of gaining meaning from spoken language or print. The National Reading Panel (NICHD, 2000) states that "reading comprehension is a cognitive process that integrates complex skills and cannot be understood without examining the critical role of vocabulary learning and instruction, and its development and active interactive strategic processes are critically necessary to the development of reading comprehension" (p. 4-1).

Comprehension is the ultimate goal of reading. We want to obtain information and understand it. It has been described as the "essence of reading" (*reading.uoregon.edu*); it is also very complex. Affected by a variety of factors and influenced by a multitude of student characteristics, comprehension is a process that is less overt than the other essentials of learning to read. We can't directly measure it, yet we do have ways to assess whether a student understands the content. We can't just teach one way to do it, because a variety of strategies come into play, depending on the text, and we can't expect all students to understand the material, because they are influenced by their own background knowledge, vocabulary, and decoding skills. It is multifaceted and complicated, yet we do have knowledge about how to teach it and teach it well.

Both reader- and text-based factors interact to create unique learning situations for each student. Consider a student whom you know. How would you describe his or her reading skills? Now think about that student reading a variety of texts. How well would the student understand a narrative story? An expository piece? How well would the student comprehend the material if it had new vocabulary words you had not yet discussed in class? If the student had a lot of background knowledge? Or no background knowledge at all?

Reading researchers Ken Howell and Victor Nolet (2000) recognize the reader-based factors and refer to them as "comprehension skills," which include decoding, vocabulary, syntax, and prior knowledge. With these skills, students have the equipment necessary to make sense of a reading passage; yet this is only half of the picture. They also refer to "comprehension strategies," which include monitoring meaning, using selective attention to text, adjusting for task difficulty, connecting text to prior knowledge, and clarifying when needed. With these strategies, students enable themselves to find the meaning of the passage and thereby develop a deep understanding of the meaning. Together, skills and strategies form the picture for complete understanding. The skills make comprehension possible and the strategies assist the process of further understanding.

TIER 1: CORE INTERVENTIONS

There are many core reading programs that are available. In some districts the reading curriculum is selected by the curriculum coordinator and the administrative team. In other districts reading specialists will be part of the decision-making process as well. In still others a team of teachers with reading expertise may also be involved. Each district has its own participants and process they use to begin selecting a new program to match the needs of the students.

Our goal is to provide you with characteristics and guidelines to consider when purchasing a new Tier 1 core program, as we did in Chapter 3. We do not include an exhaustive list of all of the Tier 1 research-based reading programs. The What Works Clearinghouse provides a list of the reading programs that they have reviewed. It is a good resource because they offer information about the program, what it entails, and the research behind it. Their website also provides helpful information about instructional ideas and methods for teachers. For the core program, it is also important to think about the proper combination of time, grouping, and assessments that will provide the greatest benefit for your students. In the following pages, we provide ideas for Tier 2 (supplemental) and Tier 3 (intensive) interventions.

TIER 2: SUPPLEMENTAL INTERVENTIONS

The interventions in Appendix C describe a variety of research-based strategies that can be used to address the five essential components in learning to read: phonemic awareness, alphabetic principle, fluency, vocabulary, and comprehension.

Guess the Word is a phonemic awareness intervention that allows students to practice by listening to you elongate the sounds in words. The *Word Sort* intervention is an activity for developing letter–sound knowledge. Students work in pairs to group words according to similar sounds. *Repeated Readings* targets fluency. In this intervention, students who are accurate but slow continue to read passages aloud until they increase the number of words read correct per minute. In *Have You Ever?* students consider new vocabulary words and apply them to their lives. *Story Mapping* is the comprehension intervention that prompts students to consider the characters, main problem, solution, and theme.

TIER 3: INTENSIVE INTERVENTIONS

The phonemic awareness intervention included in Appendix C is *Letter Puzzles*, in which students assemble letters and learn the sounds in words. *Silent e Changes* is a phonics intervention that helps students learn how words change when the letter *e* is added to the end of words. The fluency intervention, *Phrase Drill Procedure*, allows students to practice words that they misread in passages. The vocabulary intervention, *Word Associations*, is included to help students learn new words by pairing them with words they already know. Finally, the *3H Instructional Strategy* is included for comprehension. This intervention helps students to categorize questions about passages as "here, hidden, or in my head."

A NOTE ABOUT THE INTERVENTIONS

It is important to note that although some instructional interventions are listed as supplemental and others as intensive, it does not mean you can only use the interventions at those levels of support. A supplemental intervention can easily become part of your core instruction, if your core needs to be enhanced to meet the needs of more of your students (see Chapter 3). A supplemental intervention can also become an intensive intervention if done more frequently, for more time, and with more explicit support and practice. Conversely, an intensive intervention can become a supplemental intervention by using it less often, maybe just as a quick practice activity. An intensive intervention can also be used with your core by adding it to your daily activities that all students receive.

It is not necessarily the name of interventions that makes them powerful. It is how you use them and with what intensity that really will make the difference. As Joseph Torgeson (2000) stated, "To know what kind of instruction is most effective is not the same thing as knowing how much of that instruction, delivered under what conditions, will lead to adequate development of word reading . . . we must examine the intensity and duration of instruction required to eliminate reading failure in children with the most severe phonological disabilities" (p. 63).

RESOURCES

Big Ideas in Beginning Reading

reading.uoregon.edu

This website is designed to provide information, technology, and resources to teachers, administrators, and parents across the country. It includes definitions and descriptions of the research and theories behind each of the big ideas, describes how to assess the big ideas, gives information on how to teach the big ideas (including instructional examples), and, finally, shows you how to put it all together in your school.

Florida Center for Reading Research

fcrr.org

The mission of this center is to conduct basic research on reading, reading growth, reading assessment, and reading instruction that will contribute to the scientific knowledge of reading and benefit students in Florida and throughout the nation. The website provides excellent resources for teachers, administrators, and parents, including implementation guides and student center lesson activities.

International Reading Association

www.reading.org

The International Reading Association provides a network and multiple resources on teaching students to learn to read. From research and policy to teacher tools that include lesson plans, this website offers a variety of resources for teachers and administrators.

National Reading Panel

www.nationalreadingpanel.org

For more than 2 years, the NRP reviewed research-based knowledge on reading instruction and held open-panel meetings in Washington, DC, and regional meetings across the United States. In April 2000, the NRP concluded its work and submitted "The Report of the National Reading Panel: Teaching Children to Read," at a hearing before the U.S. Senate.

Vaughn Gross Center for Reading and Language Arts

www.texasreading.org

The center is committed to providing leadership to state, national, and international educators in effective reading and mathematics instruction. The center's mission emphasizes scientifically based research and instruction and is dedicated to improving reading and mathematics instruction for all students, especially struggling readers, English language learners, and special education students.

Research in reading is more extensive and widely available than research on other subject areas. The National Reading Panel's website, *www.nationalreadingpanel.org*, offers a variety of materials that you can download for free or order online. Specifically, the summary is a concise reference on each of the panel's findings. The Vaughn Gross Center for Reading and Language Arts, *www.texasreading.org*, provides many useful materials, including booklets and professional development guides. Finally, the International Reading Association, *www. reading.org*, includes helpful information on teaching reading to students.

CHAPTER 7

Written Language Interventions

Mrs. Gilbert is a fifth-grade teacher who works in an elementary school located outside of a large metropolitan area. Her class typically ranges from 23 to 27 students, with some years being bigger classes than others. Depending on student skills and needs, Mrs. Gilbert works with her teacher aide to operate interventions in the areas of reading, written language, or math. This year, there were a number of students struggling with writing and spelling. Knowing that her students would be expected to write even more next year in sixth grade, Mrs. Gilbert wanted to pinpoint their needs and provide explicit instruction to help remediate their difficulties. She started by scoring their writing samples using a writing rubric. In doing so, she noticed that four of her students needed additional instruction with sentence fluency and conventions. Three of her students needed to work more on organization and voice. She decided to work with the group that needed more support with sentence fluency and conventions. These students also struggled a bit with reading. Her aide would work with the students who needed additional support with organization and voice. These students had the mechanics down; they just needed more structure to think about and organize their writing. Mrs. Gilbert and her aide worked daily with their groups over the course of the year, with students progressing at different rates and moving to different groups as needed. They used a variety of activities and interventions, with Mrs. Gilbert ensuring explicit instruction and multiple opportunities for practice for both groups. Written language is an area of passion for Mrs. Gilbert, as she occasionally teaches an undergraduate education class at the local college. Working with college sophomores and juniors, Mrs. Gilbert is often surprised and dismayed by her students' writing abilities. As many as half of her students have struggled with writing coherent and succinct papers. She often differentiates her instruction and spends time working with students on the conventions of writing, voice, and expression for those who need it. She understands that some students are naturally gifted in writing, while others have talents in other areas, but she doesn't let that stop her from working to improve her college students' writing. The same is true for her fifth-grade class. She knew that acting now would help many of her students make progress. She didn't want them to go to college lacking the skills they need to succeed. At the end of the year, all of her fifth-grade struggling writers had made progress, some more than others, with three of the students now performing at the expected level for the end of fifth grade. These experiences, and her awareness of college student performance, motivated Mrs. Gilbert to keep working hard to get her students to be better writers, even if it meant running an extra intervention group for the course of the year.

Mrs. Gilbert, like many other teachers, appreciates the years when most students in her class are ready to learn grade-level writing skills. An average-performing class means less work, which means less planning, less time, and less stress. Of course, this rarely happens, because there are always students who require extra support to succeed. So she decides to push herself, as she pushes her students, to learn more and do more. Mrs. Gilbert has been teaching for 11 years, so this process has gotten easier as she has gathered more ideas, materials, and strategies. But she continues to look for something new, something better, something that might make that difference for a group of struggling kids. So instead of becoming exhausted, she becomes inspired, because her students make gains that surprise everyone, including herself.

WHAT DO WE KNOW ABOUT EFFECTIVE WRITING INSTRUCTION?

Teaching a child to write is an intricate process influenced by multiple aspects of the student, the instruction, and the curriculum. There are many factors involved, many aspects of the task to consider, and many student characteristics that influence the process. For these reasons, writing is complex, detailed, and sometimes difficult for students, and we know that it is important to consider the characteristics of effective instruction for writing to make an undefined process become explicit.

Graham, Harris, and Larsen (2001) identified multiple features of effective writing instruction that teachers and administrators can look for when examining programs.

Literate Classroom Environment

A literate classroom environment supports and encourages literacy and writing. It is a classroom that has letters and words on the walls, displays student writing, and uses the whole room to support student learning. There are multiple books or magazines to read and many opportunities to write about what students are learning. Students use calendars, signs, and schedules to see how words are used every day. Table 7.1 includes more ideas from the U.S. Department of Education to make your classroom environment more literate.

Daily Writing with a Range of Tasks

Daily writing with a range of tasks gives students opportunities to write on a variety of topics. They also get opportunities to write for a variety of purposes and audiences. This

TABLE 7.1. Ways to Create a Literate Classroom Environment

Student materials	Student activities
• Phone books • Dictionaries • Menus • Recipes • Labels • Signs • Printed directions • Student work • Alphabet displays	• Word/letter games • Play with alphabet letter cookie cutters or stamps • Discuss the daily schedule • Interact with magnetic letters • Label photos of students, teachers, and class activities • Explore a variety of books, magazines, books on tape, e-books • Complete daily communication notebooks

provides students with a range of tasks, experiences, and options when deciding what to write about, which accomplishes two things. One, it teaches students to write in a multitude of ways. Two, it keeps writing interesting, because the ideas are always changing and the topics are always different. Figure 7.1 includes a variety of topics that students can choose from when deciding what to write.

Make Writing Motivating

The biggest thing teachers can do to make writing motivating is give students choice when writing. By giving them options on what to write, students have the freedom to be creative and brainstorm ideas in an area in which they're interested. This can be especially effective with students who do not enjoy writing and experience difficulty with it. Students are used to being told what to write about; by giving them options, you open up a new realm to them, giving them opportunities to write about what they are thinking about, what they enjoy, and what is currently occurring in their lives.

Regular Teacher–Student Conferences

Regular teacher–student conferences are important for providing direct feedback to students for their writing, editing, and revising. These conferences are face to face, so students can learn from the teacher what they wrote well and what they need to fix. These meetings can also be used to ask guiding questions to help students think about finishing their writing with a complete ending. With this support, students know what they did well, what they need to improve, and what they need to do next.

Especially important about these conferences is that they can be very brief, only a few minutes. This allows you to quickly meet with all students, provide explicit feedback, and check in to see where each student is at with his or her progress. The quick meetings provide information about student performance and give students information about how to edit and revise their writing to make it more complete.

- If I could travel through time I would . . .
- If I were a teacher I would . . .
- The best birthday was . . .
- The worst birthday was . . .
- My best childhood memory is . . .
- My hobbies are . . .
- I want to travel to . . .
- My hero is . . .
- Describe a dream that you had recently.
- A joke that makes me laugh is . . .
- My favorite foods . . .
- When I grow up I want to be . . .
- I was most angry when . . .
- I was most happy when . . .
- I was most disappointed when . . .
- My favorite holiday is . . .
- Sometimes I wish that . . .
- What would you do if you were principal for a day?
- If you could change places with anyone, who would it be and why?
- You have an extra $1,000,000 to give away. What would you do with the money?
- Tell me about your family.
- What is something you are pessimistic about?
- What is your favorite song and why?
- What is the best advice you ever received?
- What do you think about ghosts?
- What do you think of someone who has bad manners?
- What do you think about people who take advantage of others?
- What do you think about when you can't fall asleep?
- Tell me about your best friend. Why is that person your best friend?
- If you were an animal, what kind would you be and why?
- My favorite book is . . .
- My favorite character is . . .
- If I could be any color in a crayon box, I would be . . .
- My favorite movie is . . .
- Ten things that make me laugh . . .
- A list of things I'll never do . . .
- What is something you dislike about yourself?
- What is something you do well?
- What is something you are optimistic about?
- What do you think courage means?
- What do you think makes a good friend?
- What do you think makes a happy family?

FIGURE 7.1. Writing prompts for students.

A Predictable Writing Routine

Like any subject, a predictable schedule and routine are important. When students know when writing is each day, they can prepare for it and make the most of it. If writing occurs randomly and students don't know when to expect it, it takes longer to get students ready and longer to get them actually sitting down and writing. Making it predictable means making it doable, structured, and productive. Students know the expectations, they know when it is going to occur, and they know how to follow the rules and make progress with their writing tasks.

Overt Teacher Modeling

Overt teacher modeling means showing students directly how to craft grammatically and syntactically correct sentences, complete paragraphs, and stories that have a beginning, middle, and end. It means showing students how to write and providing multiple examples and nonexamples of writing sentences, paragraphs, and stories. It also means providing students with opportunities to practice what they have learned and giving feedback on what is correct and what they need to improve. Modeling is a way to be explicit, to be straightforward, and a way to tell students exactly what you are looking for.

Cooperative Arrangements among Students

Cooperative arrangements among students provide students opportunities to work together and learn from one another. In these arrangements, students help each other plan, revise, edit, or publish their written work. These partnerships are helpful because they prompt students to assess writing and think about what to look for. They teach students how to evaluate writing, which in turn helps them to consider what to include in their own writing. These partnerships are also beneficial because students receive direct feedback from a peer regarding their writing. This provides a process for revisions and edits that can help the student improve their writing before they meet with you as the teacher.

Group or Individual Sharing

Group or individual sharing of student writing is beneficial for the same reasons that cooperative arrangements are beneficial. Students receive direct and immediate feedback from their peers. This provides information to the student that may be different, or have a different impact on the student than hearing it from you as the teacher. Sharing also provides the class, or the partner, a way to think critically about what to listen for and how to assess the other person's writing. This helps the listeners to learn the components needed in writing, so that they can use this knowledge and understanding to apply it to their own writing.

When using this strategy, it is necessary to create a safe environment for student sharing. For some students, this may be a daunting task and may not be helpful for their

---

Listening to Writing

What did you like?

What might be changed?

What is one question you have?

FIGURE 7.2. Sample student feedback sheet on listening to writing.

learning if the situation creates too much discomfort. Play it by ear according to how you know your students. Some may want to share in front of the whole class. Some may do better in small groups. And some may benefit the most from sharing with a partner, as the situation is then safer and more private. Regardless of how sharing is done, using a structured feedback sheet can be helpful for the students' listening. This provides information on how the students should respond and constrains their responses to what is listed on the paper. Figures 7.2 and 7.3 show some examples.

Instruction Covering a Broad Range of Skills

Writing is a complex process. It requires taking all that you know about reading, spelling, handwriting, and written language itself to create a coherent paragraph, story, or essay. It requires thinking, planning, writing, editing, revising, and more writing to end up with a product that is well written and appealing to the reader. It is often a process that writers can't describe themselves. Where do the ideas come from? When do the ideas come to mind? How do I pull them together? What makes the writing flow with transitions? What is the ultimate goal?

All of these questions boggle the minds of adult writers, and we try to answer these questions when teaching student writers. Writing instruction, therefore, must cover a range of skills. This includes everything from handwriting and spelling, writing conventions, and sentence-level skills to text structure, the function of writing, and planning and revising. Some researchers and teachers have referred to the two main roles of a

Peer Editing

What was the author describing in his or her story?

What are three compliments you have for the writer?

1.

2.

3.

What is one suggestion you have for the writer?

What is one question you have for the writer?

FIGURE 7.3. Sample student feedback sheet on peer editing.

writer: the secretary and the author. The writer as the secretary must ensure that grammar, punctuation, and organization are used correctly. The writer as an author, on the other hand, is responsible for selecting the ideas and combining them to make a coherent product. Table 7.2, from Isaacson (1989), highlights the differences.

Follow-Up Instruction to Ensure Mastery of Targeted Skills

Follow-up instruction is important because it provides students a way to revisit learned skills and ensure that they have mastered the content before moving on. This is some-

TABLE 7.2. Secretary versus Author Responsibilities

Secretary	Author
• Grammar and sentence structure	• Create ideas
• Punctuation and spelling	• Combine the ideas
• Organization depending on purpose	• Select and arrange the words

Note. Based on Isaacson (1989).

thing that many teachers understand. The question isn't why follow-up instruction is important, but rather, how we ensure that follow-up instruction is done systematically to ensure results.

Throughout each grade level, instruction should be provided so that students are introduced to skills, taught the skills, practice the skills, and review the skills then and later. This is something that should be delineated through your writing curriculum so that you are provided a structure for introduction, teaching, mastery, and review. Your district standards and benchmarks should outline this for you, so you are provided clear information on what to teach when, and how to review as necessary.

Integration of Writing Activities throughout Other Subjects

Integrating writing activities into other subjects allows students to practice their skills in different ways and for different purposes. By having students write in math, science, social studies, or other subjects, they learn how to apply their skills in other settings. This is an important component of creating strong writers, because students who are given these opportunities practice how to write in many different ways.

One easy way to incorporate writing into different subjects is by providing simple prompts that students write about at the beginning of each class or on a weekly basis. These prompts should be content specific and relate to what is being discussed in class. They can be used to explain math equations, describe the U.S. Constitution, explain the functions of cells, or anything else that is related to the class. This gives teachers a simple way to incorporate more writing into their classes and gives students a way to consistently practice their skills and strategies for writing.

Frequent Opportunities for Students to Self-Regulate Their Behavior during Writing

When you are presented with a task—say, writing a letter to your grandmother—you likely will desire a certain setting. Depending on your style, you may prefer your quiet office or the kitchen table with a cup of tea. You may want to be sitting on the couch with your kids with music playing in the background. You may want to sit in front of the TV, writing the words as you think of them.

Everyone has their individual preferences with regards to writing and completing tasks. Be it quiet or with noise, alone or in the company of others, in the morning or afternoon, everyone works differently under different conditions. It is important to teach students how to regulate their own behavior during writing so they can begin to notice what works for them. This includes things like working independently, arranging their space, and seeking help from others when needed.

While working quietly at one's own desk may work for many students, it may not work for all. Thus, as the teacher, you can have critical conversations about creating different environments for students and the importance of learning what works for them individually. Be sure also to provide a variety of options, so students can decide where they want to sit to write, how they want to seek help from you or other students, and what level of noise they are comfortable with. The worksheet in Appendix 7.1 can be used as a survey to get information from students regarding their preferences.

Teacher and Student Assessments of Skills and Needs

Monitoring student progress and growth with skills is critical to your teaching. It is something that you do informally every day by reviewing work, noting student comments, and making observations about what they know and don't know. As a teacher, you know your students so well that you could speak about any one of them individually for hours. This is your own version of formative assessment, or assessing their skills along the way.

Formative assessment should also be done more formally, with quick measures that assess if your students are making growth with their writing. You can provide them a monthly writing prompt and, using a rubric, note the strengths, weaknesses, and growth in their writing. You can make notes about their story ideas, grammar, punctuation, expository versus narrative skills, and many other facets of writing. By doing so, you are gathering consistent data that provide you more information about what they need to work on and what they are doing well.

Frequent Communication with Parents

As with any subject, at any grade, and with any student, frequent communication with parents is essential. Sharing information with parents can help to increase student success as parents practice newly learned skills with their children at home. This can provide even more opportunities for extensions and application across time and settings.

What can be helpful for these conversations is a consistent format for conveying information to parents. This helps everyone understand where the student is, where he or she needs to be, and what steps it will take to get him or her there. This consistency is especially important for parents who have a lot going on at home and may be dealing with other issues as well. Providing a consistent format with clear notes can be useful.

You can choose to create your own, depending on what grade level you teach and what core writing skills you are working on. The form in Appendix 7.2 is provided to give you a structure for thinking about what to include in the sheet you create. Consider your standards and benchmarks first, what skills you are currently working on, and what skills are the goal for the end of the year. Use all of that information to make a structure that assists communication between you and the parents about the student's writing skills. You can include a rubric if that makes it clearer for communication. Using a structure like a rubric can help parents easily see growth over time as well.

TIER 1: CORE INTERVENTIONS

There are many core writing programs available. Our intent is to provide you with characteristics to consider when your district is ready to purchase a new core; for more discussion of core programs, see Chapter 3. The most important factors to consider are (1) the research behind the program and (2) the match to your student needs. With both of these in mind, your curriculum team is armed to decide on a curriculum that will teach your students to write and to do it well. We offer interventions to supplement the core program at Tiers 2 and 3 for students who need additional support.

An intervention that is not listed but can be powerful when added to your core writing program is *Providing Choice When Writing*. Because writing is a difficult process for some students, it quickly becomes punishing rather than reinforcing. You may have some students who just don't want to write. For those students who need additional incentive, letting them choose what they want to write about can change the task from punishing to fun. It can provide the reinforcement they need to be more invested in writing, even though it still may be difficult. This simple strategy gets more students writing and thereby gives them the practice they need. We offer this option because it can make a big impact on students who have difficulty.

TIER 2: SUPPLEMENTAL INTERVENTIONS

We offer three instructional strategies in Appendix C for the supplemental level. *Planning Your Writing* is designed to help students plan for writing using basic questions that consider who, what, where, when, and why. *Personal Narrative Think Sheet* is a plan for thinking about writing that includes a worksheet with major story components like setting, characters, problem, events, and solution. *Student Editor Strategy* provides students a format for reading, editing, and revising the writing with a partner. Students learn how to improve their own writing and what to look for when editing others' stories.

TIER 3: INTENSIVE INTERVENTIONS

Use C-SPACE to Take Notes is a strategy that helps students plan for writing a story. Students consider the characters, setting, problem, action, conclusion, and emotion for their stories. The *Proofreading Checklist* is a structure that helps students think about what they included and what they need to improve before completing their writing. *Modeling the Writing Process* is an explicit instructional plan for teaching students how to work on one part of the writing process, like using commas. As the teacher you demonstrate exactly how and when to use commas with examples, nonexamples, and with active student responding.

A NOTE ABOUT THE INTERVENTIONS

Finally, it is important to note that although some instruction interventions are listed as supplemental and others as intensive, it does not mean you can only use the interventions at those levels of support. A supplemental intervention can easily become part of your core instruction, if your core needs to be enhanced to meet the needs of more of your students. A supplemental intervention can also become an intensive intervention if done more frequently, for more time, and with more explicit support and practice. Conversely, an intensive intervention can become a supplemental intervention by using it less often, maybe just as a quick practice activity. An intensive intervention can also be used with your core by adding it to your daily activities that all students receive. It is not necessarily the distinction of interventions that makes them powerful. It is how you use them and with what intensity that really will make the difference.

RESOURCES

LD Online

www.ldonline.org

This website provides information to help children reach their full potential by providing accurate information about learning disabilities. The site features helpful articles, monthly columns by noted experts, first-person essays, and a comprehensive resource guide. An important article about teaching writing is available on this website at *www.ldonline.org/article/6213*.

Interventioncentral.org

www.interventioncentral.org

This website offers free tools and resources to help school staff and parents. The site, created by Jim Wright, a school psychologist and school administrator from central New York, features a variety of academic and behavioral intervention strategies, information on effective teaching practices, and tools that streamline classroom assessment and intervention. Specific writing strategies are available at *www.jimwrightonline.com/php/interventionista/interventionista_intv_list.php?prob_type=writing*.

LD online (*www.ldonline.org*) is a site that includes information about effective writing instruction. The U.S. Department of Education has compiled a toolkit on creating literacy-rich environments for students with disabilities, available at *www.osepideasthatwork.org/parentkit/literacy.asp*. Finally, a great resource with many ideas for writing instruction is the article "Prevention and Intervention of Writing Difficulties for Students with Learning Disabilities" (Graham et al., 2001). Multiple strategies are provided to increase writing achievement in students.

Worksheet on Student Writing Preferences

Your Writing Style

Please read the questions and check the answer that best applies to you.

1. When you are writing, how much noise do you prefer in the room?

    ☐ None

    ☐ A little background noise like quiet music or the teacher talking

    ☐ Normal classroom noise like students talking and working together

2. What area and space would you prefer for writing?

    ☐ My desk

    ☐ The large table in back

    ☐ The special chairs

3. What would you like to do when you need help from me?

    ☐ Raise my hand

    ☐ Write on a sticky note what I need and place it on the edge of my desk

    ☐ Make a note in the margin of the paper and ask later

4. How would you like to work with other students for writing?

    ☐ Ask my partner for help when I have a question

    ☐ Ask my partner to read over what I wrote

    ☐ Ask my partner to give me specific comments about what I wrote

Use the space below to describe more about what you prefer when writing.

_____

_____

_____

_____

_____

_____

_____

_____

_____

_____

_____

_____

Student Writing Form to Share with Parents

Student Writing

Name: _____ Date: _____

Ideas for stories (original thought; keeps interest; uses language; includes details):

Organization (transitions; flow of the story; has beginning, middle, and conclusion):

Sentence construction (well crafted; vary in length; smooth transitions):

Grammar and punctuation (used correctly; spelling is accurate; edits are easily incorporated):

CHAPTER 8

Math Interventions

Sandy has attended the same school since kindergarten. She is now in the third grade and finds math to be a big challenge. In her school, third-grade math instruction focuses on subtraction with regrouping, multiplication facts, measurement, and problem solving. With daily practice, Sandy mastered subtraction with regrouping and she looked forward to learning multiplication. Her teacher introduced multiplication by having the class members work in small groups to complete word problems that required multiplying sets of items. One other girl and two boys were in Sandy's group. The boys were active during the small-group sessions, and the other girl completed most of the work for the group. After 2 weeks of small-group activities, Sandy's teacher distributed a 9-by-9 multiplication grid and told the students to fill it out based on the work they had done in small groups. Sandy was able to fill in all of the 1's and some of the 2's but none of the other numbers. The teacher gave Sandy time to work on the grid each day, but by the end of the week, Sandy did not have any more multiplication facts filled in. Sandy's teacher sent the grid home with Sandy with the instruction to complete it over the weekend as homework. When Sandy got home, she complained to her mom that the weekend homework was "impossible" and she had no idea how to complete it. Sandy did not do the homework and when her teacher asked her on Monday why she had not completed the grid, Sandy said "I did not know how."

Situations like Sandy's are not unusual, and many students struggle to become skilled in math. Compared with reading instruction, far less research has been conducted on effective math instruction. Many teachers have lamented the smaller amount of math research. Although fewer in number than those for reading, there are many good math interventions that can be used. This section will describe effective math interventions that can be used at all three levels of RTI. If you have a "Sandy" in your class, this chapter is designed to help you.

WHAT DO WE KNOW ABOUT MATH INSTRUCTION?

The U.S. National Research Council conducted a review of math instruction research. The findings were summarized in the book *Adding It Up: Helping Children Learn Mathematics* (Kilpatrick, Swafford, & Findell, 2001). The book, written by a panel of researchers with expertise in math instruction, summarizes research conducted over the preceding 30 years. The book's authors and editors worked together to identify trends and major findings from the available research. Based on their review of the available studies, the authors were able to offer several major conclusions about effective math instruction. One of the core conclusions found in *Adding It Up* is that math proficiency is something that all U.S. children must develop. In the words of the authors, "All young Americans must learn to think mathematically, and they must think mathematically to learn" (Kilpatrick et al., 2001, p. 1). The authors emphasized that math skills cannot be thought of as something that only some children will learn. Instead, effective math instruction must be included in the general curriculum of all U.S. schools, including yours!

To help you be able to provide the most effective math instruction, *Adding It Up* provided a five-part conceptual framework for how math needs to be taught. Known as *strands*, the following five math components were identified by Kilpatrick et al. (2001, p. 116) as essential for all students.

1. *Conceptual understanding*—comprehension of mathematical concepts, operations, and relations.
2. *Procedural fluency*—skill in carrying out procedures flexibly, accurately, efficiently, and appropriately.
3. *Strategic competence*—ability to formulate, represent, and solve mathematical problems.
4. *Adaptive reasoning*—capacity for logical thought, reflection, explanation, and justification.
5. *Productive disposition*—habitual inclination to see mathematics as sensible, useful, and worthwhile, coupled with a belief in diligence and one's own efficacy.

One of the points that the authors made about the five strands is that they are not independent of one another. The five strands are interdependent and all must be included in math instruction at all grade levels. At this point, you are probably wondering, "How can I help my most struggling students meet such challenging math standards?"

The five strands identified in *Adding It Up* provide a way to organize the math instruction that your students need. These strands can be linked with specific instructional needs that students have. Table 8.1 provides examples of what specific skills are included in each of the strands. Keep in mind, these examples are not exhaustive, and other skills are also included in each strand. The key thing to realize is that your students will need to be able to do all of the skills listed in Table 8.1 in order to be proficient at math. Although *Adding It Up* provided clear goals for *what* math students need to learn, there is less agreement about the *order* in which math skills should be taught. Some math skills are very important building blocks for others. For example students who don't

TABLE 8.1. Strands of Math Proficiency and Sample Skills Related to the Strands

Strand	Sample skills
1. Conceptual understanding	• Understanding that a quantity of items matches the same quantity as represented by numerals. • Understanding that some math operations make things bigger and others make things smaller.
2. Procedural fluency	• Using accurate and automatic addition, subtraction, multiplication, and division skills. • Using mathematical symbols such as parentheses, plus signs and minus signs with accuracy.
3. Strategic competence	• Using rules related to the order in which specific problems need to be completed (e.g., PEMDAS). • Using different ways of representing values such as fractions and decimals.
4. Adaptive reasoning	• Using mathematical skills for different everyday activities such as cooking and sewing. • Adapting mathematical skills for use in new settings such as stores and workplaces.
5. Productive disposition	• Using learned math skills independently. • Using learned math skills to develop additional skills for solving problems.

understand that numerals stand for quantities will have a very hard time understanding the lesser and greater values that numerals represent. In a similar way, following the standard "order of operations" using "PEMDAS" is essential for correctly solving for a variable in algebra (see Figure 8.1 for a reminder about PEMDAS).

Based on the information gathered in *Adding It Up*, the U.S. Department of Education appointed a National Mathematics Advisory Panel (NMAP) in 2006. This panel included researchers with strong expertise in mathematics and mathematics instruction. This group was charged with reviewing all the available research about math instruction and summarizing what they found. Their final report, entitled *Foundations for Success*, was published in 2008 (NMAP, 2008). The report identified six main steps that need to be taken to improve math learning in U.S. schools:

1. The prekindergarten through grade 8 math curriculum should be streamlined to emphasize a narrower set of the most critical topics.
2. There must be better utilization of what is known about how children learn, especially the benefits and importance of early intervention, conceptual understanding, fluency, automaticity, and effort in math skill development.
3. Elementary grade teachers must have strong math skills in order to teach math well.
4. Math instruction should not be purely "student centered" or "teacher centered," but must be an integration of both perspectives based on the findings of research.

The acronym PEMDAS stands for the order in which the types of math included in an equation need to be completed. The letters in PEMDAS stand for six specific mathematical notations and steps. The use of the acronym helps students (and adults) remember the order as follows:

P *Parentheses*: do whatever is in parentheses *before* any other parts of the problem.

E *Exponents*: if there are any exponents in the problem, do those next.

M *Multiplication*: next do any multiplying.

D *Division*: followed by any division.

A *Addition*: then do any addition.

S *Subtraction*: finally, do any subtraction.

In order to make the PEMDAS acronym the most helpful (like many others), some teachers and students have matched up each of the letters with a word in a short, silly sentence: "Please Excuse My Dear Aunt Sally," which many people use to recall the correct order of operations for math problems.

FIGURE 8.1. "Please Excuse My Dear Aunt Sally."

5. National assessments such as the National Assessment of Educational Progress (NAEP) should be strengthened to include emphasis on the most critical math knowledge and skills.

6. There is a need for more rigorous research about math instruction, and the findings of such research must be used to improve teaching practices.

The NMAP report provides important information about what direction elementary and middle school math instruction needs to take. A key theme in the report is the importance of early student mastery of basic math skills such as computation fluency. This conclusion is similar to findings from other recent research about math instruction such as work done by Scott Baker, Russell Gerston, and Dae-Sik Lee (2002). In a study published in the *Elementary School Journal*, these researchers summarized what was then known about effective math interventions for struggling students (Baker et al., 2002). Their findings were very similar to the NMAP report. Effective math instruction includes focusing on basic skills, teaching directly and systematically, and gathering regular data on student progress.

One of the challenges that teachers face is that students won't always learn skills in the same order. Some students—maybe one of yours—may struggle with subtraction but then quickly and easily figure out multiplication. This is why using RTI to assist students struggling with math can be so helpful. For your students who "get" certain math skills right away, Tier 1 is all they need. For your students who struggle, Tier 2 provides an important way of giving extra instruction and support. Just like any use of RTI, the key to effective use of math instruction will depend on knowing what math skills a student needs to learn. Thankfully, there are certain math instruction methods that have been shown to be effective for most learners.

Many of the instructional methods which are effective for math are the same that work in other subject areas. For example explicit and systematic instruction of math skills in a planned sequence has been shown to be very effective. And, just like other areas of learning, some students will need more instruction than others. Employing three tiers of RTI math instruction helps to ensure that all students can become proficient in math. The next section provides information about what math instruction should look like at each tier, and then intervention "recipes" that you can use at each tier will be described.

TIER 1: CORE INTERVENTIONS

The best resource on effective basic math instruction is the book entitled *Designing Effective Math Instruction: A Direct Instruction Approach* (Stein, Kinder, Silbert, & Carnine, 2006), now in its fourth edition. This book provides a very thorough explanation of how to organize and provide effective math instruction for all elementary grades as well as a summary of the research that supports the methods described in the book. Stein and her colleagues incorporate four basic elements in all aspects of the book's methods:

1. Initial assessment and progress monitoring.
2. Presentation techniques.
3. Error–correction procedures.
4. Diagnosis and remediation.

Effective Tier 1 math instruction needs to include all of the above four components. First, your student's current math skills need to be known. That information is used to determine what math skills you should teach next. Progress monitoring needs to occur on a regular basis during instruction, according to each student's risk level (for information on progress monitoring, see Chapter 4).

The presentation techniques that have been shown to be the most effective are modeling, guided practice, independent practice, and review. It is important that all of your students be engaged during the lessons. One of the best ways to ensure that all students participate regularly is for you to use signals for the students so they know when to respond as a group. Signals play an important role in group instruction because they provide a way for you and your students to communicate during instruction. Signals allow the students to know when to move forward in a lesson and let you see which students understand the lesson and which ones do not. In addition to using signals, it's important that you pace the instruction to match the needs of your students. Every lesson's pace needs to follow the "Goldilocks" rule: not too slow and not too fast, but just right for the students to follow you. In general, effective presentations of lessons will be organized, engage all students simultaneously, and build on what the student already knows.

One of the key features of effective instruction is error correction. Error correction is crucial for effective teaching because it prevents a student from learning a skill the wrong way, then having to "unlearn" the error and learn the correct method. If errors are corrected right away in the learning sequence, your students will master skills more quickly and with less frustration. Finally, diagnosis and remediation are included as instructional steps at Tier 1 because you will need to reteach some skills several times for the benefit of all students. At Tier 1, diagnosis refers to identifying problems in the moment of learning and providing adjusted instruction for the entire class. This is an application of differentiated instruction at Tier 1.

Evidence-Based Core Interventions

A number of Tier 1 math interventions are available for purchase. Generally, your school district chooses what Tier 1 interventions will be used. It is beyond the scope of this book to describe all of the currently available math Tier 1 curricula, but there are some helpful websites that provide up-to-date information about available curricula. The What Works Clearinghouse (WWC; *ies.ed.gov/ncee/wwc*), a website created with funds from No Child Left Behind, locates and summarizes information about instructional methods and materials for teachers. The site includes summary tables of findings about curricula and instruction for many subject areas. As of 2008, two sets of summary data for mathematics instruction were provided at WWC. One summary covers elementary school math, and the other focuses on middle school math. Each summary includes a table that lists the specific programs and products included in the review. There is a common table legend that indicates the trend of evidence for each program. For example as of 2008, five elementary math programs had been reviewed. Detailed information about each program reviewed can be seen by clicking on the title of the program in the summary table.

Many school districts will adopt specific math curricula for their Tier 1 interventions. As noted above, few specific Tier 1 programs have been reviewed by WWC so far. You may want to add to the Tier 1 instruction chosen at the district or school level. For this reason, two Tier 1 interventions are discussed in this chapter and included in the math intervention "recipes" in Appendix C. These two recipes are ones that can be used with a whole class of students at many different grade levels. They have been used in many research studies and found to be very effective in helping students develop math skills. The recipes are *Practice, Practice, Practice* and *Interspersing Easy and Hard Math Problems*.

Practice, Practice, Practice

This Tier 1 recipe involves providing your students with opportunities to practice computation skills (Stein et al., 2006). The reason this recipe can be useful at Tier 1 is that all core math instructional programs include teaching computation skills, and many of your students will benefit from practicing these skills. As noted above, your students need to learn many skills in order to become proficient in math. What is not known at this time is what percentage of math instruction should be devoted to computation. Despite this, it is clear that all students who go on to become proficient in math have strong computation skills, and so additional practice using addition, subtraction, multiplication, and division skills is important for all your students. The *Practice, Practice, Practice* recipe involves creating computation skills worksheets and having your students complete them on a regular basis.

The *Practice, Practice, Practice* recipe can be used with your current core (e.g., Tier 1) math curriculum, and you can select which computation skills to have students practice and in what order. In addition, mixed-skill worksheets can be developed so that your students can practice computation problems requiring the use of different operations. This can be particularly helpful for your students who perform the wrong operation (e.g., adding the numbers instead of subtracting them). The *Practice, Practice, Practice* recipe uses a free program that generates worksheets with different problems on them that you can match to the Tier 1 instruction during the course of the year (Intervention Central, 2008). The worksheet software is the Math Worksheet Generator from the Intervention Central website.

Interspersing Easy and Hard Math Problems

A second Tier 1 intervention recipe includes instructions for creating computation worksheets that include both easy and difficult math problems (McDonald & Ardoin, 2007). Having both difficult and easy math problems on the same worksheet can be helpful for your students for several reasons. First, such practice worksheets help them maintain previously learned computation skills. Second, balancing easy and hard problems allows your students to get practice with new and emerging computation skills as they work on the hard problems. Since "hard" problems will probably take your students longer to do and be "harder," the easy ones on the same page give them a break from difficult work.

Interspersing worksheets can be created at the same website where the *Practice, Practice, Practice* worksheets can be made. At this site, you create "mixed-skill" worksheets that include problems that are easy and hard for your students. The easy problems should be ones that you know they can do quickly and independently. The hard problems should be ones that incorporate skills you have recently taught. The worksheet generator at Intervention Central will organize the easy and hard problems in a random order on the worksheet. This is important because the benefit of interspersing the problems is to have your students go back and forth between easy and hard problems while they practice. Some of your students may initially do all of the hard or all of the easy problems first on a page. If this happens, tell your students they will find doing the worksheet easier if they do them in order so they get a break from the easy ones now and then, but also get the challenge of the hard ones.

TIER 2: SUPPLEMENTAL INTERVENTIONS

For many of your students, the Tier 1 math program will be what they need to make effective progress in learning math skills. Some of them, however, will need more than Tier 1 to succeed in math. For these students Tier 2 math instruction will be essential. Tier 2 math instruction is typically done with small groups (e.g., 3 to 5 students) on a regular basis. The frequency of the instruction can vary from 2 to 5 days a week, depending on how much support your students need. While ongoing research about math instruction is still needed, results from previous research provides an excellent starting point for planning your Tier 2 interventions. In their study published in *Elementary School Journal*, Baker et al. (2002) reviewed all available studies that investigated the effects of math interventions for low-achieving students. First, the authors identified all scientifically based published studies that reported the outcomes of specific math interventions. It is important to note that Baker et al. included only studies with students who were low achieving in math but who were *not* receiving special education services. The review of studies for students struggling in math but not participating in special education is an important feature of their research because it included exactly the type of students who need Tier 2 math interventions. Baker et al. identified 15 studies that described the effects of math interventions for students not in special education.

Their findings revealed that three specific Tier 2 instructional practices yielded beneficial outcomes for the students: (1) peer-assisted learning, (2) explicit instruction, and (3) providing teachers and students with student performance data and instructional recommendations. You can use these three methods regardless of the Tier 1 curriculum in place at your school. The first of these three interventions utilizes peer-assisted learning strategies (PALS), which was developed based on research conducted by Doug and Lynn Fuchs at Vanderbilt University (PALS, 2008). There is a website devoted to providing PALS resources located at *kc.vanderbilt.edu/pals*. PALS materials have been developed for both reading and math, including student materials, teacher manuals, and training videos. The materials range in cost from $15.00 to $35.00 and can be purchased using the order form at *kc.vanderbilt.edu/pals/pdfs/PALS_order_form.pdf*.

The primary means by which PALS helps struggling students is by providing them with many opportunities to practice and get immediate corrective feedback from a peer. These instructional components have been shown to be important for all stages and levels of learning; however, your students who are struggling to learn math skills are the most likely to benefit from PALS. It is important to note that PALS is a very *structured* peer-based learning system. All of your participating students need to learn the specific steps to make it work. When done correctly, your students will enjoy doing PALS work, and it will enhance their math skills. One of the benefits of PALS as a Tier 2 math intervention is that it can be done easily in your classroom because it can be used with all your students even if they are at a variety of skill development levels. It does not require "pull-out" services and personnel. PALS is most likely to help your students with math difficulties when it is used in addition to a carefully selected Tier 1 intervention.

The second math intervention method that Baker et al. (2002) found to be most effective for struggling students was explicit instruction. Specifically, their research showed that when highly explicit and sequenced math instruction was provided for struggling students, they made significant gains in math skills. Such instruction is similar to the directed and sequenced math instruction we recommended for Tier 1; however, for your students who are struggling, additional direct instruction is needed. For example let's say you have a student who has not yet learned how to add numbers with regrouping from the 1's to 10's place. This student needs you to teach how to do such addition. In the same way, if you have a student who has struggled to master the steps needed in solving word problems, you need to teach how to "translate" words into numerical equations.

The third instructional method that Baker et al. (2002) found to be helpful for struggling math students was providing data on student performance to both the student and the teacher. This finding is highly similar to findings about the benefits of regular progress monitoring for students participating in any intervention. A thorough discussion of the benefits of progress monitoring is found in Chapter 4 in this book, but the Baker et al. (2002) study showed that if you and your students review their progress regularly, it is helpful above and beyond the specific Tier 2 instruction you provide.

The benefits of weekly progress monitoring show the importance of helping your students to develop fluency—a measure of both speed and accuracy—with math skills. It is not just speed or accuracy by themselves. *Fluency* is the accurate performance of a skill within the time frame needed for that skill, so using math skills fluently means using them accurately for the purpose at hand. For example it's the ability to calculate whether you got the right change back before you leave the store. It's possible to do math too slowly, and this may mean never completing the problems. Alternatively, it's possible to do math too quickly and make many errors. Doing math fluently means going at just the right speed for the task. For some of your students, fluency practice can be an important part of Tier 2 math intervention. These students might have learned how to complete the math problems correctly, but not at the speed needed. In such cases, fluency practice can be an important part of your Tier 2 intervention.

Evidence-Based Supplemental Interventions

In order to help your students who are struggling with their math skills, you can use selected Tier 2 interventions. As with other content areas, it's important to match the selected intervention to the skills that each student needs to learn. Once each student's learning needs have been identified, a Tier 2 intervention can be used to boost those skills. You probably have a few students with multiple Tier 2 math learning needs. For those students, it's important to start with the content closest to what your student already knows, which will allow you to build new learning on top of existing skills. To assist you in helping your students struggling in math, three Tier 2 intervention "recipes" are provided in Appendix C at the back of the book: *Skip-Counting Practice, Computation Grid with M & M's,* and *Timed Practice, Practice, Practice.*

Skip-Counting Practice

Skip-Counting Practice helps students learn the size of the difference between numbers. It is based on research summarized in work by Stein et al. (2006). Many of your students will quickly learn how to count one number at a time (1, 2, 3, etc.), but some of your students probably struggle to recall how far apart specific numbers are. The distance between numbers plays a critical role in all mathematics, and helping your students master number patterns and relative distance can help them be better at many aspects of math. *Skip-Counting Practice* can be used to help your students become more skilled with number distances. To do the skip-counting activity, you will need copies of skip-counting grids as well as highlighters to mark number intervals identified by the teacher. Directions for *Skip-Counting Practice* are found on p. 205 of Appendix C.

Skip-Counting Practice can be used with small groups in your classroom. You will predetermine what counting intervals the students need to practice, and then they prac-

Count by: 3

1	2	3	4	5	6	7	8	9	10
11	12	13	14	15	16	17	18	19	20
21	22	23	24	25	26	27	28	29	30
31	32	33	34	35	36	37	38	39	40
41	42	43	44	45	46	47	48	49	50
51	52	53	54	55	56	57	58	59	60
61	62	63	64	65	66	67	68	69	70
71	72	73	74	75	76	77	78	79	80
81	82	83	84	85	86	87	88	89	90
91	92	93	94	95	96	97	98	99	100

Count by: 5

1	2	3	4	5	6	7	8	9	10
11	12	13	14	15	16	17	18	19	20
21	22	23	24	25	26	27	28	29	30
31	32	33	34	35	36	37	38	39	40
41	42	43	44	45	46	47	48	49	50
51	52	53	54	55	56	57	58	59	60
61	62	63	64	65	66	67	68	69	70
71	72	73	74	75	76	77	78	79	80
81	82	83	84	85	86	87	88	89	90
91	92	93	94	95	96	97	98	99	100

FIGURE 8.2. Sample completed Skip Counting grids.

tice by marking these intervals on the grids. All of the students in a group can practice the same intervals, or you can ask students to practice different intervals. Eight grids are provided on each page of the template. An initial practice of this activity can start with having all your students fill in the intervals when counting from 2's through 9's. Many students don't struggle with counting by 1's and 10's, but if these are intervals that your students need to practice, they can be used too. When using the Skip-Counting grid with your students for the first time, it is best if you model how to complete the activity. Such modeling incorporates direct instruction of the task for your students. Some reproducible Skip-Counting grids that you can use are found in Appendix 8.1 at the end of this chapter. Two examples of completed grids are shown here in Figure 8.2.

Computation Grid with M & M's

A second Tier 2 intervention that can help students is the *Computation Grid with M & M's*. This recipe, adapted from Stein et al. (2006), requires somewhat more preparation and materials than others in this book, but it is an effective way for your students to practice how quantities are grouped for different mathematical operations. This recipe requires a blank computation grid such as that shown in Appendix 8.1, as well as sets of 100 counting items for each of your students. The basic recipe calls for the use of 100 M & M's candies for each of your students, because candy can be an effective reinforcer for students (and teachers!). If edibles are not allowed in your school, or if any of your students cannot eat or do not like M & M's, you can use alternative counting items. For example other types of small candy or countable items such as raw beans can be used. It is important that the *Computation Grid with M & M's* recipe be used as part of your structured, sequenced math instructional program in which your students eventually show their mastery of computation facts without external counting items.

To use *Computation Grid with M & M's* you need to count out 100 sets of M & M's or other items in advance. These can be counted into zip-top plastic bags or paper juice cups. If the activity will last more than one day, using zip-top bags is recommended. It works best if you make a set of 100 items for yourself as well to use for modeling the activity for the students (and eating at the end!). You also need to decide what mathematical operation the students will practice. The blank grid in Appendix 8.2 can be used for addition, subtraction, multiplication, and division. Your students will circle what operation is being practiced on the top of the page. Once the counting sets have been created, you will give the materials to your students. In addition to the set of 100 items (candies), each of your students will need a paper plate, napkin, or paper towel on which to count out items, and a pencil to fill in the grid. In order to complete this activity so that everyone can eat the candy later, it is recommended that you and the students wash your hands immediately before and after touching the candy. Remind your students to touch only their own candy/items and not those of other students.

First, you will model how to use the M & M's to identify the correct number for each cell on the grid. You can decide whether to model all answers for one row or column, or whether to model specific sums, differences, products, or dividends. After showing students the process of grouping the number of candies or items to find the answers, give them a specified amount of time to work on completing the grid. Depending on your students' ages and skills, as well as the operation being practiced, this activity may be done in one 30-minute session, or may be completed over several sessions. Once your students can complete the entire grid with 100% accuracy in a specific period of time, they should practice these skills in other math activities.

Timed Practice, Practice, Practice

As noted above, for some of your students Tier 2 math interventions need to include fluency instruction. The best way to provide such instruction is to have students practice math problems under timed conditions and graph the number of digits or problems completed correctly (NMAP, 2008). Once they learn the routines, your students will enjoy the timed practice sessions and will be able to see their skills improve with each session. The recipe for *Timed Practice, Practice, Practice* is very similar to the one for *Practice, Practice, Practice*. The only difference is that this one is timed. There are commercial fluency interventions that incorporate timed practice of math problems, but the same intervention can be created using the Intervention Central website as well.

The process for creating the timed practice sheets is identical to the method for creating the untimed ones. The choice of what skill(s) the worksheet should include should be based on what skill(s) your students have recently learned. Timed practice sheets should include skills that they can do independently but not fluently. This means that they know the steps to complete the problems but do so slowly. The timed worksheets provide a way for your students to practice completing the problems with both accuracy and greater speed. Developing such fluency is important so that they will be able to use the skills for more complex math applications in the future. For example your students will be able to tackle multistep word problems, and eventually algebra problems, much more easily once they are fluent with basic operations. The instructions for *Timed Practice, Practice, Practice* are found in the math inverventions section.

Within a three-tiered RTI system, if your students are not (yet) successful with at least two Tier 2 interventions, they are generally referred for a comprehensive evaluation. The reason for conducting a comprehensive evaluation at Tier 3 is that the interventions used at Tier 2 have not worked and there is no reason to think they will suddenly start working tomorrow. Still, there are some important procedural aspects of Tier 2 interventions that need to be verified before a comprehensive evaluation is used. For example it's important to verify that the Tier 2 interventions were implemented correctly and thoroughly. You would not want to conclude that a specific Tier 2 intervention did not work if it was never put in place correctly. The accuracy of an intervention is known as *treatment integrity*. If the treatment integrity of the Tier 2 interventions was accurate and complete, and the student did not respond to the interventions, then it's a good idea to try something else.

The specific components of a comprehensive evaluation are covered in detail in other books about RTI (see Brown-Chidsey & Steege, 2005). Comprehensive evaluations include all the data from interventions at Tiers 1 and 2, as well as additional selected assessments such as measures of memory, emotional skills, or everyday living skills. Comprehensive evaluations must meet the criteria required by your state's special education regulations, and the comprehensive evaluation reports will be used by your school-based team to help determine whether your student is eligible for special education. It's important to know that while a comprehensive evaluation is being conducted, intervention should continue.

TIER 3: INTENSIVE INTERVENTIONS

Interventions provided while your student is undergoing a comprehensive evaluation are known as Tier 3 interventions. Such interventions often are very similar to programs used for students in special education. One of the features of intensive interventions that can play a role in the comprehensive evaluation is that they can be used as part of the diagnostic teaching described in Chapter 2. There are a few diagnostic and prescriptive math interventions that can be used as part of Tier 3 intervention and assessment (Carnine, 1997). An example of a very intensive math intervention is Touch Math (Simon & Hanrahan, 2004). Touch Math is a program that integrates direct teaching of numeral shapes with dots incorporated into the numerals. The dots are designed to help your student remember what numeral shapes represent which specific quantities. Limited research has shown that the Touch Math method is effective for students with learning disabilities, but additional research that reviews available intensive interventions for students who do not respond to Tier 2 math instruction is needed. At the present time, Tier 3 interventions usually include more intensive versions of methods used at Tier 2. Although ongoing research concerning Tier 3 math interventions will be helpful, there are some interventions in addition to Touch Math that can be used for students with ongoing math difficulties. Three intervention recipes that can be used with such students are *Flashcards, Flashcards with Folding In New Items*, and *Cover–Copy–Compare*.

Flashcards

Flashcards are one of the oldest and lowest-cost math interventions. The principles behind flashcards are repeated exposure, practice, and corrective feedback for students who struggle to master specific math skills (Cates, 2005; Shapiro, 2004). To be most effective, flashcards need to be matched to your student's current learning area and used daily with your feedback. The cards are very easy to make, and there are a number of premade cards available for purchase. You are likely to find it helpful to have a ready supply of blank 3″ × 5″ cards so you can make new flashcards as your students' learning needs change. As noted in the recipe directions, it's important that the cards be used individually at your student's specific skill level. They can also be used in a peer-based format if your students are old enough. A feature of the recipe is for you or a peer to provide feedback to the student during the flashcard drill. Immediate corrective feedback is very effective for mastery of math facts and skills. Once your student has mastered one set of flashcards, the *Flashcards with Folding In New Items* recipe can be used.

Flashcards with Folding In New Items

This recipe is very similar to the basic *Flashcards* recipe, but it includes "folding in" new math problems once students master previous ones (Shapiro, 2004). The folding component of this recipe is very much like folding in an ingredient to a cake: it must be done slowly and with care. Once your student has mastered a set of 10 flashcards, it's time to fold in new items. This is done at a rate of two new problems for every 10 cards. The new problems should be shuffled into the set of cards so as to be random during the drill sessions. Once your student has mastered the newly folded-in items, two additional new problems can be folded into that set. Folding in two new items at a time helps students to maintain fluency with the old items while building skills with the new ones. This is an excellent way to check whether your student is retaining information over time. Once a student has shown mastery of a problem, it can be removed from that set.

Cover–Copy–Compare

A final Tier 3 recipe is *Cover–Copy–Compare*. This is a fairly traditional one as well. In this recipe, your student looks at a specific problem, then covers it with a hand, writes it on the paper next to the covered one, and then compares her own answer with the original (Shapiro, 2004). This intervention works by having your student practice problems in very small chunks—one at a time—with a focus on accuracy. This recipe is well suited for your students who have problems with computation accuracy. The "compare" phase of the recipe provides them with an immediate feedback loop to know whether their answer is correct. When incorrect, students erase and write the correct answer so they practice the accurate response. *Cover–Copy–Compare* worksheets can be developed at the Intervention Central website. As with the practice worksheets, you decide what problem type the students will practice. This ensures that the items match the students' current learning need.

SUMMARY

Although there is less research about math interventions, there are studies that indicate specific interventions can be effective for most students. At Tier 1, direct instruction has been found to be very effective. For some students, Tier 1 alone is not enough, and many can benefit from Tier 2 interventions. Three main Tier 2 math intervention components have been shown to be most effective: peer teaching, explicit instruction, and regular feedback for students and teachers. Within the research, computation fluency has been identified as an important aspect of overall math skill development. For your students who still struggle after participating in Tier 2 instruction, diagnostic teaching and evaluation at Tier 3 can be a way to identify the specific nature of their math difficulties. You can use specific intervention recipes matched to the needs of learners across the three tiers. These recipes offer a way for you to support all your students in developing strong math skills.

RESOURCES

National Math Advisory Panel

www.ed.gov/about/bdscomm/list/mathpanel/index.html

The panel was commissioned by President George W. Bush to review all available research about math instruction and write a report with specific recommendations for improving math instruction. This website includes links to the full text of the panel's report as well as related documents about math instruction.

What Works Clearinghouse

ies.ed.gov/ncee/wwc

Established in 2002, WWC is a central and trusted source of scientific evidence for what works in education. An initiative of the U.S. Department of Education's Institute of Education Sciences, the WWC produces user-friendly practice guides for educators that address instructional challenges with research-based recommendations for schools and classrooms. WWC has reports about a number of specific math curricula.

Although not as large as the resources about reading, there are resources about effective math interventions. The best and most comprehensive book about math instruction is *Designing Effective Mathematics Instruction: A Direct Instruction Approach* (2006) by Marcy Stein, Diane Kinder, Jerry Silbert, and Douglas W. Carnine. It covers all aspects of effective mathematics instruction for kindergarten through grade 8. The website *www.prenhall.com/stein* accompanies the text. Scott Baker, Russ Gerston and D. S. Lee (2002) compiled a summary of the research on math interventions for low-achieving students in an article for *Elementary School Journal*. Doug Carnine (1997) has written about effective math instruction for students with learning disabilities as well. Additional information about the math recipes included in this chapter can be found in the articles listed in the references at the back of the book. More general math intervention information is available at *www.interventioncentral.org*.

Skip-Counting Practice Grids

Name: _____

Skip-Counting Practice

Count by:

1	2	3	4	5	6	7	8	9	10
11	12	13	14	15	16	17	18	19	20
21	22	23	24	25	26	27	28	29	30
31	32	33	34	35	36	37	38	39	40
41	42	43	44	45	46	47	48	49	50
51	52	53	54	55	56	57	58	59	60
61	62	63	64	65	66	67	68	69	70
71	72	73	74	75	76	77	78	79	80
81	82	83	84	85	86	87	88	89	90
91	92	93	94	95	96	97	98	99	100

Count by:

1	2	3	4	5	6	7	8	9	10
11	12	13	14	15	16	17	18	19	20
21	22	23	24	25	26	27	28	29	30
31	32	33	34	35	36	37	38	39	40
41	42	43	44	45	46	47	48	49	50
51	52	53	54	55	56	57	58	59	60
61	62	63	64	65	66	67	68	69	70
71	72	73	74	75	76	77	78	79	80
81	82	83	84	85	86	87	88	89	90
91	92	93	94	95	96	97	98	99	100

Count by:

1	2	3	4	5	6	7	8	9	10
11	12	13	14	15	16	17	18	19	20
21	22	23	24	25	26	27	28	29	30
31	32	33	34	35	36	37	38	39	40
41	42	43	44	45	46	47	48	49	50
51	52	53	54	55	56	57	58	59	60
61	62	63	64	65	66	67	68	69	70
71	72	73	74	75	76	77	78	79	80
81	82	83	84	85	86	87	88	89	90
91	92	93	94	95	96	97	98	99	100

Count by:

1	2	3	4	5	6	7	8	9	10
11	12	13	14	15	16	17	18	19	20
21	22	23	24	25	26	27	28	29	30
31	32	33	34	35	36	37	38	39	40
41	42	43	44	45	46	47	48	49	50
51	52	53	54	55	56	57	58	59	60
61	62	63	64	65	66	67	68	69	70
71	72	73	74	75	76	77	78	79	80
81	82	83	84	85	86	87	88	89	90
91	92	93	94	95	96	97	98	99	100

Computation Grid

Name: _____

Computation Grid

Circle operation: Addition   Subtraction   Multiplication   Division

	1	2	3	4	5	6	7	8	9	10
1										
2										
3										
4										
5										
6										
7										
8										
9										
10										

Graph for Timed Practice, Practice, Practice

Name: _____ Skill: _____

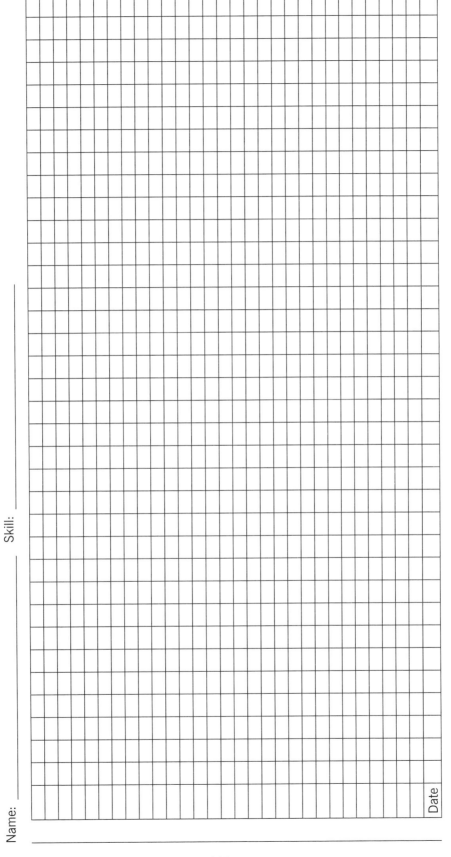

Date

CHAPTER 9

Behavior Interventions

A few years ago I (Louise) was asked to teach a seminar at the University of Oregon for students who were in our general education teacher training program. The focus of this weekly get-together was how best to teach elementary school students who were receiving services in special education. These teachers-to-be wanted to know more about teaching the most challenging students, anticipating that this would better prepare them for their general education classrooms. Before our first class I sought advice from my colleague, Joan, who had been teaching elementary students in special education for almost 30 years. She had a well-deserved reputation as an expert in her field and was often called upon to do district-level training for special education teachers. I asked her how she would summarize the job of a special education teacher. She turned to me and without hesitation said, "Your job is to manage the behavior so that you can deliver the instruction. Period." Simple, profound, and right on. It was a great answer that made the point that even the best academic interventions will flop if the students are not paying attention.

I'm sure more than a few of you are reading this and thinking, "Boy, is that ever the truth. If only I could stop student so-and-so from acting out every time I introduce an academic activity, he or she might actually learn something." Now, I know that Joan was talking about her students in special education, but what I later learned by working as a school psychologist, and you probably learned in your first year of teaching, was that some of your students in general education are also very demanding and have behaviors that you need to manage. Maybe you've had the experience of referring a student to the school psychologist for an evaluation, only to be told before the ink on the assessments had dried that your student does not qualify for special education and you are responsible for managing his or her behavior and delivering instruction. Probably not your best day, but I hope that you did get some help from the team regarding how to manage the student's behavior. Unfortunately, at this point it is more common that many teachers in general education get little or no help, making this a defining moment early in their careers.

In this chapter it is our intent to give you some guidance and offer practical solutions for managing unwanted student behavior in your general education classroom. In keeping with the theme of the book, this chapter will frame these interventions within an RTI model. In other words, we will give you "recipes" for behavior management and align them with the three tiers of an RTI system. That being said, it is worth noting that among academicians there is still some discussion about which behavior interventions belong in which category: Tiers 1, 2, or 3 (Hawken, Vincent, & Schumann, 2008). We do not presume to have a definitive answer to this so we will move forward with the understanding that this chapter should be (1) useful to you, the classroom teacher, and (2) make some sense within the tiered system of RTI. Just bear in mind that the choice of interventions needs to reflect each individual situation you face.

Let's take a few moments to go over what we do know about managing student behavior in schools. The information that follows has been gleaned from many sources and many studies. At the end of this chapter you will find a list of resources that will guide you to the people who have helped us to understand so much about student behavior in schools. One clear "truth" that has emerged is that behavior is best managed by using a prevention model grounded in positive interaction between adults and students (Walker et al., 1996). It sounds simple enough, but so many of us struggle to implement it. Let's take a closer look: Prevention implies that you'll want whatever you're going to do to be in place before the first student comes in and has a chance to behave in a way that you would rather he didn't. Notice the last phrase, "in a way that you would rather he didn't." This really requires the student to know what your preferences are. A student who doesn't know your preferences may decide to get up and visit with a neighbor because that's what he did in his last class. Think of how unfair and unwelcoming it would be in the first week of school to turn around and publicly scold him for this behavior. In a prevention model you're going to have to make sure that you clearly state your rules in a positive way, teach them to the students, post them on the walls, and review them from time to time so that all students (including the ones who just moved in) understand what is expected of them.

Whenever I talk about proactive classroom rules it always makes me think of play dates. As a mother of a 10-year-old I have experienced my fair share of them, and I am constantly in awe of other parents who just open their front doors and tell my visiting child to "go on upstairs and find Billy/Johnny/José/Ricky—he's playing in his room." They wave blithely from the doorstep as I back my car out of their driveway saying a little prayer that my son, who does not know their house rules, will not unintentionally violate every one of them in the first 15 minutes of his visit. If he does, he will spend half of the play date being corrected and embarrassed, and I will be branded as yet another psychologist who can't raise her own child, let alone anyone else's. Yikes.

It probably won't surprise you that when the play date is at my house, I spend the first 5 minutes with my son and his friend going over the house rules. Things like which rooms are okay for playing in, pillows must stay on the beds, and outside playing is usually better than inside. This ensures that we are all on the same page and there won't be any "gotcha" moments for our young visitor. I also try to state the rules in a positive way. I didn't say, "Don't go in this room" or "Don't hit each other with the pillows." Instead I said, "These two rooms are for playing in, and pillows must stay on the bed." See the difference? Subtle, but powerful. When you write up your class rules try to make sure that you state them in a positive way. Environments that are full of positive energy are always best for young and old alike.

TIER 1: CORE INTERVENTIONS

In the world of RTI your proactive introduction of three to five positively stated class rules is considered Tier 1, or green, intervention. This is something that all students should receive and you will find that it helps to suppress many unwanted student behaviors. However, there is more to this first green intervention. Do you remember the example above with your student on the first day getting up to visit neighbors because he was allowed to do that in his last class? Well, it certainly adds confusion to the situation when rules vary dramatically from class to class. The more closely you and your colleagues align your classroom rules, the more success you will have with student behavior management.

It is also very helpful (and part of a Tier 1 behavior system) to include all parts of the school in your positive, proactive environment. Perhaps you have had the experience of walking into the school cafeteria during a student lunch period and thinking, "I sure am glad I don't have to eat in here!" Chances are your student cafeteria is either loud and chaotic, or deathly quiet. You have the "no-rules" version or the "super-duper negatively stated rules that will only be broken over my dead body" version. The cafeteria would benefit from having similar expectations to what you have in your classroom. In addition to the cafeteria, other places that benefit from Tier 1 core behavior expectations are the hallways, playgrounds, and school buses. When these places are under control in a positive, proactive way, your students will come back to your room with fewer issues and more ready to learn. You will find that closely aligning the rules from your classroom across all areas will greatly increase the student behavior that you want, and decrease what you don't want.

Other Tier 1 (green) interventions include the techniques you use to manage the behavior of your class. For example maybe you pay close attention to the seating arrangements. Having students' desks in groups will facilitate group work; however, it may also encourage off-task socializing. Having students' desks in a semicircle will increase your visibility to each of them and may help to encourage participation and discourage off-task behavior. When you are arranging your students' desks, you should consider how well you can move between the students and around them in order to provide praise, assistance, and proximity as needed. You'll need to weigh the plusses and minuses of this in your room. Taking into consideration individual behavior and how well you manage it may help inform your decision about the arrangement of the desks.

Praise can be a powerful classroom management tool. In order for it to work, it is important that praise be specific and meaningful. For example let's say that your student

Sarah often runs out of time when it comes to finishing her seatwork, but today she hands it to you on time. This is a perfect opportunity to praise her for a behavior that you would like to see more of. So you say, "Sarah, nice job turning in your seatwork before the time limit." This is a positive and specific statement that will encourage on-time work completion not only from Sarah but also from those around her who heard your praise. However, if you make the all-too-common mistake of saying "Nice job, Sarah," then it's too general. It will not have the desired effect of encouraging Sarah to continue the behavior, and the other students will miss the point entirely. When offering praise, keep in mind: positive, specific, and meaningful.

Keeping students engaged during independent seatwork or whole-group instruction can be a challenge. If these work times are too long, you're in trouble. If transitions between the activities take too long, you're in trouble. If during independent seatwork, a student has to raise his hand and $w \ldots a \ldots i \ldots t \ldots$ (zzzzzzzz) for you to come over, you're in trouble. A recipe for shortening transition times appears at the end of this chapter. As for waiting with hands raised for help, here's a great idea that I'll pass along to you. I saw a third-grade teacher use a very simple yet effective tool that eliminated waiting with hand raised. She had taken a $3'' \times 5''$ red index card and a $3'' \times 5''$ green index card and glued them together, back to back. She then laminated them and gave one to each student in the class. Students were instructed to have the card, green side up, on their desks during independent seat work. She taught her students that if they had a question then they were to mark the question on their work (such as circling problem number 5) and flip their green card over to red. The critical piece in this example is that students were taught to continue working (after flipping the card to red), with the understanding that the teacher would be over shortly to help with the problem that had stumped them. This resulted in no raised hands, no students staring off into space while waiting for help, no waving of hands to attract more immediate attention, and no visiting with neighbors to kill time. That room ran like a Swiss watch. In addition, you could have students use the red/green card to respond to whole-group questions. These would have to be questions with yes-or-no answers, and students would respond by holding their card up so that you could see it and turning to the color that corresponded with yes (green) or no (red). It's a way of quickly checking for understanding across the class.

Another "truth" in the area of student behavior in school is that good social skills lead to better relationships with peers and teachers. Wouldn't it be nice if all children came to school having learned how to listen respectfully to adults, follow directions, take turns, share, play nicely with others, be able to take the perspective of others, and be kind to their fellow students? That's Lake Wobegon, not reality, right? Right. And yet you don't need some researcher to tell you that the closer all students come to having these skills, the more smoothly your school and classroom will run. This is why a good social skills training program should be part of any Tier 1 core behavior program. You can't control what your students come in with, but you can control what they leave with. The social skills program that you use should be designed for all students to receive lessons in class as part of their weekly routine. These programs should provide opportunities to role-play and practice the skills that are being taught. Several of these programs are mentioned at the end of this chapter.

TIER 2: SUPPLEMENTAL INTERVENTIONS

If you have your Tier 1 interventions in place and running smoothly, will that solve all of the behavior problems? No, but it will go a long way to reducing the number of problems that you will have. In a class of 30 you will almost certainly have three to five students in your classroom who will need more help managing their behavior. This brings us to Tier 2. Tier 2, or yellow, interventions are usually designed to accommodate small groups of students. For example there may be a *Check-In, Check-Out* intervention already in place to which you send four of your students each day. The small-group format contributes to the easy, low resource allocation goal of Tier 2 interventions. You'll want your Tier 2/yellow interventions to already be in place, ready for you to access easily and quickly. Ideally, you will want your student to have access within a week of the need becoming known. You don't want to get bogged down in multiple team meetings or student assessments in order to offer your student a Tier 2 behavior intervention. Why? Because if the student has to wait for help, you may find that his or her behavior goes from bad to worse fairly quickly. This makes everything more difficult in the moment and in the future. So don't wait; jump right in.

TIER 3: INTENSIVE INTERVENTIONS

This brings us to the third and final tier. Tier 3, or red, interventions will most likely be necessary for one or maybe two of your students (in a 30-student class). Tier 3 interventions are different from Tiers 1 and 2 in that they require more school resources, more of your time, and are almost always customized for that particular student. We have intentionally not included any recipes for Tier 3 behavior interventions because students who require Tier 3 behavior intervention typically have complex behavior patterns that have developed over time, usually as a result of their interactions in both the home and school environments. In very general terms, however, the two main reasons that children act out are (1) to get something pleasant, or (2) to avoid something unpleasant. You will need to have a person on your behavior team who has been trained to think of behavior in functional terms, that is, antecedent → behavior → consequence. This specialist will guide you in examining the environment and the behavior in terms of function. In other words, what does the child get for the behavior? What sets him off? Why does he keep doing it? And of course, what can we do to alter this student's behavioral chain of events for the better? To help find answers to these questions, a school psychologist or other behavior specialist may undertake what is known as a functional behavioral assessment (FBA) of the student in Tier 3. The results of the FBA can be used to guide you and your team in crafting an appropriate behavior intervention for your student.

Tier 3 interventions also involve the family to the greatest extent possible. Typically, these are the students for whom nothing else has worked, and Tier 3 is the last stop before a referral to a different placement. These students are at very high risk for academic failure, leading to delinquency, drug use, and dropping out. It is also true that by the time they reach Tier 3 you will already have tried Tiers 1 and 2 with them. Who could blame you if you were fed up and tired of the whole thing? At this point in the process you must dig deep and ask yourself what is at stake. A child's future is. You can do it—it's one of the reasons you took the job. Don't make the mistake of thinking that these students will be better off somewhere else. In most cases they won't. They know you and have a connection (however fragile it may be) to you and the other students in the class. Starting over is never easy even in the best of circumstances. Use your team, collaborate on these Tier 3 recipes, and remember, even in the darkest moments—never give up on a child.

No chapter on RTI would be complete without a reference to monitoring progress. Just like you did with the academic interventions, you will need to collect some data before you begin the intervention and some as you go along. With behavior we have no test scores to reference, so you'll have to go with things like direct observations, tallies from point cards, or office discipline referrals. The recipes that follow include suggestions for how best to measure and graph your student's behavioral progress. Don't forget to check our website, *www.rticlassroom.org* (coming by Fall 2009) from time to time to find helpful tools that you can download and use.

RESOURCES

National Technical Assistance Center on Positive Behavior Interventions and Supports

www.pbis.org

Click on the tab that says "On-Line Library." From that page you will find links to "Resource Links" and "PBS in Your State." Both of these links are very helpful. You may find that looking up your state facilitator under "PBS in Your State" and contacting him or her will put you on the fastest track to establishing a PBS system in your school or district.

First Step to Success

First Step to Success, by Walker et al. (1997), is a proven collaborative home–school program that teaches challenging children how to get along with others and engage in schoolwork. This is a very good Tier 2 intervention for students in K–3. Everything that you need to work with three students comes in one starter kit for less than $200. More students can be served by purchasing a resupply kit for less than $50. Published by Sopris West (*store.cambium-learning.com*).

Second Step

www.cfchildren.org/programs/ssp/overview

Second Step is a violence prevention program that integrates academics with social and emotional learning. It is research based and covers students from preschool through eighth grade. A kit for one grade can be purchased for a little less than $200.

Systematic Screening for Behavior Disorders

The Systematic Screening for Behavior Disorders (SSBD), by Walker and Severson (1992), can be used to screen and identify students who may be at risk for developing behavior disorders. This kit incorporates teacher opinion as well as some direct observations. Sopris West/ Cambium Learning sells an SSBD kit that can be used over and over again, and includes a video training tape. This kit can be purchased for your elementary school for just over $100. Talk to your team about this option.

Michigan Positive Behavior Support Network

Michigan Positive Behavior Support Network has a link to several forms for conducting a functional behavioral assessment (FBA). They are designed for a specialist to work with a teacher on how to collect and analyze behavior data in order to create an appropriate intervention for that student. Log on to *www.bridges4kids.org/PBS/index.htm* and then select "Functional Behavioral Assessments (FBA)."

Responding to Problem Behavior in Schools: The Behavior Education Program (Crone, Hawken, & Horner, 2004) is an excellent "how-to" book that specifically targets students in Tier 2. The Behavior Education Program (BEP) can be added to your existing schoolwide behavior program. The BEP is designed to be used with students who demonstrate persistent, but not dangerous, patterns of problem behavior. These are the students who are not responding well enough to the schoolwide behavioral expectations. This book also provides some good ideas on how to identify students who would benefit from Tier 2 behavior interventions.

Safe and Healthy Schools: Practical Prevention Strategies (Sprague & Walker, 2004) provides a very straightforward step-by-step approach to structuring your school in a way that will minimize unwanted student behavior. This book includes information on positive behavior support, school safety, and bully prevention.

Strong Kids series (Merrell) is a social and emotional learning curriculum for children in grades 3–8. *Strong Start* and *Strong Teens* are companion programs that target students in K–2 and 9–12, respectively. One advantage of this program is that one book covers three grades and costs only $34.95. This price includes a CD-ROM that makes it easy for you to print out all of the handouts and lessons. More information is available from Brookes Publishing (*www.brookespublishing.com*).

Effective School Interventions, Second Edition: Evidence-Based Strategies for Improving Student Outcomes (Rathvon, 2008) is a practical source of additional interventions that have been demonstrated to improve the classroom learning environment, academic achievement, and student behavior and social competence.

Reducing Problem Behaviors in the Elementary School Classroom: A Practice Guide (Epstein, Atkins, Cullinan, Kutash, & Weaver, 2008). This project was funded by a Federal Grant and the panel consisted of researchers from various parts of the United States and one elementary school principal. Every behavior intervention recipe in Appendix C has been defined by the Institute of Education Sciences as having a "strong" level (the highest rating possible) of evidence for practice. The full guide can be downloaded from *ies.ed.gov/ncee/ wwc/pdf/practiceguides/behavior_pg_092308.pdf*.

Secondary Tier Interventions and Supports (Hawken, Adolphson, MacLeod, & Schumann, 2008) gives a thorough overview of what is necessary for Tier 2 behavior intervention. The book itself is a necessity for any school-based behavior team. The information is cutting edge, and the contributors are all top-notch experts in their fields.

CHAPTER 10

RTI with English Language Learners
Instructional Considerations

English language learners (ELLs) make up one of the fastest-growing groups of students in the United States. Often, teachers ask how RTI can be used with ELL students. Diane Haager and others have shown that RTI practices have been helpful for ELL students. Despite this evidence, there are a number of considerations teachers need to know before using RTI with ELL students. Consider the following example.

> Nadia is a third grader who moved to the United States from Russia with her family 1 year ago. While in Russia, Nadia attended school intermittently, depending on whether her family needed her to watch her younger siblings. Once she was in the United States, Nadia enrolled in the second grade and participated in additional English instruction for 30 minutes per day. During her time in Russia, and continuing into the family's migration to the United States, Nadia's family spoke only Russian at home. By the end of second grade, Nadia's English had improved, but her overall school achievement was well below the second-grade expectations. At the beginning of third grade, Nadia's teacher was very concerned about her school achievement and asked to meet with the school's intervention team to make a referral to special education. The team leader set up a meeting and explained to the teacher that the team would consider what types of interventions might work for Nadia, noting that a referral to special education might not be the best solution.

Nadia's situation exemplifies the difficulties faced by children who are English language learners. They are expected to attend school and make progress, but they may not have much prior exposure to English, and school may be the only place in their daily lives where English skills are needed. Despite this reality, national and state education policies emphasize and/or require students to master English, and ELL students are often required to participate in English-only instruction and assessment. In addition, there are many different ELL instructional practices in use in U.S. schools, and not all of these practices are grounded in research. How can you help your ELL students be successful?

LEARNING ENGLISH IS IMPORTANT

Learning English is important for students in the United States as well as in other countries. English is the most widely used language in the United States and it is an important language for business and culture in other parts of the world as well. In some countries outside of the United States, learning English is required of students as a second or third language. In the United States, second language instruction is not universal, but it is important that all students learn English to a basic level of competency. One of the most important things for everyone to remember about learning English (or any second language) is that it takes time. In addition, there are developmental steps in second language learning that have a big effect on how well your students can use the language for school tasks. One of the best descriptions of the steps involved in language learning was provided by Jim Cummins in 1981. He noted that there are two major components to language learning; he called these BICS and CALP.

BICS: Basic Interpersonal Communication Skills

BICS are the most basic language skills that allow a student to communicate orally with others. BICS include knowing important nouns and a few phrases that can be used to express basic needs such as "Can I go to the bathroom?" BICS typically develop before other language skills and are very important for daily functioning. Most of the time, BICS can develop in oral form over a few days or weeks in a setting where the second language is used regularly. Often, your students will learn BICS in English from their classmates as well as from interactions with you and other adults. It is estimated that children can master BICS in about 1 to 2 years of exposure to English at school. Keep in mind that such learning covers only very basic English and does not include the skills necessary to use English for writing or other school assignments.

CALP: Cognitive Academic Language Proficiency

By comparison, CALP includes advanced language skills necessary for thinking, writing, and working in a second language. CALP skills include learning the details of the language's spelling, grammar, usage, and advanced vocabulary terms. CALP is essential for higher-level success in school, especially at the secondary and postsecondary level. Because CALP includes mastery of far more language information, it takes much longer to develop. If your ELL students receive regular English instruction as part of their daily school activities, they are likely to develop CALP in 5 to 7 years. Mastery of CALP requires daily instruction in all elements of English as well as ongoing opportunities to use English as part of school and extracurricular activities (Cummins, 1981).

TIME IS OF THE ESSENCE

It is obvious from the above descriptions that learning English as a second language is a time-consuming process. Your students who start school already fluent in English have had about 5 years of learning and practice in mastering this language. Your students who come to school and do not yet know English, or don't know it very well, are at a significant disadvantage from the native English speakers. The reality of learning any language is that it takes time. If your students start out knowing English, the focus of instruction can be exclusively on other things. But if your students come to school not proficient in English, and all instruction is given in English, they will need time to learn the language in order to use it in school and elsewhere (Gersten et al., 2001) . One of the major challenges that you and your ELL students face is how to find time to include English instruction in an already full school schedule. This is a double-bind because for any other instruction to be effective, your students must have the chance to learn the language(s) used in the school. For this reason, finding ways to help your ELL students learn English as well as other subjects is very important.

RTI AND ELL INSTRUCTION

The good news is that effective ELL instruction fits very well with RTI. RTI practices can be used to teach and support your ELL students in the same ways that they can be used with all your students. The remainder of this chapter provides information about the benefits of using RTI to help ELL students from diverse cultures and language backgrounds. As we explain, RTI and ELL are really a perfect match because RTI is language and culture neutral; it puts the focus on what your English language learners can do, not what they cannot do; and it allows individualization of language instruction.

RTI Is Language and Culture Neutral

One of the features of RTI that makes it ideal for use with ELL students is that it is language and culture neutral. It is basically a procedural scaffold for helping your students meet specific goals and can be used with any goal. That means it can be used in any language, with any culture, and with any set of learning expectations. All cultures around the world have some form of expectations for their children. Such expectations shape the methods used for child rearing, informal and formal education, and transitional supports provided to children as they become adults. RTI includes identifying, monitoring, and adjusting the processes used to support a society's children as they mature. For this reason, it does not depend on any particular language, set of learning expectations, or values.

The neutral aspect of RTI is important to consider when using it with your students from diverse language and cultural backgrounds. Not all cultures have exactly the same expectations of their children. For this reason there are differences in the learning expectations of children in different parts of the world as well as in different regions of the United States. Even though all U.S. states now have explicit learning standards, these are not identical in all 50 states, and these standards may not be accepted by all those who send their children to your school. For this reason, an important first step in using RTI with children from diverse backgrounds is to discuss with their parents and other family members what your state's learning expectations (i.e., standards) are. Most parents who have chosen to enroll their children in a public school want them to be successful there. For ELL students, learning and using English for reading, writing, and other activities is often a major goal of school attendance. Some of your students' families may not agree with the state's standards, and other school options exist. While there are mandatory school attendance laws in all 50 U.S. states, parents are allowed to use private, parochial, and home-school options to meet these laws.

After discussing your state and/or school learning standards with your students' families, it is important to consider how these standards fit with the linguistic and cultural backgrounds of your school's community. Often, there are unique values or goals for children in specific communities that go beyond what your state or school require. Sometimes, parents are interested in ensuring that these values are not ignored or discriminated against at school. For some families, maintaining the child's first language is an important learning goal. Usually, this goes beyond your school's standards, but it is important for you and other school personnel to know whether the community expects ELL students to maintain their first language while they learn English, or whether English will become the primary language.

Within RTI practices, there is no "rule" or mandate that instruction be only in English or that U.S. values be exclusive. RTI calls for identifying a student's beginning (i.e., baseline) skills, choosing an intervention (i.e., instructional plan) and implementing it, and monitoring progress to see whether the instruction is working. RTI can be used with any goal, in any language, for any set of values or learning standards. RTI *does* require that there be agreement among the participants about the specific goal(s), intervention, and progress measurement. You play a critical role in making this agreement happen. Once such agreement is reached, RTI practices can be used to support all your students, including those who are learning English. Given that the goal for most children who are learning English is to master English, using RTI to support this learning is very effective.

RTI Focuses on What ELL Students Can Do

One of the reasons that RTI is effective for supporting ELL students is that it focuses on what your students *can* do, and not on what they cannot do. For example within an RTI framework, all of your students, including ELL students, participate in universal benchmark screenings three times a year. These screenings provide data that show how each of your students is doing in relation to the school's and state's learning standards. The benchmark data are used as part of the process to identify which of your students need additional help to meet the learning goals. Your students who are still learning English are likely to perform below the benchmark goal on the universal screenings because such screenings are usually conducted in English. It is appropriate to include your ELL students in the screenings because otherwise it would be hard to know whether they have met the goal yet. But it is also important to recognize that your students who are still learning English will need additional instruction in English as well as the skills included in the learning standard.

RTI Allows Individualization of Language Instruction

The major benefit of RTI practices for ELL students is that it allows for you to individualize instruction on the basis of students' needs. Consider this: Your students are likely to come to school with diverse backgrounds in a number of school topics (e.g., dinosaurs or art). Those who are learning English will have different levels of English proficiency when they begin each school year. For this reason it is important to gather baseline data on your ELL students' English skills so that the right instruction can be provided. But sometimes it is also crucial to gather data concerning your students' native language skills because knowing how the student is doing in both languages will help you to design the best instruction. A helpful resource concerning instructional support for ELL students is available from the U.S. Department of Education's Institute of Education Sciences (IES). This publication, entitled *Effective Literacy and English Language Instruction for English Learners in the Elementary Grades* (Gersten et al., 2001), provides a synthesis of research concerning how best to help your ELL students. It offers five main suggestions to support all students who are learning English:

1. Screen for reading progress and monitor progress.
2. Provide intensive small-group reading intervention.
3. Provide extensive and varied vocabulary instruction.
4. Develop academic English.
5. Schedule peer-assisted regular learning opportunities.

The above five core recommendations for ELL students incorporate a number of basic RTI practices. For example the first recommendation calls for screening all ELL students and monitoring their progress in learning to read English. The second recommendation is to use small-group instruction to support ELL students in developing English reading skills. The other three recommendations all fit RTI instructional practices for students participating in Tier 2 and Tier 3 activities. In general, the big idea for helping your ELL students is to use RTI practices to provide the instruction they need to learn English as well as other skills.

GENERAL GUIDELINES

In order to help ELL students succeed, you can use specific practices that incorporate RTI activities. One of the core underpinnings of effective instruction for your ELL students is to recognize they will need English instruction alongside other instruction. As noted above, providing English instruction in addition to the regular lessons will take more time, and adjustments to your students' schedules may be needed. There are six main things that you can do to help provide the most effective programs for ELL students:

1. Screen students to identify their language development in both English and the first language.
2. Provide English instruction as well as other skills instruction.
3. Monitor the students' progress in both English as well as skills learning.
4. Adapt English instruction first to see whether that helps.
5. Adapt skills instruction second.
6. Consider learning difficulties in both languages.

In past years, many ELL students were thought to have a learning disability when they had difficulties in school. Over time, it has become clear that for many of these students, the problem is that they are still learning English and they *do not* have a learning disability. The above six steps are designed to ensure that your ELL students receive effective English instruction as part of their school programs so that they have the greatest chance of meeting the learning standards.

The above steps utilize RTI methods in that they include universal screening, specific instruction, progress monitoring, and program review as part of both English and content instruction. When you use such steps, it is possible to identify whether an ELL student makes effective progress with specific instruction. These steps are set up so that your ELL student(s) would be considered for referral to special education *only* if they do not make progress with high-quality instruction in English and content areas. Basically, you can use RTI to test the hypothesis that your student would benefit from targeted English instruction in order to succeed in school. If your student makes effective progress with the combined ELL and content instruction, then success is found. If your student does not show progress after the use of specific English and content-area instruction, then the consideration of a learning disability is appropriate.

Screen Students

In order to know what type of instruction your students need, some type of screening assessment must be conducted. Your ELL students should participate in the schoolwide RTI screenings just like all students will. The difference for your ELL students is that they should participate in a second language skills screening as well, which will provide information about general language development and what type and level of English instruction is needed. Published materials have been developed to screen ELL students as part of overall RTI activities; however, such resources are generally available only in a limited number of other languages. Spanish is fast becoming the second most used language in the United States. For this reason, several publishers have Spanish versions of commonly used screening assessments. Both the DIBELS and AIMSweb reading assessments are available in Spanish (Good & Kaminski, 2001; Harcourt Assessment, Inc.,

2008). If your ELL students speak Spanish, either DIBELS or AIMSweb materials can be used for screening them.

The Spanish DIBELS is known as *Indicadores Dinámicos del Éxito en la Lectura*, and these can be downloaded for free at the DIBELS website (*https://dibels.uoregon. edu*). The Spanish AIMSweb reading assessment program is available for purchase from the AIMSweb website (*www.aimsweb.com*). These Spanish screening materials offer a way to compare students' progress in English and Spanish language and reading development. This is important because there are patterns in how students develop proficiency in first and second languages. Plus, by having screening data for both languages, you can know what types of instruction are needed in English and other skills.

At this time, published screening materials are widely available only in English and Spanish. Educators have created translations of certain assessments, such as the DIBELS, in other languages for research or small-scale applications. If you have ELL students who speak a language other than Spanish, the best thing for you to do is to work with the ELL teachers in your district to locate the appropriate materials. It's also possible to create translations of these assessments into other languages. It is important that the translation, use, and interpretation of any assessment must be done only by those who are absolutely fluent in the desired language as well as English.

Provide Instruction

Once screening data have been gathered from ELL students, the next step is to provide instruction. Just like with other applications of RTI, reviewing screening data for your ELL students involves looking for the skills the students have mastered and figuring out what they need to learn next. Also similar to other RTI practices, your ELL students should be organized into small instructional groups that will work on targeted English development skills. Such groups should include 4 to 6 students, and the group's instructional goals should be clearly identified. Once you have developed an instructional plan you should identify an appropriate progress measure.

Monitor Progress

For your students who are at the very early stages of learning English, the DIBELS or AIMSweb Test of Early Literacy are very good progress measures to use. These measures provide indications of specific English language and reading skill development. For more advanced ELLs, other assessments that measure advanced applications of English, such as grammar and complex reading comprehension, could be used. As with other uses of RTI, you should monitor your ELL students' progress weekly. Such monitoring will offer information about the effectiveness of the English instruction and whether your students' program needs to be changed. A complete description of progress monitoring procedures is included in Chapter 4 of this book. In general, progress data need to be collected for a minimum of at least three data points before your students' progress can be reviewed. ELL students should have the opportunity to learn from at least two distinct English language curricula before a decision is made to consider other reasons for school difficulties such as a learning disability.

Adapt English Instruction

If your student's progress data indicate that she is not making desired progress in learning English skills, the next best step is to adapt the English instruction. Changing her English instruction first follows from the general idea of testing the hypothesis that ELL students must first learn English in order to succeed in U.S. schools. By changing the English instruction, you can identify whether different ELL instruction helps her in both English and the content areas. It's a good idea to pay attention to how all your ELL students are doing on a regular basis. By reviewing data from all your students who receive ELL instruction, it's possible to identify how effective the ELL instructional program is as a whole. If only one or two of your ELL students are struggling, it makes sense to change only their programs. But if all your ELL students are not doing well, it makes sense to review the ELL curriculum and determine whether it is the most effective available. The What Works Clearinghouse has reviews of ELL curricula that can provide information about programs that your school is considering.

Adapt Skill Instruction

If changes in the English instruction do not lead to improvements in your student's school progress, then it is time to modify the content-area instruction. Changes in math, science, or social studies instruction allow you to use basic RTI steps to help your student. As with other uses of RTI, your changes could include increasing the duration, frequency, or group size for a specific skill area. Your student's progress in learning the skill should be monitored with a measure matched to the skill being taught. If your instructional changes result in your student's showing improved performance in that skill area, then it will be clear that she needed different content-area instruction. If your student still does not make satisfactory progress, then it may be an indication that she has a more chronic difficulty such as a learning disability.

Consider Referral

If your ELL student does not begin to make progress toward improved English and content-area skills once RTI practices are put in place, it may be appropriate for you to consider a referral for either a comprehensive language assessment or for special education. Consideration of such referrals should occur only *after* you have followed the above steps with integrity. This means that the selected ELL and content-area instruction must be used exactly as designed, and that regular progress data must be collected. If, *and only if*, accurately implemented instruction with accurate progress data indicate that your student has not responded to the interventions, then your RTI team can consider the possibility that your student may need to be referred for a comprehensive evaluation (Haager, 2007).

There are two types of comprehensive evaluations that may be helpful for your ELL students who have not responded to interventions. The first type is a comprehensive language evaluation, which is typically conducted by a speech and language pathologist, ideally one who is bilingual in English and the same language as the student. If it's not clear what your student's overall language skills are in English and the first language, a comprehensive language evaluation should be done. This evaluation will provide information concerning whether there is a language development problem in one or both languages. If your student's general language skills are known, then a comprehensive psychological evaluation can be conducted.

The psychological evaluation process relies on language skills for certain aspects of assessment. For this reason, it is unlikely to be helpful if your student's language skills are not well developed enough for him or her to participate in the evaluation. Your RTI team will want to look closely at the data and think about whether there is enough information about the student's overall English skills and language development for a psychological evaluation to be useful. If your student's language skills are not known, then a language evaluation will be much more useful. In order for either type of comprehensive evaluation to be helpful, there must be clarity about the student's current language skills. In general, the most helpful information to support students who are learning English will come from data collected during instructional activities. For this reason, the best use of the RTI team's effort is in selecting, using, and reviewing scientifically based English language teaching programs. As a classroom teacher, you can support them in using effective English teaching programs.

APPLICATIONS AND SUMMARY

If we return to the case of Nadia, we can apply the information included in this chapter about how best to support ELL students. In Nadia's case, the team leader was right to suggest that a referral might not be the best next step. Here is how Nadia's situation unfolded.

> Nadia's teacher participated in a schoolwide RTI team meeting at which data from her school progress during the first 6 months of the year was discussed. The teacher shared that Nadia had participated enthusiastically in all lessons, but she did very poorly on all the chapter tests. Her teacher noted that Nadia seemed to get along very well with her classmates and that she talked often with the other students during class activities and on the playground.
>
> The RTI team identified several parts of Nadia's situation that could affect her school progress. They noted that she had been exposed to English for a very limited time, and only at school or other events with school friends. In addition, they pointed out that she appeared to be on track for developing BICS with her peers, but that she had not yet had enough time to develop the CALP skills needed for school assignments, especially written work. The team asked the teacher what type of English language instruction Nadia received, and the teacher reported that she did not know because the ELL teacher pulled the students during the language arts block.

Together with Nadia's teacher, the team decided they needed more information about Nadia's school performance and English development. They decided to do the following:

1. The teacher contacted the ELL specialist and asked for a description of the ELL lessons as well as information about Nadia's Russian skills. The ELL teacher reported that despite her limited formal schooling, Nadia's Russian was quite good. She described the ELL instruction program and noted the importance of the students' learning the English letters and phonemes.

2. Together with the ELL teacher, they chose to monitor Nadia's English progress using the DIBELS Nonsense Word Fluency (NWF) measures on a weekly basis. Since Nadia's BICS skills were developing strongly, the ELL teacher suggested that the classroom teacher conduct the weekly NWF assessments so that she could see how Nadia progresses.

3. The two teachers agreed that Nadia would attend ELL sessions during science lesson time instead of during language arts; this would ensure that she did not miss the chance to benefit from the classroom-based English instruction.

4. The team decided to review Nadia's progress after 3 weeks and determine whether the planned activities were helpful.

5. At the 3-week review, the teacher was pleased to report that Nadia was making stronger progress in learning English as seen in her weekly NWF scores. In addition, she had shown gains in other classroom activities, including written assignments.

In Nadia's case, a referral for special education did not turn out to be the best thing to do next. Instead, the team used the RTI process to develop a plan to support Nadia with targeted instruction and weekly progress monitoring. Had Nadia been referred, she might have participated in an evaluation that could have been very inaccurate due to her new and emerging English skills. Instead, she received English instruction that supported her language and content-area skills.

This chapter has provided information about how RTI can be used to support students who are learning English. RTI is very well matched to the needs of ELL students because it allows teachers and the specialists who work with them to implement specific English language instruction and to monitor student progress. Given the growth of Spanish-speaking ELL students in the United States, Spanish assessment and instructional materials have been developed to assist with RTI practices. These materials allow teachers to screen, monitor, and review student progress in the development of both English and Spanish. Since many U.S. students speak languages other than Spanish, additional materials for more diverse languages need to be developed. Luckily, RTI practices are language neutral and can be used to support all ELL students.

RESOURCES

AIMSweb Spanish Version

www.edformation.com/measures/s-reading

AIMSweb offers Spanish versions of its reading assessments. These can be purchased for classroom use.

Fostering Academic Success for English Language Learners: What Do We Know?

www.wested.org/policy/pubs/fostering

This document by Robert Linquanti is found on the website of Wested, a nonprofit research, development, and service agency. WestEd enhances and increases education and human development within schools, families, and communities.

Indicadores Dinámicos del Éxito en la Lectura (IDEL)

https://dibels.uoregon.edu

The Spanish version of DIBELS provides an easy way to measure Spanish-speaking ELL students' progress in learning to read in both Spanish and English. It can be downloaded for free at the DIBELS website.

Teaching Literacy in English to K–5 English Learners

dww.ed.gov/priority_area/priority_landing.cfm?PA_ID

This website, run by the U.S. Department of Education's Doing What Works Clearinghouse, provides videos, slide shows, and tools for teaching reading to K–5 English learners. The site is based on five research-based recommendations: screen and monitor students' progress; provide small-group reading interventions; provide vocabulary instruction throughout the day; develop academic English competence beginning in primary grades; and schedule regular peer-assisted learning opportunities, including structured language practice.

A great deal of research has been conducted about the best instructional practices for students who are ELLs. One of the more important summaries of this research was written by Jim Cummins in 1981. His article, "Empirical and Theoretical Underpinnings of Bilingual Education," in the *Journal of Education* provides the core framework for understanding BICS and CALP. More recently, the U.S. Department of Education has put together resources that teachers can access at *ies.ed.gov/ncee*. Diane Haager has pointed out that there are important considerations for teachers when using RTI with ELL students. More resources for RTI practices appropriate for ELL students are certain to be developed in coming years.

CHAPTER 11

If You're Working in a DIBELS System, This Chapter Is for You

At this point you may be asking yourself, why is a chapter on DIBELS stuck toward the back of a book on RTI? We actually have a good explanation for this. Schools that use an RTI model must screen all students several times throughout the year (benchmarking) so that the students who are not "where they should be" can be given an intervention. From previous chapters in this book you now know that an RTI model also requires that we monitor students' progress and document how well the intervention is working. DIBELS, a measure of early literacy skills in K–6, was actually created and researched with benchmarking and progress monitoring in mind. This makes DIBELS an excellent choice for managing the early literacy strand of any RTI system. That being said, it is also true that millions of students in the United States are "DIBELed" three times a year, and a large percentage of their teachers don't know why, nor do they know what to do with the information that comes from those benchmarking sessions—certainly this is *not* the fault of the teachers. We felt that this was an unfortunate situation and have included this chapter on DIBELS to educate and empower those of you working in schools that suffer from this systemic glitch.

This chapter is not meant to convert any newcomers to DIBELS. It is not meant to sell you DIBELS (which actually is free anyway). If you are not working in a system that uses DIBELS, you might safely skip this chapter as it will have less relevance for you. If you are working in a DIBELS system, then at a minimum all of your students are being assessed for early literacy skills three times a year using the DIBELS measures. For many schools this means that three times per year (fall, winter, and spring) a district team of DIBELers comes into your school and pulls your students across the day until they all

138

have been assessed. After that, it's possible that you never hear another word and are left to wonder what that was all about. If this sounds like your system, don't be discouraged. You are not alone and it is easily fixed. Monitoring students three times a year is a good first step toward establishing a solid DIBELS system. After reading this chapter you will be better able to advocate for access to your students' scores because you will understand the power of these data to help you help all your students become readers.

What are DIBELS measures? They are 1-minute measures of early literacy skills that can be used to gauge whether a student is on track for becoming a reader. The types of early literacy skills that are being assessed are phonemic awareness (can a child hear, blend, and segment the sounds in words?), alphabetic principle or phonics (can a child see the symbol we call *b* and know that it says the sound "buh"?), and fluency, which is closely linked to comprehension. This chapter does not go into detail about the measures or other DIBELS-specific information. Instead, we assume that you are interested in this chapter because you teach reading and know that your students are being assessed three times per year with the DIBELS measures. This chapter is intended to be a practical guide in how to access the information available to you once those student scores have been entered into the DIBELS database at the University of Oregon (not every school uses this database; some use Wireless Generation, so check with your administrator if you're not sure).

When your students get "DIBELed" three times a year, this is known as *benchmarking*. After benchmarking, the data are entered into the DIBELS database and sit there until someone wants to take a look. Generally speaking, the people who have access are the district stakeholders such as the director of curriculum, the director of special services, and the district superintendent. There is a good chance that your principal also knows how to access the data, but a surprising number do not. What you may not know is that you also have access to it. All you need to have is a username and password, which you can probably get from your principal and certainly get from your within-district DIBELS person. After you get the log-in information, you will be ready to pull up your data and see how your students are doing. You'll want to view these reports first so that you can look to see which of your students (and how many) would benefit from additional support.

To log on to the site the easy way:

1. Go to *https://dibels.uoregon.edu*.
2. Click on "DIBELS Data System."
3. On the left side of the page you will need to enter your username and password.
4. Once you are logged in, you will see a menu of options on the left.

Now you are ready to use the powerful graphing features of the DIBELS website. This will let you easily monitor your students' early literacy skill acquisition and see whether your instruction is effective in getting them where they need to be by the end of the year. A good place to start is the "Reports Menu." From here you will be able to find your class lists, individual performance profiles, and class progress graphs.

CLASS LIST REPORT

To generate reports:

1. Click on "Reports."
2. Scroll down about halfway.
3. Look for "Class Reports."
4. Select "Class List Report."
5. Choose the assessment period. Which benchmark do you want to look at? If you are looking during the fall, then you only have data for the fall. However, if it's the spring, you will have three different sets of data (fall, winter, and spring). Make sure you select the one that you are interested in.

This takes you to a grid like the one in Figure 11.1 that will enable you to look at your students and their DIBELS scores. You will see the student name, their scores on the DIBELS measures, and in the far right column you will see "Instructional Recommendation." Instructional Recommendations come in three levels (and corresponding colors). Level 1 is Low Risk/Benchmark, which tells us that the student is at grade level and on track for becoming a reader. We like to think of this level as green, or "good to go." Level 2 is known as Some Risk/Strategic, and additional intervention is recommended. Level 2 is often thought of as being yellow, or "caution." Level 3 is At Risk/Intensive; that is, the student needs substantial intervention. We think of Level 3 as being red, as in "red alert—something *must* be done."

If you are teaching students who are in third grade or higher, you will see that your students are ordered from lowest scores (intensive) to highest scores (benchmark) based on instructional recommendation. This is done in order to place emphasis on the most

Name	Oral Reading Fluency			Instructional Recommendation
	Score	Percentile	Status	
Melissa	63	10	At Risk	Intensive—Needs Substantial Intervention
Sandra	72	15	At Risk	Intensive—Needs Substantial Intervention
Camille	83	21	At Risk	Intensive—Needs Substantial Intervention
Lars	88	24	At Risk	Intensive—Needs Substantial Intervention
Bryan	105	39	Some Risk	Strategic—Additional Intervention
Vanessa	106	40	Some Risk	Strategic—Additional Intervention
Harrison	107	41	Some Risk	Strategic—Additional Intervention
Madison	119	54	Low Risk	Benchmark—At Grade Level
Stuart	122	57	Low Risk	Benchmark—At Grade Level
Howard	130	64	Low Risk	Benchmark—At Grade Level
Anthony	131	65	Low Risk	Benchmark—At Grade Level
Adam	135	69	Low Risk	Benchmark—At Grade Level
Amanda	139	73	Low Risk	Benchmark—At Grade Level
Jacob	141	74	Low Risk	Benchmark—At Grade Level

FIGURE 11.1. Sample of a partial fourth-grade DIBELS Class List Report.

at-risk students, because they are the most in need of attention. If your students are in K–2, you will see that there may be more than one DIBELS score for each student and that there are still only three instructional recommendations given (benchmark, strategic, and intensive). This is because in K–2 there are more measures used than just ORF, which is what is used from third grade on. For K–2 the computer program that keeps all of the data and generates the reports takes into consideration the scores on the different measures and weights each one according to importance for that grade and benchmark period. From this, one instructional recommendation is given. It is best to use this recommendation as a general guide and use an Instructional Grouping Form to create student groups based upon need for support—for example, students with similar levels of skill deficit in alphabetic principle may be grouped together. You can access the Instructional Grouping Form through the DIBELS data system at *https://dibels.uoregon.edu*.

INDIVIDUAL STUDENT PERFORMANCE PROFILE

Another very useful report that you can easily generate and print (it's really handy to have during parent–teacher conferences) is the Individual Student Performance Profile. Here's how to find it:

1. Once you are logged in, go to the top of the screen and click on "Reports."
2. Scroll down and near the bottom of the page you will see "Student Reports."
3. Just beneath that, click on "Individual Student Performance Profiles."
4. Choose your class and click on "Download Report Here."
5. This will pull up your entire class in *alphabetical* order.
6. Each student will have his or her own page with a clean break before the next student. Each student page contains his or her DIBELS history from kindergarten through sixth grade. The gray horizontal boxes are the benchmarks or goals for the student. The solid black dots are the student's actual score during that assessment period. If you see empty black circles, those are progress monitoring data and you are ahead of the game (more about this coming up). Warning: If you do plan to use these for parent–teacher conferences, make sure that you can explain each of the measures in terms of the early literacy skills. Also, if a child is doing poorly, be ready to describe with detail the intervention he or she is receiving. An example of this report can be seen in Figure 11.2.

CLASS PROGRESS GRAPH

Another powerful graph is the Class Progress Graph. You can use this to see at a glance how much progress your class has made from the beginning to middle to end-of-year benchmarks. This can be particularly helpful if you are interested in seeing how far your lowest-performing students have come during the time that you've had them. Here's how to find it:

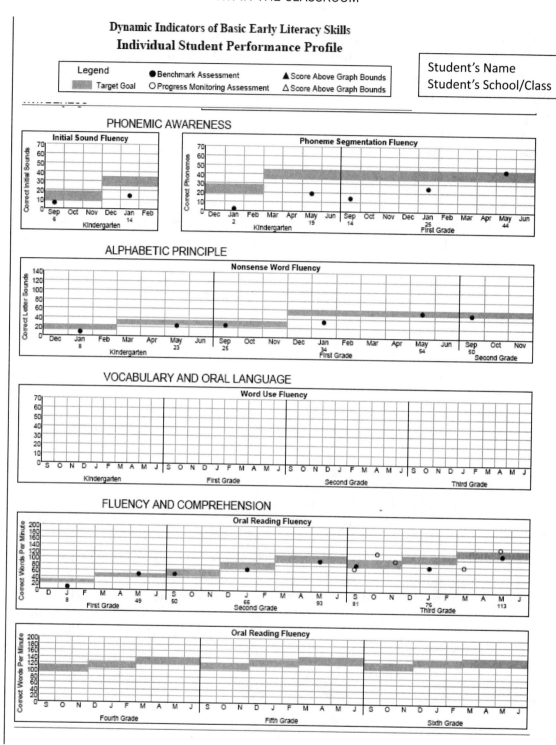

FIGURE 11.2. Sample of a DIBELS Individual Student Performance Profile for a third grader. Copyright 2007 University of Oregon Center on Teaching and Learning, College of Education. All Rights Reserved. Reprinted by permission.

1. Go to "Reports."
2. Halfway down you will see "Class Reports."
3. Just below that, click on "Class Progress Graph."
4. Select your class and click on "Download Report Here."

You will see your students ranked from lowest to highest on the fall benchmark scores with a circle. If there have been subsequent benchmarks, for example if it's spring, you will see that there also will be a box and a diamond for winter and spring, respectively.

An example of a third-grade year-end Class Progress Graph is shown in Figure 11.3. You will notice that two students on the left-hand side of the graph, Javier and Daniel, are higher up and don't fit the pattern of the rest of the class. This is because neither Daniel nor Javier was assessed in the fall. Javier has only one data point, and that is for the spring benchmark. Daniel has two data points: one for the winter and one for the spring benchmarks. Students with missing data will always appear on the far left side of the graph.

So, let's review. You have now been introduced to your Class List Report, your Individual Student Performance Profile, and the Class Progress Graph. We think that these

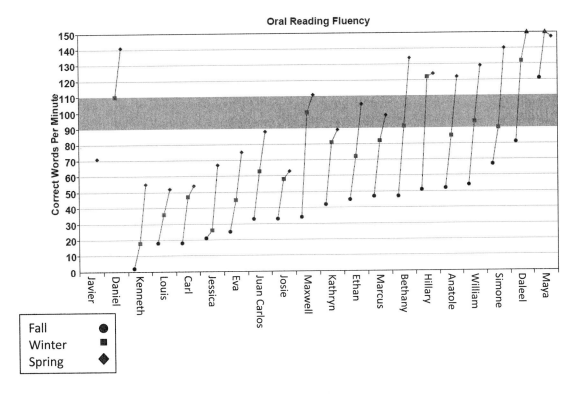

FIGURE 11.3. Sample of a third-grade DIBELS Class Progress Graph. Copyright 2007 University of Oregon Center on Teaching and Learning, College of Education. All Rights Reserved. Reprinted by permission.

three are the best places to start. Of course, there is much more information that you can pull from the DIBELS data system, but we believe that if you are just beginning, nothing beats these three for giving you useful information in a few easy steps. This is not the end of the story, though; in fact, it is only the beginning. If you have several students who score in the at-risk range (and most of us do), then you will need to work with your grade-level literacy team to group students by need and carve out time for these groups to receive an appropriate intervention.

PROGRESS MONITORING WITH THE DIBELS DATA SYSTEM

You may have noticed that the information you've gotten so far all revolves around the benchmark scores. This is a good place to start, but it is not sufficient if you are going to monitor how well your students are doing in their intervention groups. You'll need much more frequent assessments of the students' growth in order to make instructional decisions in a timely manner. These frequent assessments or check-ups are usually referred to as progress monitoring, which is an essential part of any RTI system. Chapter 4 goes into much more detail about the "why" of progress monitoring; this chapter covers the "how" of progress monitoring specifically within the DIBELS data system.

"I have my students in intervention groups and I want to know how well they're doing. How can I monitor their progress efficiently and store the data in a way that is easy for me to retrieve and interpret?" Good question. Let's start with how you will gather the data. Different schools and teams handle this differently. Some teachers like to know how to give the DIBELS measures themselves so that they can collect data any time they wish and are not reliant on others to do it for them. Other teachers feel that they already have enough to do and would like to delegate this responsibility to a select group of people within the school building. Obviously, this will be something that you and your team will need to decide before you can establish a good system for progress monitoring. If you choose to use a select group of adults within the building, one thing to think about will be the time commitment. Think about your class list. How many of your students are "intensive"? If you are like many teachers, probably 15 to 20% of your students are in that category. This means, assuming a class of 30, that approximately four to six of your students should be progress monitored every week. Depending upon the grade that you teach this will take approximately 15 to 25 minutes. If there are three classes in your grade level, then you will need a person to assess for 45 to 75 minutes per week. Consider the following example.

Ms. Howell is a second-grade teacher who has five students who score in the red/at-risk zone. All five students are receiving an intervention to target their skill deficits and need to have their progress monitored weekly so that Ms. Howell can determine whether their progress is sufficient. If these students are still weak on alphabetic principle (which is best measured with DIBELS–NWF), then they will be assessed using a 1-minute NWF probe. However, as second graders they also need to be building some fluency with connected text, and this is best measured using a DIBELS–ORF passage. This measure takes another minute. So each of Ms. Howell's five students will require 2 minutes of assessment per week, and roughly 2 additional minutes per student will be taken up just getting each student into a quiet situation where you can assess them. Doing the math results in five students getting 4 minutes each, equaling 20 minutes total. Remember, this is 20 minutes of adult time. Each individual student was pulled away for only 4 minutes.

Classes or groups can be assessed on different days so you can spread out that adult's daily time commitment. For example maybe you have a music teacher or an office assistant who is able to spend 30 minutes per day three days a week monitoring your students' progress. This would allow for 90 minutes total, which in the previous scenario would be sufficient to complete all three grade-level classes each week. Some schools ask retired teachers to help, others ask parents. There may be an educational assistant (EA) who has some time available, or you could ask the school psychologist. In other words, there are many ways to approach this, and it's up to you and your team to decide what will work best given the available resources.

Now if you've been paying attention (and we're sure you have), you'll be thinking to yourself, well, that's great—we do have an EA who is willing to do this, but how are we going to train her to administer and score these measures? There are several ways to go, the most obvious being to ask the district to lend you some of the folks who normally conduct the DIBELS benchmark assessments and have them train you. Your principal may be able to arrange this and thus keep cost to a minimum. However, you should keep in mind that these benchmark assessors probably have not been trained to be trainers and therefore won't have any of the necessary training materials. This would be the *least desirable* option.

A less obvious but very effective way to acquire the skills is through online trainings. These can be accessed 24/7 and you don't have to schedule it. Of course, if you'd like to have someone come and provide training in person, there are several very good organizations that will do that. They will also be able to help you with much of the data entry and interpretation. This is really the best way to go if your school or district has the resources. For more information on training options, go to *www.dibels.org*.

So now we fast-forward and assume that you have several people who are trained to collect DIBELS progress monitoring data within your building. We also assume that the materials have been downloaded for free from the DIBELS website (or purchased as ready-made kits from Sopris West) and made available to the data collectors. What they will do is administer the measures and record the student scores on the front of the DIBELS student booklets. After this has been done someone needs to enter the score into the DIBELS data system. This should probably be you because it will give you a chance to become very familiar with your students' progress each week. The rest of this chapter guides you through the mechanics of entering the scores into the DIBELS database.

After you are logged onto the DIBELS data system:

1. Click on "Data Entry."

2. Choose the second option: "DIBELS Progress Monitoring." Think of this as opening a file drawer.

3. Choose "Grade-Level Monitoring" or "Out-of-Grade Monitoring," depending on what measures you're using (e.g., using first-grade measures with a second grader would be Out-of-Grade Monitoring).

4. If you get no students listed, that means that none of your students have been identified for progress monitoring. If you do have students in there already, skip to step 6.

5. You'll need to select (add) students for progress monitoring, and you will probably find that you do not have access to this function with your teacher user name and password. If this is the case then ask the person who gave you your username and password to direct you to a person who *can* select and add your students for progress monitoring. The person will need to have access to the "administration" menu on the DIBELS data system. At least one person in each school building should have that access. Once your students have been added, proceed to step 6.

6. Now you should be able to click on "Enter/Edit Progress Monitoring Data" and you will get a menu that asks you if you'd like Grade-Level Monitoring or Out-of-Grade Monitoring. Out-of-Grade Monitoring is an option for students who are so low in grade-level material that you don't expect to see much growth in that material. Therefore, the DIBELS folks have created a way for you to drop down and monitor progress using measures that are below the student's current grade level. For the purpose of getting started we will guide you through the basic Grade-Level Monitoring option.

7. Now you will be asked to choose the time of year. The system offers you the choices of "Beginning of the Year," "Middle of the Year," "End of Year," and "Summer School." Click on the time of year that best matches your school schedule. If it turns out that you've chosen the wrong time of year, it's easy to go back to the previous screen and select a different time of year. This will become obvious once you have the screen open in front of you and are trying it yourself.

8. Find the student *and* find the DIBELS measures that you have scores for. Enter his or her scores in the appropriate boxes. Scroll down to see more places to enter the other measures. Teachers of lower grades will have more options because there are more measures for those students.

9. Once you have all the day's data entered for a few students, you can go to the top of the page and select "Hide Tests Without Scores" to reduce the amount of scrolling and searching that you may be doing.

10. When you are finished, scroll to the bottom of the page and select "Submit Scores."

11. You have now added the students' scores to both the progress monitoring graphs and the individual student performance profile.

12. Pulling up and printing out the progress monitoring graphs is a pretty easy step. First you'll need to go to the progress monitoring section (open that file drawer!)

and then click on "Student Progress Monitoring Graphs." This should pull up all of your students who have progress monitoring data entered. You can choose to print just one or all of them. You can also see at a glance how well your interventions are working. These are really good graphs to share with your grade-level team and/or the person who is running the intervention group, if it is not you. You will almost certainly find it helpful to sit down for 30 minutes a week with colleagues and discuss student progress and brainstorm ways to continue helping all of the students who are not making sufficient progress.

Figure 11.4 is an example of progress monitoring graphs for one kindergarten student. You can see that this student was monitored on three separate measures (ISF, PSF, and NWF). As you look at this, remember to ask yourself how much progress is enough. Given the current rate of progress, is that student going to catch up and meet the target goals? When looking at the student's scores for initial sound fluency (ISF) you see that the September score of 14 puts the student right on track for year-end success, and an additional assessment in December put that child above the aimline (22). January's score was a little bit below (17), and that's the last time the child was assessed for ISF. Moving down to view the phoneme segmentation fluency (PSF) measure we see that the student started quite low (0), but quickly popped up in March to scores over 25, meaning this student made quick progress with PSF. The student followed a similarly steep trend line in nonsense word fluency (NWF). Beginning in October, this student received two 15-minute sessions, Monday–Friday, of a research-validated early literacy intervention program aimed at kindergarten and first-grade students. You can see from the graph that the intervention made a difference for that child.

We encourage you to share this chapter with all of your literacy team members so that they too can learn how to use this system to create and print helpful graphs and track student progress.

RESOURCES

Dynamic Measurement Group is the research organization that created DIBELS. They have also created and researched versions in French (IDAPEL) and Spanish (IDEL). You can go to their website and find lots of information for parents, teachers, and administrators. If you are interested in the research behind these measures, you can also find the published journal articles that pertain to DIBELS on their website (*www.dibels.org*). There are several other DIBELS resources available if you would like to dig deeper into analyzing and using the student data. DIBELS is also available using a small hand-held device that allows you to input the student data directly into your computer. This eliminates quite a bit of work on your part. This system (mCLASS: DIBELS) is available from a company called Wireless Generation, and they have come up with some very interesting ways to help you collect, analyze, and use your student data. You can find out more at *www.wirelessgeneration.com* (and while you're there, check out the link to their *free* reading program—it's amazing).

Dynamic Indicators of Basic Early Literacy Skills
Progress Monitoring Graphs

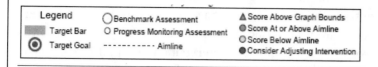

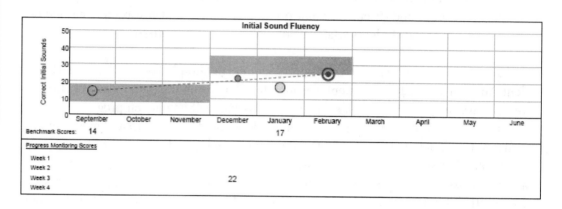

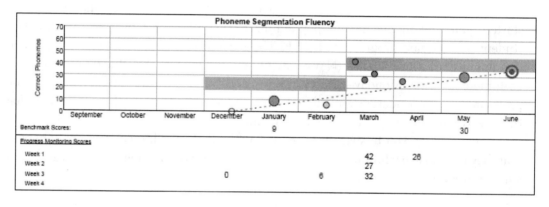

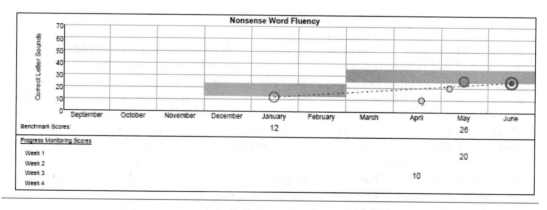

FIGURE 11.4. Sample of DIBELS Progress Monitoring Graphs for a kindergarten student. Copyright 2007 University of Oregon Center on Teaching and Learning, College of Education. All Rights Reserved. Reprinted by permission.

CHAPTER 12

This All Sounds Great, but How Am I Supposed to Fit It into My Schedule?

Scheduling and Logistics

MANAGING YOUR TIME

Think for a moment about your typical weekend schedule. Does it make you think of free time and relaxation? Or does it make you think of balancing errands, kid activities, and getting things done for work? While you may be one of the lucky ones who seems to have time to get things done, you more likely are a busy person trying to fit it all in. And that's okay. Participating in activities and getting things done with family is the stuff of life. While it can be crazy at times, it is rewarding.

Now, we could use this as a format to complain about the problem. "There is never enough time," we could say. "I wish there were 30 hours in a day"; "How am I going to fit all of this in?"; "Isn't there ever time for myself?" While we all tend to have these thoughts once in a while, those people who choose to make it work, even given all of their responsibilities, have the most success. Think about the difference between the ideal time and actual time. Ask yourself the following questions:

- How do you prioritize the family activities?
- What stays and what goes when there is a time crunch?
- How do you make those decisions of what to do and what to exclude?

The above example is included to help us think about priorities, planning, and scheduling in our personal lives. Although these situations do look different than planning and scheduling at work for the school day, the ideas are the same. Often, there is never enough time in the school day to fit in all of the activities. We are constantly balancing a variety of activities with limited time. There are assemblies, visitors, or special events that can detract from the day. There is an emphasis on improved performance in all academic areas, not just reading. There needs to be time for specials like art, music, library, computer lab, and P.E. With all of the above, how do we create school schedules that work?

In an RTI system, there inevitably needs to be more time devoted to intervention groups. We expect that the core curriculum will be meeting the needs of 80% of our students. This still leaves 20% of kids who require additional support. These 20% may be at a strategic level or they may be at an intensive level. Students at an intensive level will require even more time than those at a strategic level to close the gap and catch up to their peers. Thus we are attempting to now find even more time during the day to fit the intervention groups in.

It is not an easy task, but it is a doable task. Yes, there is more time required of the school day to provide students the instruction they need. Yet school after school and district after district are revamping their schedules and making it work. They're assessing their needs, prioritizing their goals, adding some here, and subtracting some there to find the time to run intervention groups and fit it all in.

FINDING THE TIME

Briarwood School is an elementary school in a suburban area. There are 600 students in grades K–6 who attend Briarwood. In the past, this school had mostly high-performing students who did not require much additional support. In recent years the population of Briarwood has been changing, and there are more students in need of additional instruction. Because of this changing demographic, the principal and school leadership team decided to start using an RTI system. They took a year to attend trainings, make plans for interventions, determine assessment tools, and share the ideas of RTI with the whole staff. They realized that all of the ideas resonated with their beliefs. The school was grounded on the belief that all students can learn, assessment should be linked to intervention, and support should be provided earlier rather than later. But the $64,000 question remained: What would it look like? How would the planning and logistics play out? They realized they had to start by looking at the schedule. To make the easiest transition, they decided not to modify the schedule much at all. Instead, they had the advisory period also act as an intervention period. Those students requiring additional instruction went to an intervention group. Students who were successful in the core curriculum went to the advisory. To reduce discrepancies between the students, all the classes were still referred to as the "advisory class." The only difference was that some students received additional instruction in reading or math if they attended the intervention group.

Figure 12.1 represents the general schedule for Briarwood School. Differences by grade level are not reflected here.

1st period	8:05–8:55
2nd period	9:00–9:50
Advisory period	9:55–10:15
3rd period	10:20–11:10
First lunch	11:15–12:00
Second lunch	12:05–12:50
4th period	12:55–1:45
5th period	1:50–2:40
6th period	2:45–3:35

FIGURE 12.1. General schedule for Briarwood School.

PLANNING FOR CHANGE

Take a moment and think about some of the meetings you have been a part of lately. What thoughts come to your mind? If it was a productive meeting, what made it so? If the meeting could have been organized differently, what would have made it more effective? We have likely all participated in meetings that have been quite productive, and also meetings that have seemed like a waste of time. Think about what characteristics you appreciated about the last effective meeting you attended.

Now compare your list to the questions in Figure 12.2. What is similar? What is different? Think about what specifically made the meeting effective, safe, respectful, and

- Is the meeting structured with a purpose, process, and expected outcomes?
- Does the meeting follow a clear outline?
- Are all of the designated participants present?
- If not, is there a clear plan for relaying information to absent participants?
- Is it clear why all participants are involved?
- Is there a designated facilitator?
- Is there a designated leader?
- Is there a designated timekeeper?
- Is there a designated recorder?
- Is the goal of the meeting clear?
- Is everyone given an equal opportunity to participate?
- Are people recognized for their involvement in the meeting?
- Are people allowed to ask questions or voice their opinions?
- Is there an action plan to complete after the meeting?
- Is there a way to ensure follow-through with the action plan?
- Is there a follow-up meeting scheduled if necessary?

FIGURE 12.2. Questions to consider for meetings.

honest. If you were to attempt to hold another meeting with the same conditions, what would you absolutely want to ensure exists?

STRUCTURING THE MEETING

You probably can think of many different types of meetings, ones that were organized and efficient, or ones that were unstructured, yet still productive. Those meetings that were planned well, but left some issues unaddressed. Those meetings where the discussion was fantastic, but you left with no plan of action. And those meetings that you dreaded and left, feeling displeased afterwards.

Often a meeting fails not because participants do not want to accomplish the objectives or work together as a team, but because there is a lack of structure to run the meeting. By bringing people together without established norms or objectives, the goals may not be met. Individuals may not understand their roles, and thus may not participate. People may leave feeling unheard, dissatisfied, and unmotivated to be involved in the next meeting. A clear outline and structure can change that.

THE ACTION PLAN

Pine Tree Elementary was in its first year of implementing RTI. Despite the fact that it was quite a change from old practices, the transition was smooth and relatively easy. The RTI leadership team attended trainings to learn about the rationale and implementation, the principal helped the team present the information to the rest of the staff, and most teachers were in agreement about the new model of providing support. Although all transitions have their ups and downs, the process overall seemed to be going over well. Once the school had a deeper understanding of RTI, the principal started to hold grade-level data meetings designed to review student data, make decisions about setting up additional support, and problem solve as a team. The conversations in these meetings were impressive. Teachers were bringing great questions to the table, the grade levels were working together to think about interventions, and the principal was there to support and guide teachers through the process. People left these meetings feeling good. Quality discussions were happening and teachers felt like they were heard. An outside observer would be able to see the qualities of the meetings that made them feel effective. But the question was, were they really effective? While the meetings were productive in terms of discussion, team building, and leadership, there was one crucial piece missing: the action plan. Each teacher left the meetings without a designated responsibility. Without a task, it was easy for there to be no follow-up. Yes, teachers talked about setting up interventions, and yes, sometimes they did. Yes, teachers said they would call parents, and yes, sometimes they did. Yes, teachers said they would monitor data on individual students, and yes, sometimes they did. But most of the time, most people did nothing. Not because they didn't want to, but because life gets in the way. The teachers walked away with a great conversation and that was it. Without these plans, follow-up was difficult. The principal couldn't really hold individuals accountable, because nothing was ever decided. Teachers left excited, but quickly forgot about the meeting as they moved on to the next week. It was nobody's fault, yet it was everybody's fault. Great conversations, but no action. What was happening to the students in the meantime?

By year 2 of RTI implementation, the principal realized what was occurring. At first he thought it was just because year 1 was a transition year and most teachers were just learning about the process. When the fall of year 2 came, though, he saw similar patterns in his staff. At this point he knew something needed to change, and he had the willingness and insight to recognize that his meetings were not as organized as they could be. He saw quality discussion, but knew that teacher practices needed to change. From that point on, he structured the meetings with an outline. He gave people roles like recorder and timekeeper. And most importantly, each teacher left with a designated responsibility, which would be discussed at the next meeting when follow-up decisions would be made. While there were still ups and downs, from that point on teachers fulfilled their tasks and were able to come back and talk about what worked and what didn't. This is where a lot of the real learning occurred.

Appendix 12.1 at the end of this chapter is one example of an action plan that can be completed at the end of a meeting.

DECISION-MAKING FRAMEWORK

This is why it is useful to use a plan that works for the culture of your school. A change in the schedule takes time to prioritize, plan, and decide on as a school. During a process like this, it is helpful to have a decision-making framework to work from. A decision-making framework is a set of general steps that allows the team to move forward in a structured and organized way. Many decision-making frameworks exist; some are more detailed and in depth, some are simple. The framework provided in Figure 12.3 is one option. It is a set of steps that allows teams to consider their principles, use them to set guidelines for change, and review options as they are discussed.

The steps in Figure 12.3 are straightforward and outline a clear plan for how a decision can be made. The steps are not necessarily insightful, or provide you anything that you have not heard of before. Yet they are effective because they are delineated and clear. By using a framework, a team can reach a decision more easily and more efficiently. It allows participants to know the purpose of the meeting and the process that will get them there.

Step 1 is identifying the principles that guide the school's actions. *Webster's Dictionary* defines *principle* as a "basic generalization that is accepted as true and can be used as the basis for reasoning or conduct" (*Merriam-Webster Online Dictionary*, 2008). Principles form the foundation of practice because they are overarching ideas that provide a picture of how the school can operate. They are general in nature and offer a structure

1. Identify your guiding principles as a school.
   - Consider what truths you operate from.
2. Determine guidelines for change.
   - What are the "must haves," the "maybes," and the unnecessary components?
3. Brainstorm options.
   - List all of the possible options that exist.
4. Evaluate the options.
   - What are the pros and cons of each option?
5. Reach consensus.
   - Consider how this will be accomplished. A vote? A majority decision?
6. Plan the decision.
   - Determine the time, resources, and tools necessary for success.
7. Implement the decision.
   - Do it with 100% effort and execution.
8. Evaluate the decision.
   - What's working? What could be improved?

FIGURE 12.3. Decision-making framework.

to work from. Principles naturally are fleshed out through goals, plans, and actions. They are the guiding force behind school decisions.

Step 2 is determining the guidelines for the school schedule. What components of the schedule are "non-negotiables"? What subjects will stay regardless of what changes occur? These are core classes like reading, writing, and math. There may be other classes your school considers essential as well, like art, music, and P.E., while others may consider these optional.

Next consider the "maybes," the components that are good to include, but may not be essential according to your principles. Finally, consider what can be deleted from the schedule. Are there components that people agree can be changed? Are there classes that people believe can be erased from the daily routine?

As you were reading the previous paragraph, it is possible you were thinking, "Well, how does that work? We all have different views and opinions on what is necessary, negotiable, and easily deleted." And you're correct. This can be a smooth process, but it won't always be an easy process. The schedule is the one constant that affects everybody's day, and changing it carries huge implications for all staff in the school.

This is where Step 3 comes in: Brainstorm all possible options. This means anything. The point of this activity is to get people thinking creatively and freely. To do so, there must be a safe, easy method for brainstorming. Participants have to feel like they can say anything and know that it won't be judged or ridiculed. This allows people to think more freely.

Brainstorming can be done verbally in a small group, with one person acting as the recorder. This option typically works best when all members of the group are comfortable around one another. This process can also be accomplished by asking participants to write their ideas anonymously and turn them in to one person to record them. There are other ways this task can be accomplished as well. The point of this step is that there are no guidelines, limits, or rules about what can be said. With total freedom, any option is possible, and out of all of these options, one idea may just make perfect sense.

Now that all of the ideas are on the table, Step 4 comes in: Evaluate the options. What are the pros and cons of each? It helps to have a team work through this step, as there may be a lot of options to review. Defining the activity as listing two pros and two cons of each option can make it more manageable.

The team reviews each idea and lists the pluses and minuses, advantages and disadvantages, until they get through all of the options. It is important that this be done with all of the brainstormed possibilities, regardless of how illogical some of the ideas may seem. In this way, all of the ideas are given credit, and all are equally reviewed as possibilities for implementation. This supports the freedom and flexibility in creating them.

Step 5, reaching consensus, completely depends on who is involved in the decision-making process and who has been designated decision-making responsibilities. In some cases, the leadership team pulls together the options with pros and cons from the staff, but ultimately the principal and assistant principal decide. In other situations, the principal may be more directly involved with brainstorming and listing pros and cons, but the district administrative team ultimately makes the decision. It is likely that the principal is part of the district administrative team, but also possible that he or she does not ultimately get to vote. In other schools, the principal and leadership team decide together, after reviewing all of the options. Finally, it can be possible that the whole staff participates in voting.

It is clear that there are many variations that can occur, and many outcomes that can result. It depends on who is directly involved in the decision-making process. Regardless of the decision-making process used, it is important to be clear, straightforward, and honest with all of the issues. This helps participants who are engaged in reaching consensus have an accurate picture of the implications.

Step 6 is the planning. A critical factor in any major change is the timing. At what point do we plan to implement this change, and how long do we have to plan for it? These are important questions, as they allow the RTI team to consider how much time is needed before a change in the schedule can occur. Some schools may take 3 months to plan, for example, if the modifications are easily accepted by staff and require only small changes to daily plans. Some schools may need a year to plan, for example, if there are larger implications for teachers' schedules and more people will be affected.

It is important to consider the implications for staff. How much time do we need to adequately meet as a team and plan accordingly? It may take 3 months because we have the time to meet frequently. It may take 3 months because the changes are small and easily adopted by staff. It may take 3 months because the principal has led a school through similar changes before and is familiar with the process. At the other end, it may take a year to plan because many staff will be affected. It may take a year because building staff consensus will take that long. It may take a year to plan all of the details and iron out all the kinks.

Regardless of how long it takes to plan, "planning the planning time" is important. Make sure enough planning time exists. Don't rush a change without considering all of the implications. Allow the team enough time to work together and create options. Take more time than not, and know that it is good to do that instead of rushing through the process. By doing so, you are helping to ensure that the planning will be thoughtful, supported, and productive throughout the process.

MAKING IT WORK

All they wanted was a half hour. Thirty minutes to provide additional instruction to students who needed interventions. A little slice of the day to give students what they need, whether they were struggling with concepts or they were advanced beyond the curriculum. The RTI team thought this was a great way to slowly make changes to the schedule and provide teachers the time they need to work with students. Thirty minutes does not sound like a lot, but it was. The team was facing other priorities within the school schedule that were difficult to get rid of. Core subjects, lunch, P.E., and specials already filled the day. The staff were unable to see how anything could be deleted from the schedule without upsetting certain teachers or causing a firestorm from parents. How would they find a half-hour in a day already packed with classes and activities? Because of the ramifications and complexities surrounding the change, the RTI team decided to take a year to plan for the schedule modifications. With this amount of time, they had multiple opportunities to meet, solve problems, brainstorm, present ideas to the rest of the staff, go back to the drawing board, and come back again with new options. A year seemed like a long time, but they knew they needed it to make this work. In their meetings, they asked the hard questions and tried to be creative in their thinking. They tried to come up with many variations, so the pros and cons could all be weighed. By the time May came around, the team finally had some viable options. These options were based on their principles as a school, their impact on all staff, and the need to give students the support they required. The team was able to take 5 minutes from here, 10 minutes from there, until they were able to find the extra half-hour that was needed. In the end, not everyone was happy, but most people understood the rationale and final option that was selected. For some, it was an easy transition. For others, it was more difficult. But the team felt it was a success, not because certain people were pleased, but because they had spent the time to work through a process and do it well. They remembered where they had started and knew that the school had come a long way.

Step 7 is where the action comes in. It is time to implement the decision and see how it all plays out. While there may be foreseeable areas of concern, there also may be some surprises. Some things may go more smoothly than expected, while other unexpected issues may arise. Regardless, now is the time for it to all happen, both good and bad, easy and difficult. It is important during this time to take note of what positive outcomes occur, what issues arise, and what questions result. There can be a designated person to take note of the pluses, minuses, and questions and date them so the school has a running record of implementation. This is useful information that can be used formatively, as the implementation is occurring, to make changes as needed. This is also good data to have for summative decisions as the team looks back and assesses the overall impact of the new schedule.

Throughout the whole process, it is important to do two things as a RTI leadership team: Remind people there will be bumps in the road and that communication will be open and honest. The bumps may be bumps, but they are okay and expected. Communication will be open and frequent so people are aware of what is occurring. By giving staff information, they are kept involved in the process. This can do a lot to answer questions and address concerns.

Ideally, we would all appreciate if the changes in our lives were smooth transitions. Sometimes this is the case and other times not. In a year when the schedule has been altered, many staff may be affected or few staff may be affected. Until the change occurs, it can be difficult to predict all of the outcomes, so it may not be smooth sailing for a while. People may understand this logic, but when you're in the middle of it, it is difficult to keep that in mind. Reminding teachers that there will be ups and downs can be very helpful.

Communication also will be kept open and frequent, so that all staff are aware of the events and accurately informed of what's occurring. This seems logical—we like to assume that if a major change will be implemented, we will be informed. Yet sometimes life gets in the way. The information may get to people, but it's late, or confusing, or misconstrued.

So what is the best way to convey this information to the school? The answer is: It depends on multiple factors, including:

- Magnitude of the change
- Complexity of the change
- Number of people affected
- The specific staff that are affected
- Level of staff buy-in
- When the change will occur
- How the change will occur

Given that every school is its own living, breathing environment, each atmosphere is different. Each school has different factors to contend with and different issues to address. With these realities, a schedule alteration may be an easy change for some and a huge jump for others. It is important to consider the factors listed above and choose the best method of presenting the information.

Why is this important? Choosing an appropriate method of presenting the information is critical because it helps prevent rumors. It helps people to feel informed, so there is less guessing and fewer conversations that center around negative comments. And it

- What are the positive outcomes? Successes? Celebrations?
- What are the aspects that can be improved?
- Does anything need to be changed for next year?
- How do we make changes for next year?
- How did the changes evolve from September to June?
- How were staff affected over the course of the year?
- What responsibilities do we have in the fall to sustain implementation?
- What have we learned overall from the whole process?

FIGURE 12.4. RTI leadership team questions.

continues to validate that teachers are valued staff members whose voices are heard. It helps people to feel like a part of the process, even if they are not directly involved with the RTI leadership team.

The final step (Step 8) is to evaluate the decision. What's working? What can be improved? First, this can be done formatively, that is, on an ongoing basis. If the team is meeting once a month, they can easily discuss what is going well and what may need to be changed. This may lead to smaller changes in the schedule depending on how things are going for the school. These are great opportunities to open it up for honest conversations, allow staff to take their concerns to the RTI team, and support the process of brainstorming and problem solving as issues arise.

Second, this can be done summatively, at the end of the school year. Now that the team has information from the first year of implementation, there can be a meeting to review data and make plans for the following year. These are the fun meetings, the ones where you get to look back, remember what occurred, and start talking about next year (knowing that summer vacation is here). Some questions that the RTI leadership team can use to guide the discussion are in Figure 12.4.

SCHEDULES

Changing the schedule is a complex task because each grade is affected in a different way. It's not a task where if the times, classes, or order of classes is changed, each grade is affected the same. Grade levels typically operate very differently from one another, so each class can access the library, computer lab, lunchroom, playground, gym, art, and music at different times. They also operate differently because they are teaching different subjects at different times, depending on the ages of the students. Thus one change in second grade can look completely unlike the same change in fifth grade.

The schedules in Appendix 12.2 at the end of this chapter are presented as examples from other elementary schools as they adopted an RTI model and had to fit additional instructional time into the school day. Because each grade level is affected differently, multiple grade levels are included. The schedules are only a few examples of what exists. They represent how daily activities have played out differently depending on the district principles, priorities, and beliefs.

Schedules are better described through explicit examples, rather than just concepts. It is helpful to see what other schools have done in this transition and how they made it work. This does two things. One, it shows that yes, it can be done. Other schools have actually found the time to change their practices for RTI implementation. Two, it provides multiple options to consider, so teams can learn from others. Instead of reinventing the wheel, the schedules shown here can help schools make the wheel roll a little bit easier. Then the transition can be a smooth one on the highway, instead of a bumpy one on the back roads.

SUMMARY

When we talk about any big initiative, it is easy to talk about the concepts and difficult to talk about the day-to-day reality. This is the biggest complaint of most teachers. They get many ideas thrown at them on professional development days, but few ideas for applying them in the school day. Our goal with this chapter is to provide some insight into how other schools have made RTI work, given their limited time and resources. Although it may be difficult, it is doable with the right planning, time, and support. We hope that you take some of the ideas listed in the chapter, modify them as needed, and make them work for your school.

Action Plan Form

Action Plan				
Action steps	Target date	Person responsible	Resources needed	Completed?
1.				
2.				
3.				
4.				
5.				

Schedules

Schedule 1: Kindergarten

Breakfast	8:00–8:30
Class begins	8:30–8:40
Announcements	8:40–8:45
Calendar and morning meeting	8:45–9:00
Phonemic awareness activity	9:00–9:10
Whole-group writing	9:10–9:30
Whole-group reading	9:30–10:00
Reading curriculum	10:00–10:30
Literacy centers	10:30–11:00
Intervention groups	11:00–11:20
Lunch and recess	11:25–11:55
Story read-aloud	11:55–12:10
Rest, read, or write	12:10–12:35
ESL instruction for ELLs	12:10–12:35
Writer's workshop	12:35–1:10
Specials	1:10–1:40
Math	1:40–2:15
Choice time or recess	2:15–2:45
End of day	2:45–3:00

Schedule 2: First grade

Planning time	8:15–8:45
Class start	8:45–8:50
Phonics activity	8:50–9:05
Reading: literacy centers and small-group instruction	9:05–10:10
Recess	10:10–10:25
Math	10:25–11:10
Spelling	11:10–11:30
Lunch and second recess	11:30–12:10
Specials: art, music, library, guidance	12:10–12:50
Intervention groups	12:50–1:20
Written language	1:20–2:05
P.E.	2:05–2:40
Science/social studies	2:40–3:25
Line up for buses	3:25–3:35

Schedule 3: Second grade

Prep time	8:00–8:30
Students arrive	8:30–8:40
Math	8:40–9:40
Intervention groups	9:40–10:10
Recess	10:10–10:30
90-minute core reading	10:30–12:00
Lunch	12:00–12:30
Art, music, computer lab, or guidance	12:30–1:15
Writing block	1:15–2:15
Science or social studies	2:15–3:00
P.E.	3:00–3:30
Get ready to go home	3:30–3:45

Schedule 4: Third grade

Intervention groups	8:00–8:30
90-minute core reading	8:30–10:00
Recess	10:00–10:15
Writing	10:15–11:00
Spelling	11:00–11:20
Lunch and recess	11:20–12:00
Math	12:00–12:45
Science	12:45–1:30
Art, music, library, computer lab	1:30–2:30
P.E.	2:30–3:00
Social studies	3:00–3:45
End of day	3:45–3:50

Schedule 5: Fourth grade

Homeroom	8:20–8:30
Reading	8:30–9:40
Intervention groups	9:40–10:10
Math	10:10–11:10
Lunch	11:10–11:30
Recess	11:30–11:50
Art, music, library, computer lab	11:50–12:40
Written language	12:40–1:40
Science/social studies	1:40–2:20
P.E.	2:20–3:00
Study hall/guidance	3:00–3:30
End of day	3:30–3:40

APPENDIX A

RTI Readiness Checklist

Implementation of RTI: Self-Assessment Tool

This self-assessment tool is intended to assist schools/districts wanting to determine "next steps" toward implementation of a multi-tiered ***response to intervention*** approach for meeting the learning needs of ALL students. The tool addresses five broad indicators along with specific indicators/subtopics for each.

The tool could be completed by each staff member in order to formulate a school profile and/or be used to stimulate group conversations. To determine "next steps," it is important not only to gauge the current implementation status of each item, but to also determine its relative priority. A basic planning format has been provided at the end of the checklist on which specific actions around the top priority items can be documented.

Some basic underpinnings of this systemic approach:

- It relies on the premise that all students receive research-based and standards-driven instruction in general education.
- The learning of all students is assessed early and often (ongoing progress monitoring). Assessment is focused on direct measurements of achievement and behavior.
- If there are concerns about student progress, increasingly intense tiers of intervention are available to groups or individuals.
- Individual student data gathered through the process may be used to determine appropriateness of a special education referral (e.g., in the case of students who do not respond adequately to intervention or who require ongoing intensive intervention in order to sustain growth) and as part of a comprehensive evaluation for determination of eligibility.

Response to intervention is ...
Response to intervention is an approach that promotes a well-integrated system connecting general, compensatory, gifted, and special education in providing high-quality, standards-based instruction/intervention that is matched to students' academic, social–emotional, and behavioral needs. A continuum of intervention tiers with increasing levels of intensity and duration is central to RTI. Collaborative educational decisions are based on data derived from frequent monitoring of student performance and rate of learning.

The overarching purpose of RTI implementation is to improve educational outcomes for all students.

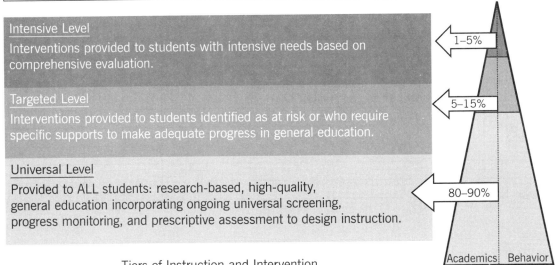

Intensive Level
Interventions provided to students with intensive needs based on comprehensive evaluation.

Targeted Level
Interventions provided to students identified as at risk or who require specific supports to make adequate progress in general education.

Universal Level
Provided to ALL students: research-based, high-quality, general education incorporating ongoing universal screening, progress monitoring, and prescriptive assessment to design instruction.

1–5%

5–15%

80–90%

Academics Behavior

Tiers of Instruction and Intervention

APPENDIX A.2

Priority Rating:			Indicators of RTI Implementation	Level of Implementation:			
Low	Medium	High		(1) Do not do this in our school	(2) Starting to move in this direction	(3) Making good progress here	(4) This condition well established
			I. EFFECTIVE STUDENT INTERVENTION/ PROBLEM-SOLVING TEAM IN PLACE				
			Use of problem-solving and data-driven decision-making processes at the school, classroom, and individual student levels				
			Function as a problem-solving team to address the needs of groups or individuals				
			Shared responsibility among general educators and specific program-area specialists (e.g., special education, ELA, G/T, Title)				
			Focus on student outcomes vs. eligibility (team's main purpose is not special education referral)				
			Use of universal screening and prescriptive assessment for instruction				
			Use of progress monitoring techniques				
			Coaching and peer collaboration				
			Collaboration between educators and parents				
			II. HIGH-QUALITY, STANDARDS-BASED CURRICULUM AND RESEARCH-BASED INSTRUCTION (80% SUCCESS RATE) IN GENERAL EDUCATION, ESPECIALLY IN THE AREAS OF:				
			Reading: Addresses five components (phonemic awareness; decoding/phonics/word recognition; fluency; vocabulary; comprehension) in an explicit, systematic, intensive manner with fidelity and sufficient duration				
			Writing/spelling				
			Math: Addresses four essential domains (problem solving; arithmetic skill/fluency; conceptual knowledge/ number sense; reasoning ability)				
			Behavior				
			Other:				
			Other:				
			Other:				
			Other:				

(cont.)

Priority
Rating: Level of Implementation:

Low	Medium	High	Indicators of RTI Implementation	(1) Do not do this in our school	(2) Starting to move in this direction	(3) Making good progress here	(4) This condition well established
			III. PRESCRIPTIVE/ONGOING ASSESSMENT PRACTICES IN PLACE				
			Universal screening system to assess strengths and challenges of all students in academic achievement, talents, and behavior				
			Structured data conversations occurring to inform instructional decisions				
			Direct measurements of achievement and behavior (learning benchmarks) that have a documented/predictable relationship to positive student outcomes				
			Progress monitoring that is systematic, documented, and shared				
			Data management system in place (technology support)				

Low	Medium	High		(1)	(2)	(3)	(4)
			IV. LEVELS OF INTERVENTION IDENTIFIED AND RESOURCES ALLOCATED				
			A range of research-based instructional interventions for any students at risk of not reaching their potential, including those identified as gifted/talented or those already experiencing academic failure (systematic model in place such as three-tiered approach, pyramid of interventions, etc.)				
			Utilization of both a standard protocol approach to providing interventions to groups of students with similar needs and an individual approach of providing interventions to any student with unique needs				
			Informed as to the frequency, intensity, and duration of an intervention that is needed for effectiveness				
			System in place to evaluate research-based interventions as to integrity/fidelity of implementation				
			Flexible groupings according to specific intervention needs				
			Allocation of staff to provide various interventions (flexible uses of staffing across all roles)				
			Availability of instructional programs/materials				

(cont.)

Priority Rating:				Level of Implementation:			
Low	Medium	High	**Indicators of RTI Implementation**	(1) Do not do this in our school	(2) Starting to move in this direction	(3) Making good progress here	(4) This condition well established
			V. ONGOING, JOB-EMBEDDED PROFESSIONAL DEVELOPMENT THAT ADDRESSES RELEVANT AREAS ESSENTIAL TO EFFECTIVE IMPLEMENTATION OF RTI AND IMPROVED STUDENT OUTCOMES				
			Across all staff/roles				
			Involves families				
			Includes follow-up (e.g., coaching, professional dialogue, peer feedback, etc.)				
			Professional development addresses relevant areas such as:	No development in this area	Area minimally addressed	Ongoing focus in this area	Extensive development in this area
			Collaborative decision making (e.g., professional learning communities)				
			Effective use of data, including that gathered through ongoing progress monitoring, in making instructional decisions				
			Collaborative delivery of instruction/interventions				
			Research-based instructional practices, including supporting materials and tools				
			What constitutes "interventions" vs. "accommodations and modifications"				
			Prescriptive and varied assessment techniques				
			Progress monitoring techniques				
			Parent engagement strategies				
			Other:				
			Other:				
			Other:				

Action Plan

Date _____

Indicator or Subtopic	Specific Actions	Resources	Timeline	Who Is Responsible?	Evidence of Change

Planning Team: _____

Reproducible Planning Forms

Student Progress and Request for Assistance

Teacher completes this side and puts in school psychologist's mailbox or brings to next team meeting.

Teacher: _____

Student: _____

Date: _____

Reason for concern:

_____

_____

Universal interventions already in place—circle Y or N below.
See green (Tier 1) intervention recipes for descriptions.

	Available?	Used by student?	Comments
Establishing Classroom Expectations	Y/N	Y/N	_____
Managing Transition Time	Y/N	Y/N	_____
Practice, Practice, Practice	Y/N	Y/N	_____
Other _____	Y/N	Y/N	_____
Other _____	Y/N	Y/N	_____

Most recent scores in area of academic concern (CBM refers to curriculum-based measurement):

	CBM or Quiz	CBM or Quiz	CBM or Quiz	CBM or Quiz
Date	_____	_____	_____	_____
Student score	_____	_____	_____	_____
Class average	_____	_____	_____	_____

Top three reasons why you think student is not making progress:

1. _____
2. _____
3. _____

Date of your last parent contact: _____ Phone or in person? _____

Topics discussed: _____

_____

```
                  low ———————————→ high
Level of urgency:   1    2    3    4    5
```

Best days and times to meet: _____

_____   _____
Teacher signature   Date

Student Planning Form

Teacher and school psychologist or team complete this side together.

Student Progress

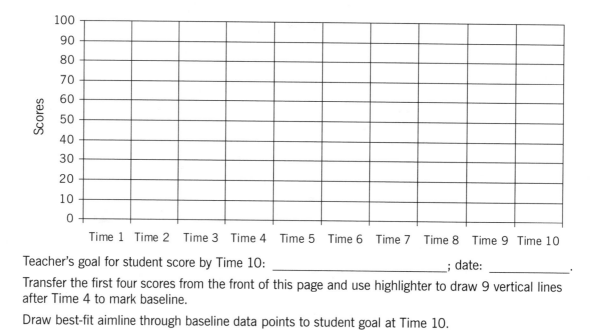

Teacher's goal for student score by Time 10: _____ ; date: _____ .

Transfer the first four scores from the front of this page and use highlighter to draw 9 vertical lines after Time 4 to mark baseline.

Draw best-fit aimline through baseline data points to student goal at Time 10.

What to look for on your graph:

- If four consecutive data points are below the aimline, the intervention should be modified or changed. Contact the school psychologist.
- If four consecutive data points are above the aimline, continue with the recommended intervention.
- If four consecutive data points are both above **AND** below aimline, continue to collect data to determine intervention effectiveness.

Intervention/tier	Date started	Date stopped	Why stopped?
1.			
2.			
3.			

Intervention Options and Planning: Reading/Tier 2 (Yellow)

Teacher and school psychologist or team complete this form together.

Teacher: _____ Date: _____

Student: _____

Reason for concern: _____

See yellow (Tier 2) intervention recipes: Choose one and circle.

Guess the Word	Have You Ever?
Word Sort	Story Mapping
Repeated Readings	Other: _____

Materials or assistance needed:

_____

_____

_____

_____

Start date for implementation: _____

How often will the intervention be used? _____

School psychologist will observe, provide performance feedback, and review data points with teacher on:

_____   _____
Time and date   Time and date

Notes:

_____

_____

_____

_____

_____

_____

_____

_____

_____

_____

_____

_____   _____
Teacher signature   School psychologist signature

Intervention Options and Planning: Reading/Tier 3 (Red)

Teacher and school psychologist or team complete this form together.

Teacher: _____ Date: _____

Student: _____

Reason for concern: _____

See red (Tier 3) intervention recipes: Choose one and circle.

Letter Puzzles   Word Associations

Silent e Changes   3H Instructional Strategy

Phrase Drill Procedure   Other: _____

Materials or assistance needed:

_____

_____

_____

_____

Start date for implementation: _____

How often will the intervention be used? _____

School psychologist will observe, provide performance feedback, and review data points with teacher on:

_____   _____
Time and date   Time and date

Notes:

_____

_____

_____

_____

_____

_____

_____

_____

_____

_____

_____

_____   _____
Teacher signature   School psychologist signature

Intervention Options and Planning: Writing/Tier 2 (Yellow)

Teacher and school psychologist or team complete this form together.

Teacher: _____ Date: _____

Student: _____

Reason for concern: _____

See yellow (Tier 2) intervention recipes: Choose one and circle.

Planning Your Writing   Student Editor Strategy

Personal Narrative Think Sheet   Other: _____

Materials or assistance needed:

_____

_____

_____

_____

Start date for implementation: _____

How often will the intervention be used? _____

School psychologist will observe, provide performance feedback, and review data points with teacher on:

_____   _____
Time and date   Time and date

Notes:

_____

_____

_____

_____

_____

_____

_____

_____

_____

_____

_____

_____   _____
Teacher signature   School psychologist signature

Intervention Options and Planning: Writing/Tier 3 (Red)

Teacher and school psychologist or team complete this form together.

Teacher: _____ Date: _____

Student: _____

Reason for concern: _____

See red (Tier 3) intervention recipes: Choose one and circle.

Use C-SPACE to Take Notes   Modeling the Writing Process

Proofreading Checklist   Other: _____

Materials or assistance needed:

_____

_____

_____

_____

Start date for implementation: _____

How often will the intervention be used? _____

School psychologist will observe, provide performance feedback, and review data points with teacher on:

_____   _____
Time and date   Time and date

Notes:

_____

_____

_____

_____

_____

_____

_____

_____

_____

_____

_____

_____   _____
Teacher signature   School psychologist signature

Intervention Options and Planning: Math/Tier 1 (Green)

Teacher and school psychologist or team complete this form together.

Teacher: _____ Date: _____

Student: _____

Reason for concern: _____

See green (Tier 1) intervention recipes: Choose one and circle.

Practice, Practice, Practice   Other: _____

Interspersing Easy and Hard Math Problems

Materials or assistance needed:

_____

_____

_____

_____

Start date for implementation: _____

How often will the intervention be used? _____

School psychologist will observe, provide performance feedback, and review data points with teacher on:

_____   _____
Time and date   Time and date

Notes:

_____

_____

_____

_____

_____

_____

_____

_____

_____

_____

_____   _____
Teacher signature   School psychologist signature

Intervention Options and Planning: Math/Tier 2 (Yellow)

Teacher and school psychologist or team complete this form together.

Teacher: _____   Date: _____

Student: _____

Reason for concern: _____

See yellow (Tier 2) intervention recipes: Choose one and circle.

Skip-Counting Practice   Timed Practice, Practice, Practice

Computation Grid with M & M's   Other: _____

Materials or assistance needed:

_____

_____

_____

_____

Start date for implementation: _____

How often will the intervention be used? _____

School psychologist will observe, provide performance feedback, and review data points with teacher on:

_____   _____
Time and date   Time and date

Notes:

_____

_____

_____

_____

_____

_____

_____

_____

_____

_____

_____

_____   _____
Teacher signature   School psychologist signature

Intervention Options and Planning: Math/Tier 3 (Red)

Teacher and school psychologist or team complete this form together.

Teacher: _____ Date: _____

Student: _____

Reason for concern: _____

See red (Tier 3) intervention recipes: Choose one and circle.

Flashcards   Cover–Copy–Compare

Flashcards with Folding In New Items   Other: _____

Materials or assistance needed:

_____

_____

_____

_____

Start date for implementation: _____

How often will the intervention be used? _____

School psychologist will observe, provide performance feedback, and review data points with teacher on:

_____   _____
Time and date   Time and date

Notes:

_____

_____

_____

_____

_____

_____

_____

_____

_____

_____

_____   _____
Teacher signature   School psychologist signature

Intervention Options and Planning: Behavior/Tier 1 (Green)

Teacher and school psychologist or team complete this form together.

Teacher: _____ Date: _____

Student: _____

Reason for concern: _____

See green (Tier 1) intervention recipes: Choose one and circle.

Establishing Classroom Expectations   Other: _____

Managing Transition Time

Materials or assistance needed:

_____

_____

_____

_____

Start date for implementation: _____

How often will the intervention be used? _____

School psychologist will observe, provide performance feedback, and review data points with teacher on:

_____   _____
Time and date   Time and date

Notes:

_____

_____

_____

_____

_____

_____

_____

_____

_____

_____

_____

_____   _____
Teacher signature   School psychologist signature

Intervention Options and Planning: Behavior/Tier 2 (Yellow)

Teacher and school psychologist or team complete this form together.

Teacher: _____ Date: _____

Student: _____

Reason for concern: _____

See yellow (Tier 2) intervention recipes: Choose one and circle.

The Good Behavior Game   Peer Tutoring

Check-In, Check-Out   Other: _____

Self-Monitoring

Materials or assistance needed:

_____

_____

_____

_____

Start date for implementation: _____

How often will the intervention be used? _____

School psychologist will observe, provide performance feedback, and review data points with teacher on:

_____   _____
Time and date   Time and date

Notes:

_____

_____

_____

_____

_____

_____

_____

_____

_____

_____

_____

_____   _____
Teacher signature   School psychologist signature

Intervention Options and Planning: Behavior/Tier 3 (Red)

Teacher and school psychologist or team complete this form together.

Teacher: _____ Date: _____

Student: _____

Reason for concern: _____

Referral for Functional Behavioral Assessment (FBA)
Other: _____

Materials or assistance needed:

_____

_____

_____

_____

Start date for implementation: _____
How often will the intervention be used? _____

School psychologist will observe, provide performance feedback, and review data points with teacher on:

_____   _____
Time and date   Time and date

Notes:

_____

_____

_____

_____

_____

_____

_____

_____

_____

_____

_____

_____   _____
Teacher signature   School psychologist signature

APPENDIX C

Intervention Recipes for Reading, Writing, Math, and Behavior

READING

WRITTEN LANGUAGE

MATHEMATICS

BEHAVIOR

PHONEMIC AWARENESS

Recipe: Guess the Word

Purpose:	To help students begin to hear the individual sounds in words.
Research Base:	Chard and Dickson (1999).
Ingredients:	Picture cards.
Prep Time:	20 minutes.
Activity Time:	10 minutes.
Preparation:	1. Collect a stack of cards with pictures that represent simple CVC words.
	2. You can make your own by finding pictures on the Internet, printing them, and pasting them on cards.
	3. Gather a large stack so that you can vary the words each time you do the activity.

Activity

1. Have students sit in a circle and place picture cards in the middle.
2. Say: *I am going to say the name of one of the pictures in snail talk. I want you to look at the pictures and guess which one I am saying.*
3. Listen: *"BBAAATTT." What picture am I saying?*
4. Have the students respond as a group first.
5. Ask individual students after the group has responded a few times.
6. Monitor progress with Phoneme Segmentation Fluency.

ALPHABETIC PRINCIPLE

Recipe: Word Sort

Purpose:	To practice letter sounds by sorting words.
Research Base:	Florida Center for Reading Research (2006).
Ingredients:	Words with similar sounds cut into pieces and containers labeled with the sounds.
Prep Time:	20 minutes.
Activity Time:	10–15 minutes.
Preparation:	1. Determine what sounds the students are learning.

2. Create individual words that contain the letter sounds and cut them out and laminate.
3. Gather containers where students can place the words.
4. Label the containers with the sounds students are learning. Short and long vowel sounds are one example.

Activity

1. Place students in partners.
2. Instruct students to place the words in the correct container by sound.
3. Students take turns with their partner and continue until all the words have been sorted.
4. Walk around during the activity and ask students to explain why they are putting the words in the containers that they are.
5. Monitor progress with nonsense word fluency (DIBELS).

FLUENCY

Recipe: Repeated Readings

Purpose:	To increase reading fluency in students who are accurate but slow readers.
Research Base:	Rashotte and Torgesen (1985).
Ingredients:	Reading passages that the student can read with 95% accuracy and a stopwatch.
Prep Time:	10 minutes.
Activity Time:	10 minutes.
Preparation:	1. Determine what grade-level passages the student can read with 95% accuracy.
	2. Gather a selection of these passages.
	3. Find a stopwatch or other timer.

Activity

1. Have the student read the passage for 1 minute. Note the rate.
2. Set a goal that is 20% above the initial rate of the student.
3. Mark the goal so the student knows what to aim for.
4. Inform the student to reread the passage.
5. Have the student keep rereading the passage until the goal is met.
6. Make this fun for the student by tying the goal to a reward.
7. Emphasize improvement rather than "reading as fast as you can."
8. If the student is easily able to reach the goal that is 20% higher, increase the goal so you can continue to monitor the progress.
9. Monitor progress with Oral Reading Fluency.

VOCABULARY

Recipe: Have You Ever?

Purpose: To practice new vocabulary words by tying them to personal experiences.

Research Base: Beck, McKeown, and Kucan (2002).

Ingredients: Set of new vocabulary words and prompts for students to consider.

Prep Time: 30 minutes.

Activity Time: 15 minutes for grades 1–3 and 30 minutes for grades 4–6.

Preparation:
1. Determine what new vocabulary words the students are learning.
2. Collect a sample of these words. Five words is a good place to start.
3. Create prompts that include the new vocabulary words and personal experiences.

Activity

1. Describe the new vocabulary words: *Today we are going to talk about new vocabulary words and think about how they apply to your lives. The new words are examples* (console, defend, elaborate, *and* encourage).
2. Present the prompts to your students, for example: *"Describe a time when you would (console) your brother or sister," "Explain when you would (defend) your friend at school," "Talk about a time when you would (elaborate) in class,"* and *"Describe a time when you would (encourage) your classmate."*
3. Give students time to write about each prompt.
4. Ask students to share what they wrote and explain their reasoning.
5. Younger students can orally share what they are thinking.
6. Check for understanding by asking multiple students to share.
7. Define the new vocabulary word and explain it to the class.
8. Ask students to rewrite their answer if they did not initially know the meaning of the word.
9. Repeat the process with each word.
10. Monitor progress with weekly vocabulary tests.

COMPREHENSION

Recipe: Story Mapping

Purpose:	To increase comprehension by providing a method for identifying the main elements in stories.
Research Base:	Gardill and Jitendra (1999).
Ingredients:	Narrative story and story mapping worksheet.
Prep Time:	20 minutes.
Activity Time:	15 minutes for grades 1–2 and 30 minutes for grades 3–6.
Preparation:	

1. Select a narrative story to show in front of the class.
2. Make a transparency or use a document projector to show the story to the class.
3. Go to *interventioncentral.org* and click on "Intervention Ideas." Scroll down to the "Reading Comprehension" section and click on "Advanced Story Map." Then click on the "Advanced Story Map" link included in the intervention description.
4. Print the story map and make copies for each student.

Activity

1. Preview the story with students: *Today we are going to talk about* [title of the story here]. *We are going to look for the main parts together using the story map worksheets.*
2. Explain the parts of the story mapping worksheet.
3. Together identify the important characters, main problem, solution, and theme. Complete the parts of the worksheet as a class.
4. Provide time for error correction to ensure that students understand the main components.
5. Instruct the students to read a new story independently. Have them identify the main components on their own.
6. Monitor progress with Maze comprehension assessment (AIMSweb).

READING RECIPES—Tier 3

T3

PHONEMIC AWARENESS

Recipe: Letter Puzzles

Purpose:	To practice blending individual sounds in words.
Research Base:	Florida Center for Reading Research (2006).
Ingredients:	Individual letters that are laminated; paper and pencils.
Prep Time:	20 minutes.
Activity Time:	20 minutes.
Preparation:	1. Print letters, cut, and laminate.
	2. Gather paper and pencils.
	3. Create a list of words that include the letter sounds that students are learning.

Activity

1. Scramble the letter pieces on the table.
2. Have the students assemble the puzzles by matching the pieces.
3. Once the word is complete, the student says the word.
4. The student writes the word on a sheet and illustrates the word.
5. To save time, use the puzzle pieces available on the Florida Center for Reading Research website (*fcrr.org*).
6. Monitor progress with Nonsense Word Fluency.

ALPHABETIC PRINCIPLE

Recipe: Silent e Changes _____

Purpose:	To practice blending sounds in words when the letter *e* is added to the end.
Research Base:	Florida Center for Reading Research (2006).
Ingredients:	Student sheet with two columns titled "Short vowel" and "Silent *e*"; word cards that have silent *e*; words on them and folded so the *e* is hidden; and pencils.
Prep Time:	20 minutes.
Activity Time:	20 minutes.
Preparation:	1. Create sheets with two columns titled "Short vowel" and "Silent *e*."
	2. Create word cards by cutting out words and folding them so the *e* is hidden.

Activity . . . .

1. Put the students in partners.
2. Explain the directions to the class: *You will be working with your partner. You each take a turn picking a word card. Once you pick the card, read it when the flap is folded back. Then read it again with the flap pulled forward. When you have read it both ways, you will write the words in the column where they belong. For example, I read the word with the flap folded back and it says* rip. *Then I pull the flap forward ant read the word again. Now it says* ripe. *I will write the word* rip *in the column that says "Short vowel" because here the* I *says its short vowel sound. I will write the word* ripe *in the column that says "Silent* e*" because now the sound of the* I *has changed because of the silent* e.
3. Students take turns reading the word cards that have the silent *e* folded back.
4. Then they read the word again once the silent *e* has been folded to the front.
5. Students write the words in the correct columns after they say them out loud.
6. The activity continues until all the words are read.
7. To minimize preparation time, you can skip the word cards and just say the words out loud and write them on the board. Add the silent *e* to the end of the word. Students talk in partners as words are presented and write the words in the appropriate columns on their sheets.
8. Monitor progress with flashcard drill of regular short- and long-vowel words.

T3

FLUENCY

Recipe: Phrase Drill Procedure

Purpose:	Increase reading fluency by allowing student to practice misread words.
Research Base:	O'Shea (1984).
Ingredients:	Reading passage and highlighter.
Prep Time:	10 minutes.
Activity Time:	20 minutes.
Preparation:	1. Collect passages that the student reads with 85–95% accuracy.
	2. Get a highlighter.

Activity

1. Instruct the student to read the passage.
2. Highlight any words read incorrectly.
3. Point to each highlighted word and read them to the student.
4. Instruct the student to read the word back to you.
5. Instruct the student to read the sentences with the words they read incorrectly three times aloud.
6. If a sentence contains more than one word read incorrectly, have the student read each word in isolation first, before reading the sentence aloud three times.
7. Monitor progress with Oral Reading Fluency.

VOCABULARY

Recipe: Word Associations ———————

Purpose:	To practice new vocabulary words as they are introduced.
Research Base:	Beck, McKeown, and Kucan (2002).
Ingredients:	Set of new vocabulary words and list of questions that target the new words.
Prep Time:	20 minutes.
Activity Time:	20 minutes.
Preparation:	1. Select new vocabulary words that will be addressed in the lesson.
	2. Create a list of questions to associate with the new words.

Activity . . . .

1. Write the new vocabulary words on the board: *The new words are examples* (discussion, struggle, duties, *and* unusual).
2. Ask students to indicate which word goes with the description you provide (examples: *Which word goes with responsibility? Which word goes with "out of the ordinary"? Which word goes with difficulty? Which word goes with conversation?*).
3. For each pairing, ask students why they picked the word they did.
4. Do this with individual students or the whole class.
5. Monitor progress with weekly vocabulary tests.

READING RECIPES—Tier 3

T3

T3

COMPREHENSION

Recipe: 3H Instructional Strategy

Purpose:	Teach students to use a mnemonic to remember how to answer different types of comprehension questions.
Research Base:	Graham and Wong (1993).
Ingredients:	Reading passages with comprehension questions and notecards.
Prep Time:	30 minutes.
Activity Time:	30 minutes.
Preparation:	1. Create an outline with the three types of question–answer relationships: "Here," "Hidden," or "In My Head." Describe each category.
	2. Gather reading passages with a variety of comprehension questions.

Activity

1. Provide the outline describing the three types of questions to students.
2. Describe the differences between answers that are found "Here," that are "Hidden," or that are "In My Head."
3. Read a passage together.
4. Look at each of the comprehension questions.
5. Together decide where the answer is, using the 3H strategy (Here, Hidden, or In My Head).
6. Instruct the students to write "Here," "Hidden," or "In My Head" next to each comprehension question.
7. Repeat this activity with different passages and different comprehension questions.
8. Students can do this independently with the new passages.
9. For additional support, have students orally recite the description of the three H's or write down what the three H's represent on notecards.
10. Monitor progress with weekly comprehension tests.

Recipe: Planning Your Writing

Purpose: To help students plan for writing.

Research Base: Englert, Raphaet, Anderson, Anthony, and Stevens (1991).

Ingredients: Question cards and a writing topic.

Prep Time: 10 minutes.

Activity Time: 30 minutes.

Preparation:
1. Create question cards that contain the following prompts:
   a. What is my topic?
   b. Who am I writing for?
   c. Why am I writing this?
   d. How can I group my ideas?
   e. How will I organize my ideas?
2. Provide space on the question cards for students to write their answers so they can easily reference them.

Activity

1. Provide cards that contain the questions.
2. Provide a selection of writing topics.
3. Provide examples as you teach the steps explicitly.
4. Walk students through the steps as they plan for their writing.
5. Monitor progress by evaluating their answers to these questions over time. Look for depth, detail, and specifics that will guide them in their writing.

T2

Recipe: Personal Narrative Think Sheet

Purpose:	To provide a structure for students as they plan their writing.
Research Base:	Isaacson (2004).
Ingredients:	Paper, pencils, Personal Narrative Think Sheet.
Prep Time:	20 minutes
Activity Time:	30–40 minutes.
Preparation:	1. Make copies of the Personal Narrative Think Sheet. The example is provided below.
	2. Walk through the steps and think about how you will explain each section.
	3. Create an example to model to the students.

Activity

1. Model how to use the Personal Narrative Think Sheet as a whole group.
2. Explicitly teach how to complete each section of the think sheet.
3. Allow students time to work alone or with a partner in planning a story.
4. Hold brief check-in meetings to see how students have used the think sheet.
5. Monitor progress with story starter probes and a writing rubric.

Personal Narrative Think Sheet

Topic: _____

1. Search all memories:

   The time when . . . .

   The time when . . . .

   The time when . . . .

2. Choose one story to tell.
3. Play it in your mind (like a video).

4. Where did it happen?	8. What happened?
5. Who was there?	9. What were my feelings?
6. What did I see?	10. How did it end?
7. What did I hear?	11. Why do I remember this? Why is it important?

From *RTI in the Classroom: Guidelines and Recipes for Success* by Rachel Brown-Chidsey, Louise Bronaugh, and Kelly McGraw. Copyright 2009 by The Guilford Press. Permission to photocopy this form is granted to purchasers of this book for personal use only (see copyright page for details).

Recipe: Student Editor Strategy

Purpose: To give students a format for reading, revising, and editing with a partner.

Research Base: Graham, Schwartz, and MacArthur (1993).

Ingredients: Paper, pencils, and Student Editor Strategy checklist.

Prep Time: 20 minutes.

Activity Time: 30–40 minutes.

Preparation:
1. Copy the Student Editor Strategy directions for each student.
2. Make two copies of the stories the students wrote so each partner has a copy.
3. Pair students before the activity. You can place either those with high and low skills together or those with similar skills together.
4. Walk through the steps so you can explain the directions to the class.

Activity

1. Explain how to use the checklist by describing each part of the worksheet.
2. Model using the checklist with a story and a partner in front of the class.
3. Put students in pairs.
4. Give the pairs two copies of their stories.
5. Walk the students through each part of the worksheet. See the example.
6. Meet with each pair briefly during the process.

Notes

1. You can pair students with high and low skills together. If done this way, understand that the students with higher skills will then need to receive feedback from you or another student with higher skills so they can benefit from the activity.
2. You can pair students with similar skills together. If done this way, make sure that you provide more support to the students with lower skills so they can be successful with the revision process.

Student Editor Strategy

1. Listen and read along as the author reads.
   a. One student reads while the other follows along.
2. Tell what it was about and what you liked best.
   a. One student paraphrases what he or she just read. Once this is complete, the students switch roles. The other student reads out loud and paraphrases.
3. Read and make notes about:
   a. Was it clear?
   b. Is there anything that is hard to understand?
   c. Are there enough details?
   d. Where can more information be added?
4. Talk about your ideas with the writer.
   a. Discuss the ideas and share questions and answers.
5. The writer makes revisions to his or her work.

WRITTEN LANGUAGE RECIPES—Tier 2

T3

Recipe: Use C-SPACE to Take Notes _____

Purpose:	:	To provide a structure for students in planning a story.
Research Base:	:	MacArthur and Graham (1993).
Ingredients:	:	1. C-SPACE planning sheets.

  a. C = characters; S = setting; P = problem; A = action;
     C = conclusion; E = emotion.

  2. Pencils.

Prep Time:	:	15 minutes.
Activity Time:	:	30 minutes.
Preparation:	:	1. Create sheets that have the mnemonic C-SPACE going down the left side of the page.

Activity . . . .

1. Teach students to use this planning mnemonic when thinking about writing.
2. Model its use and provide examples.
3. Ask students to provide ideas as you are demonstrating the mnemonic.

Notes . . . .

1. Make it a game by dividing students into groups. Have each group think of their own stories using the mnemonic.
2. Provide points to each group for their details under each category.
3. Monitor progress with a story starter probe and writing rubric (AIMSweb).

Recipe: Proofreading Checklist _____

Purpose: To provide students a format for checking their writing when they are finished.

Research Base: Graham, Harris, and Larsen (2001).

Ingredients: Paper, pencils, checklist, overhead of sample story.

Prep Time: 10 minutes.

Activity Time: 30–40 minutes.

Preparation:
1. Make copies of the Proofreading Checklist.
2. Think about how to explain each part of the checklist to your students.

Activity . . . .

1. Explain how to use the checklist by describing each part.
2. Model using the checklist with a story. Take a sample story you have written and show the students how to use the checklist with the story.
3. Describe what to do if one of the items cannot be checked off: *If you come to a part of the checklist and you realize you need to make some changes in your story, go back and fix what you need to. Ask a partner if you have questions first and then ask me second if you still need help.*
4. Provide an explicit plan for students when they feel they cannot check off one of the components because it is not complete in their writing.

Proofreading Checklist	
Used a planning sheet to think of ideas	
Have a beginning, middle, and end	
Double-check spelling	
Formed letters correctly	
Used periods, commas, question marks, and exclamation points as needed	
Capitalized beginning letters and proper nouns	
Have a partner read over and give feedback	

Recipe: Modeling the Writing Process _____

Purpose: To provide instruction that is clear, straightforward, and explicit.

Research Base: Adapted from Isaacson (2004).

Ingredients: Paper, pencils, overhead, overhead pens.

Prep Time: 30 minutes.

Activity Time: 30 minutes.

Preparation:
1. Prepare an overhead with the steps of the writing component you are going to teach.
2. Create multiple examples and nonexamples to show the students.
3. Rehearse the simple, repetitive language that you will use in class.

Activity . . . .

1. Model each step of the concept you are teaching. Example: *Today we are going to learn when to use commas. Commas are used in many ways. We are going to focus on one of these ways today.*
2. Think aloud as you write on the overhead: *One way that commas are used is to separate nouns in a list. If you have multiple nouns in a sentence, they need to be separated with commas.*
3. Use simple, repetitive language. Examples: *Separate nouns in a list*, and *Use commas between each noun.*
4. Ask questions to keep students engaged. Example: *What are some lists of nouns you can think of? Where would you put the commas? Would you put commas here or here?*
   a. Let the students offer their ideas. Compare the ideas.
   b. Check their understanding of important points.
5. Follow the model, lead, and test format.
   Examples:
   a. *Watch me. Commas go here, here, and here because they separate the nouns in this list.*
   b. *Now let's do it together. Look at this sentence. There are nouns here. Let's put the commas where they belong. Here, here, and here.*
   c. *Now it's your turn. Look at this sentence. Where do the commas go?*
6. Provide multiple examples and nonexamples to illustrate the concept.
7. Monitor progress with a writing probe looking for use of skill taught.

Note . . . .

Note about intensive interventions for writing: Because the writing process is complex, the interventions listed above are not intended to be exhaustive and comprehensive. The interventions primarily focus on the writing process itself. At the intensive level of instruction, you can easily encounter students who are not yet ready to focus on the writing process, because they have not mastered the basic skills of grammar, spelling, or handwriting. In these cases, it is crucial to focus on the component skills first, so that students can make progress in the basic skill areas before moving on to the process of writing. Thus, even though interventions on grammar, spelling, and handwriting are not included, start with those areas first for students who need it. Once mastered, instruction can move to targeting the writing process.

Recipe: Practice, Practice, Practice _____

Purpose:	To help students develop accuracy with basic computation skills.
Research Base:	Stein, Kinder, Silbert, and Carnine (2006).
Ingredients:	Computation problems matched to students' independent practice level.
Prep Time:	5–10 minutes.
Activity Time:	10 minutes per worksheet (this time can be adjusted as needed by your students).

Preparation:

1. Identify what computation skill students most need to practice (e.g., addition, subtraction, multiplication, or division).
2. Go to the following website: *www.interventioncentral.org.*
3. In the section labeled "Online Tools" click on "Math Worksheet Generator" on the right-hand side of the page.
4. When the new math page loads, click on the computation skill(s) you want students to practice (e.g., addition, subtraction, multiplication, division, mixed skills).
5. Click on the specific skill(s) you want included in your practice worksheet.
6. At the bottom of the page choose how many columns, rows, and what size font you want students to use.
7. Click on "Single Skill Computation Probe."
8. Once you click on the button to create the probe, your browser should create and load a new tab or page with the teacher (answer) key first. Once this page is loaded, click on the text at the very top of the page which says "Click for Student Worksheet."
9. Another new tab or page will load. This is the one you want to print for the students. Print as many copies as you need for the students, or print one copy and then make photocopies.
10. Print a copy of the answer sheet onto an overhead transparency.

Activity . . . .

1. Give worksheet to students and say: *Today we are going to practice _____. You have 10 minutes to finish the paper I am handing out.*
2. Give students 10 minutes to complete the page, then say: *Pass your worksheet to a classmate. I will put the correct answers on the overhead. Mark your classmates' answers correct or incorrect.*
3. When finished correcting answers say to students: *Pass the worksheet back to its owner. Look at your correct and incorrect answers. Fix the ones you got wrong.*
4. After students have corrected their answers, collect the worksheets so you can review them and record the student's scores.

Recipe: Interspersing Easy and Hard Math Problems ___

Purpose:	To provide practice opportunities solving known and new problems.
Research Base:	McDonald and Ardoin (2007).
Ingredients:	Easy and difficult math problems.
Prep Time:	5–10 minutes.
Activity Time:	10 minutes per worksheet.
Preparation:	

1. Identify what computation skills students have mastered and what ones the students need to practice in order to master (e.g., addition with regrouping, subtraction without regrouping).

2. Go to the following website: *www.interventioncentral.org.*

3. In the section labeled "Online Tools" click on "Math Worksheet Generator" on the right-hand side of the page.

4. When the new math page loads, click on the button labeled "Mixed Skills."

5. Click on the specific skill(s) you want included in your practice worksheet.

6. At the bottom of the page choose how many columns, rows, and what size font you want students to use.

7. Click on "Single Skill Computation Probe."

8. Once you click on the button to create the probe, your browser should create and load a new tab or page with the teacher (answer) key first. Once this page is loaded, click on the text at the very top of the page that says "Click for Student Worksheet."

9. Another new tab or page will load. This is the one you want to print for the students. Print as many copies as you need for the students, or print one copy and then make photocopies.

10. Print a copy of the answer sheet onto an overhead transparency.

Activity . . . .

1. Give worksheet to students and say: *Today we are going to practice math problems. Some of the problems are easy and some will be hard. You have 10 minutes to finish the paper I am handing out.*

2. Give students 10 minutes to complete the page, then say: *Pass your worksheet to a classmate. I will put the correct answers on the overhead. Mark your classmates' answers correct or incorrect.*

3. When finished correcting answers say to students: *Pass the worksheet back to its owner. Look at your correct and incorrect answers. Fix the ones you got wrong.*

4. After students have corrected their answers, collect the worksheets so you can review them and record the students' scores.

Recipe: Skip-Counting Practice

Purpose:	To help students master the intervals between whole numbers.
Research Base:	Stein, Kinder, Silbert, and Carnine (2006).
Ingredients:	Enough Skip-Counting Practice Grid templates for each student (see Appendix 8.1, p. 117).
	Enough highlighters for each student.
Prep Time:	5 minutes.
Activity Time:	10 minutes.
Preparation:	1. Write in the number by which to count for each grid.
	2. Make enough copies of the Skip-Counting Practice Grid template for each student.
	3. Make a transparency of the handout to use on an overhead projector.

Activity

1. Give each student a grid template and a highlighter.
2. Say to students: *Today we are going to practice skip-counting. On the sheet I just gave you, there are eight boxes with numbers in them. At the top of each box is the number by which to count. You are going to use your highlighter to highlight the next number when counting by the number for that box. Let's do the first one together. Look at the overhead projector.*
3. Use an overhead marker and say to students: *Watch as I highlight the numbers when I count by 3's. First I highlight 3, then 6, then 9. Raise your hand to tell me what number comes next.* Call on a student who raised a hand and highlight 12 if correct. If the student says a number other than 12, say: *That is not the correct number. Twelve is the next number when counting by 3's. Let's try another one. Raise your hand to tell me what number comes next.* Continue this process with students until the grid is complete.
4. Say to students: *Now you are going to do the rest of the worksheet on your own. Use your highlighter to mark the correct number sequence for each number at the top of the grid boxes. If you need help, raise your hand and I will come to help you.* Give students about 10–15 minutes to highlight numbers. Walk around the room and check on progress and ensure all students are engaged.
5. At the end of the work time, say to students: *Put your highlighters down and look at the overhead. We are going to review the answers together.* Place completed overhead of worksheet on projector and say to students: *Raise your hand to tell me what number comes next.* Call on a student who raised a hand and highlight the number on the overhead, if correct. If the student says an incorrect number, say: *That is not the correct number. _____ is the next number when counting by ____'s. Let's try another one. Raise your hand to tell me what number comes next.* Continue this question and response with students until the worksheet is complete.
6. Collect student worksheets to review and record their answers.

Recipe: Computation Grid with M & M's

Purpose: To help students see and apply knowledge about quantities to master computation facts.

Research Base: Stein, Kinder, Silbert, and Carnine (2006).

Ingredients: Enough blank Computation Grids for each student.

100 M & M's candies (or other small countable shape) for each student.

Food service sanitary gloves.

Paper cups or small zip-top bags.

Paper plates or other sanitary surface on which students can count out sets of candies.

Pencils.

Prep Time: 30 minutes.

Activity Time: 30 minutes.

Preparation:

1. Make enough copies of the Computation Grid (Appendix 8.2, p. 118) for each student.
2. Make an overhead transparency of the Computation Grid.
3. Using sanitary food-service gloves, teacher counts out sets of 100 M & M's or other candy or counting objects into cups or small zip-top bags.
4. Have students (and teacher) wash and dry their hands with warm soap and water before starting this activity.
5. Check to verify that no students in the group have an allergy to any foods being used for the activity. Substitute candies or counting objects can be used as needed.
6. Identify what operation students will complete for the grid (e.g., addition, subtraction, multiplication, division).

Activity

1. Distribute Computation Grids, sets of 100 candies/objects, and pencils to each student.
2. Say to students: *We are going to fill out this grid with* (choose one) [addition, subtraction, multiplication, division] *answers. You will use M & M's to help you with this. You will be able to eat the candy at the end of the activity, but if you eat it now you will not have enough to finish your work.* Some students may figure out that if they start with the 10 × 10 column and row and work "backward" they can eat as they go, and if they discover this, it's okay to complete the grid that way.
3. Say to students: *Look at the overhead. I will show you how to do the first row. One* [plus, minus, multiplied by, divided by] *one is* [1 or 0]. Set out candies on overhead to show answer. Say: *I know this because when I* [add, subtract, multiply, divide] *one and one candies, I get* [1 or 0]. *Now you are going to do the rest of the worksheet on your own using the candies I gave you. Remember, don't eat the candy until the end, or you won't have enough to finish.*
4. Watch students as they group items and fill in the grid; provide corrective feedback as needed and have students correct errors as they go along.
5. Set a predetermined stop time (e.g., 30 minutes) and remind students how much time they have left at intervals during the activity. At the end of the work time, check each student's work and have them correct any remaining errors. If students are not done with the grid, it can be completed at another time.
6. When activity is completed, allow students to eat the candy.

Recipe: Timed Practice, Practice, Practice

Purpose: To help students build fluency with basic computation skills.

Research Base: National Mathematics Advisory Panel (2008).

Ingredients: Computation problems matched to students' independent practice level.

Timer or stopwatch.

Graph on which students can enter the number of correct answers (see Appendix 8.3, p. 119).

Prep Time: 5–10 minutes.

Activity Time: 2 minutes per worksheet.

Preparation:

1. Identify what computation skill students most need to practice for the purpose of developing fluency (i.e., accuracy plus speed).
2. Go to the following website: *www.interventioncentral.org.*
3. In the section labeled "Online Tools" click on "Math Worksheet Generator" on the right-hand side of the page.
4. When the new math page loads, click on the computation skill(s) you want students to practice (e.g., addition, subtraction, multiplication, division, mixed skills).
5. Click on the specific skill(s) you want included in your practice worksheet.
6. At the bottom of the page, choose four columns, five rows, and medium-size font. For the timed version of this activity, it is important that the same number of items be used for each timed session.
7. Click on "Single Skill Computation Probe."
8. Once you click on the button to create the probe, your browser should create and load a new tab or page with the teacher (answer) key first. Once this page is loaded, click on the text at the very top of the page which says "Click for Student Worksheet."
9. Another new tab or page will load. This is the one you want to print for the students. Print as many copies as you need for the students, or print one copy and then make photocopies.
10. Print a copy of the answer sheet onto an overhead transparency (optional).

Activity

1. Say to students: *Today we are going to practice _____. I want you to do the problems as accurately and as fast as you can. You will have 2 minutes to finish the paper I am handing out.*
2. Hand out worksheet and say to students: *Do not start until I say begin.*
3. Once all students have their worksheets, say: *Begin.*
4. Begin your timer and give students 2 minutes to work on the problems, then say: *Stop. Pass your worksheet to a classmate. I will put the correct answers on the overhead or read them out loud. Mark your classmates' answers correct or incorrect. Write the number of correct answers on the top of the page.*
5. When finished correcting answers, say to students: *Pass the worksheet back to its owner. Take out your math graph and fill in the number correct for today. Be sure to write today's date at the bottom of the graph. When you are done, put your graph away.*
6. Say: *Now, look at your correct and incorrect answers. Fix the ones you got wrong.*
7. Collect student worksheets and graphs.

Recipe: Flashcards

Purpose:	To build student fluency with computation facts.
Research Base:	Cates (2005); Shapiro (2004).
Ingredients:	Blank 3″ × 5″ flashcards.
	Sets of math computation problems.
	Marker.
Prep Time:	20 minutes.
Activity Time:	10 minutes.

Preparation:
1. Identify sets of 10 math computation problems that the student needs to master.
2. Write one math problem on one side of each card.
3. Write the answer to each problem on the other side of the cards.

Activity

1. Sit facing the student and hold up the problem side of each card.
2. Say to student: *We are going to work on some math facts. You will say the answer to the problems on these cards.*
3. Hold up the first card and say: *What is the answer to this problem?*
4. If student says the correct answer, say: *Good.* Go on to next card.
5. If student does not respond in 5 seconds, tell the student the answer and go to the next card.
6. As student gives answers place the cards in separate piles according to correct and incorrect answers.
7. Repeat drill five times in a row for all cards.
8. After five practices with all the cards, set aside the cards the student has gotten correct on all five practices.
9. Sit facing the student and hold up the problem side of each card the student previously answered incorrectly. Say to student: *Now we are going to practice only the ones that were incorrect.*
10. Hold up the first card and say: *What is the answer to this problem?*
11. If student says the correct answer, say: *Good.* Go on to next card.
12. If student does not respond in 5 seconds, tell the student the answer and go to the next card.
13. As student gives answers place the cards in separate piles according to correct and incorrect answers.
14. Repeat drill five times in a row for all cards.
15. Repeat drill five times in a row for all cards the student missed on the first five drills.
16. Use this drill daily until the student answers all cards correctly during five consecutive drills.

Recipe: Flashcards with Folding In New Items _____

Purpose: To build and maintain students' fluency with computation facts.

Research Base: Shapiro (2004).

Ingredients: Blank 3″ × 5″ flashcards.

Sets of known and new math computation problems.

Marker.

Prep Time: 20 minutes.

Activity Time: 10 minutes.

Preparation:

1. Use the Recipe for Flashcards found on p. 208 of this book.

2. Once the student has mastered all of the items in a set of 10 problems, create an additional set of flashcards with new math problems. Write one new math problem on one side of each card; write the answer to each new problem on the other side of the cards.

3. Shuffle the set of mastered problems and remove two randomly selected cards; replace the removed cards with two of the new (unknown) problem cards.

Activity . . . .

1. Sit facing the student and hold up the problem side of each card.

2. Say to student: *We are going to work on some math facts. You will say the answer to the problems on these cards.*

3. Hold up the first card and say: *What is the answer to this problem?*

4. If student says the correct answer, say: *Good.* Go on to next card.

5. If student does not respond in 5 seconds, tell the student the answer and go to the next card.

6. As student gives answers place the cards in separate piles according to correct and incorrect answers.

7. Repeat drill five times in a row for all cards.

8. After five practices with all the cards, set aside the cards the student has gotten correct on all five practices.

9. Sit facing the student and hold up the problem side of each card the student previously answered incorrectly. Say to student: *Now we are going to practice only the ones that were incorrect.*

10. Hold up the first card and say: *What is the answer to this problem?*

11. If student says the correct answer, say: *Good.* Go on to next card.

12. If student does not respond in 5 seconds, tell the student the answer and go to the next card.

13. As student gives answers place the cards in separate piles according to correct and incorrect answers.

14. Repeat drill five times in a row for all cards.

15. Repeat drill five times in a row for all cards the student missed on the first five drills.

16. Use this drill daily until the student answers all cards correctly during five consecutive drills.

17. Once the student masters all 10 cards in the blended set (eight known plus two unknown), repeat with new folded-in items.

T3

MATHEMATICS RECIPES—Tier 3

Recipe: Cover–Copy–Compare

Purpose:	To provide students with errorless practice of computation skills.
Research Base:	Shapiro (2004).
Ingredients:	Computation problems matched to students' instructional learning level. Pencil.
Prep Time:	5–10 minutes.
Activity Time:	5 minutes per worksheet.
Preparation:	

1. Identify what computation skill students most need to learn (e.g., addition with regrouping, multiplication).
2. Go to the following website: *www.interventioncentral.org.*
3. In the section labeled "Online Tools" click on "Math Worksheet Generator" on the right-hand side of the page.
4. When the new math page loads, click on the computation skill you want students to practice.
5. Click on the specific skill you want included in your Cover–Copy–Compare Worksheet.
6. At the bottom of the page select the number of columns, rows, and font size appropriate for the student.
7. Click on "Cover–Copy–Compare Worksheet."
8. Once you click on the button to create the probe, your browser should create and load a new tab or page with the student worksheet.
9. Print as many copies as you need for students, or print one copy and then make photocopies.
10. Print a copy of the answer sheet.

Activity . . . .

1. Give worksheet to student and say: *Look at the math problems on this page. We are going to work on math problems and then compare your answer to the correct answer. This activity is called "Cover–Copy–Compare."*
2. Say the first problem out loud to the student. For example, if the problem is 2 + 4 = 6, say: *This problem shows that 2 plus 4 equals 6.*
3. Say to the student: *Watch while I do one.* Place your hand over the correct answer and write the answer in the blank space provided.
4. Say to student: *I wrote _____ here because it is the answer to the problem _____. Now I will remove my hand and check my answer. I can see that my answer is correct.*
5. Say to student: *Now it is your turn to try one.* Point to next problem and say: *Read this problem out loud to me.* After student reads problem, say: *Now cover the problem with your hand and write the correct answer in the space.*
6. After student has written answer, say: *Remove your hand and check your answer.*
7. If student's answer was correct, say: *Good. Now you will do the rest of the problems on this page.*
8. If student's answer was incorrect, say: *That answer is incorrect. The correct answer is __ because* (read number sentence) *__ equals __. Let's try another one.*
9. Repeat Steps 5–6 until student answers at least one problem correctly, then go on to Step 7.
10. Once student has completed all problems, review the answers and check to see whether they are correct. If any answers are incorrect, repeat Steps 3–7, modifying directions as needed, and collect worksheet.

Recipe: Establishing Classroom Expectations _____

T1

Purpose:	To establish an orderly and positive classroom environment by teaching and reinforcing rules and routines.
Research Base:	Kern and Clemens (2007); Sugai and Horner (2002).
Ingredients:	A list of three to five positively stated rules visibly diplayed in the classroom. If your building already has these in place, align your classroom rules with the building rules.
Prep Time:	20 minutes.
Activity Time:	15 minutes.
Preparation:	1. Know ahead what the rule categories will be, and what the expectations will be within those categories. For example your rules may be: Be Respectful, Be Responsible, and Be Safe.
	2. Determine what the expectations will be. If you want to involve your students you can cover this in the procedure section and have them brainstorm the classroom expectations with the group.

Activity ....

1. Introduce the three to five positively stated rules to the students. Show them where they will be posted.
2. Spend sufficient time going through what each rule looks like in the classroom. For example if one of the rules is "Be Respectful," you might explain that the expectations are: Eyes on the Speaker, Ears Listening, Inside Voices, Kind Comments—these should be written on your classroom sign. Make sure students know what to do and what not to do. Give ample time for practice.
3. Practice behavioral expectations daily for the first few weeks. After that, reserve 10 minutes per week for review and practice.
4. You may reinforce students for following the rules with points or tokens. For example have a Mason jar and a stock of marbles in the front of the room. When you observe a student following the rules, give specific praise to the student and place a marble into the jar. When the jar is full, the class will have earned a predetermined reward such as a popcorn party or extra recess.
5. For students who struggle with following the rules, you can provide an individual daily reinforcement program for them and allow them to earn rewards such as a preferred activity, line leader, sitting near the teacher, or something similar.

BEHAVIOR RECIPES—Tier 1

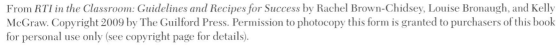

Recipe: Managing Transition Time

Purpose:	To increase time for learning and decrease class disruption by teaching students to move smoothly and quickly from one activity to the next.
Research Base:	Kuergeleis, Deutchman, and Paine (1980); Doyle (1986).
Ingredients:	1. A list of three to five positively stated classroom rules (can be pictures for younger children): these must be visible to all students.
	2. Have the materials for the next lesson ready before the transition begins.
	3. Stopwatch or a kitchen timer that can count down and beep when time is up.
Prep Time:	Plan on 10 minutes the first time you teach it and no more than 3 minutes to review the expectations on an as-needed basis.
Activity Time:	2–3 minutes.
Preparation:	1. Identify a transition time that seems to either take too long and/or be too disruptive—for example, coming in from recess and being ready for the lesson.
	2. Before you begin this intervention, time this transition period for 3 to 4 days and write down those times. These will be your baseline data.

Activity . . . .

1. Introduce your students to the concept of transition time. Explain that when it takes too long to transition, the class loses valuable time for learning.
2. Describe and demonstrate exactly what you expect students to do (and not do). It's okay to have some fun with this part.
3. Once you know they understand, you can introduce the concept of it being a game of "beat the clock." This clock part is optional, but you will find that it can make the transition more fun and effective. You should set the timer for slightly less time than the average time it took them in baseline. Each day you can reduce it by a minute or two until you have them completing the transition in the time that you think is reasonable.
4. Keep track of class progress somewhere visible to all, such as the board. Provide incentives for improving time as needed.

Recipe: The Good Behavior Game
(A Cooperative Approach)

T2

Purpose: To reduce unwanted classroom behavior using a game that allows students to work together to gain group rewards.

Research Base: Barrish, Saunders, and Wold (1969); Harris and Sherman (1973); Medland and Stachnik (1972).

Ingredients:
1. Your three to five positively stated classroom rules, taught previously.
2. A place on the board to record points.
3. On the board create two categories; one category has a smiley (☺) face at the top and one category has an unhappy (☹) face at the top. You could refer to them as Mr. Happy and Mr. Sad. Feel free to name them in a way that communicates the emotion and makes sense within your classroom culture.

Prep Time: 5 minutes.

Activity Time: Start with one time that is particularly challenging—for example a circle time activity that lasts for 20 minutes. Let the students know that the behavior game is only going on during that time. You can gradually expand the time as students get better. You may also limit this to small-group time if you need to manage challenging behaviors during those activities.

Preparation:
1. Make sure you tally the number of unwanted behaviors or the number of times you observed your classroom rules being broken for several sessions *before* you implement the good behavior game.
2. Continue collecting that information (data) and track it on your graph.

BEHAVIOR RECIPES—Tier 2

Activity

1. Let your students know about the new game that will help the classroom run more smoothly and also give them information about how it will work. Make sure to cover what the rewards will be, such as extra recess, extra computer time, choice of a game, a 15-minute video or a special class project (drawing), or extra read-aloud story time.
2. Be specific about when the game is being played and when it will be over.
3. Explain that if you see a student doing a good job of following one or more of your classroom rules (hands being raised, eyes on you, etc.) then you will put a hatch mark under the ☺ column. However, if a student is breaking one of the classroom rules, you will make a hatch mark under the ☹ column.
4. At the end of the designated game time, add up each column. If ☺ has the most points, then the students have earned their reward. If ☹ has the most points, then explain that they didn't make it today, but they can try again tomorrow.

Recipe: Check-In, Check-Out

Purpose:	To increase student engagement with school and schoolwork.
Research Base:	Hawkin and Horner (2003); Todd, Campbell, Meyer, and Horner (2008).
Ingredients:	1. Existing personnel trained, assigned, and available to provide supplemental mentoring to these identified students. Person must be available to meet with the student at the start and end of each day.
	2. A card for the teacher to record points on, which the student will take back to the mentor.
	3. System to graph the daily points earned by the student (see Appendix 4.1, p. 72).
	4. System of rewards and consequences in place.
Prep Time:	As long as you have an existing Check-In, Check-Out program already in place in your building (this should be established at the beginning of the school year), then there is very little prep time. Fifteen minutes of initial teacher time will be needed to meet with the student and explain the program.
Activity Time:	The student will need to spend approximately 5 minutes with the mentor right before class starts, and 5 minutes with the mentor at the end of the day. The teacher and the student will also spend 3–5 minutes per day assigning and discussing points.
Preparation:	1. Create a point card for the student that targets the specific behaviors that you want to correct. For example, you may be monitoring behavior during reading and math worksheet completion with a point scale of 1 to 5.
	2. If the student stays on task for reading the entire time and complies with your requests, then you may give the full 5 points.
	3. Let the mentor know that you will have a new student starting in one week.

Activity

1. Begin using the points card before mentioning anything to the student so that you can record 1 week of baseline data.
2. After 5 days of baseline data are collected, meet with the student and the mentor to explain the program. Use this time also to discuss what kinds of rewards the student would like to earn.
3. Begin the program the next school day by having the student check in with the mentor just before class begins.
4. The mentor will check to make sure that the student is ready to start his or her day. Do they have necessary materials (pencils, eraser, notebooks, homework, etc.)?
5. The mentor will give the student the point card and will assign check-in points based on how prepared the student was. The student goes to class prepared and already has had one positive interaction with an adult at the school.
6. The classroom teacher continues with the card and at the end of the day the student goes back to the mentor to check out.
7. The mentor reviews what went well and what needs more work. The mentor and student will discuss how many points have been earned toward a specific reward that the student is trying to earn.
8. It's very important that the mentor stay positive with the student. He or she will tell the student that even if it was a bad day, tomorrow is a chance to start again.

BEHAVIOR RECIPES—Tier 2

Recipe: Self-Monitoring

Purpose: To teach students how to monitor and manage their own behavior. To illustrate the concept, we have chosen to target the behavior of talking out.

Research Base: Piersel (1985).

Ingredients:
1. An index card taped to desk.
2. Two columns with headings of "I talked out" and "I wanted to talk out, but didn't."
3. A silent signal that can be used by the student to let the teacher know he needs help. This could be something as simple as a card that is red on one side or an object that the student is allowed to put on his desk.
4. Optional rewards such as stickers, line leader, and so forth.

Prep Time: 3 minutes.

Activity Time: Choose a time of day when the student has difficulty staying on task—start with smaller blocks of time and work up, keeping in mind that having your student feel successful will increase the power of this intervention.

Preparation:
1. For 1 week during the most challenging period of the day, record the number of times the student talked out. It's okay to choose only one subject, or one particular time of day if you prefer.
2. Record this baseline data on the progress monitoring form found in this book.

Activity

1. Explain to your student that you will be teaching him how to monitor his talk-outs so that he can have fewer, spend more time learning, and earn rewards for doing so. Instruct him to mark the appropriate column on the index card throughout the lesson.
2. Meet with him right after that session to discuss his self-monitoring card. Track percentage of "I talked out" and percentage of "I wanted to talk out, but didn't" on your progress monitoring graph. Provide incentives to student for improvement.

Recipe: Peer Tutoring

Purpose:	To motivate students to learn *and* increase their social skills.
Research Base:	Rohrbeck, Ginsburg-Block, Fantuzzo, and Miller (2003); Cohen, Kulik, and Kulik (1982).
Ingredients:	A script of prompts and lists of skills for the tutor, a daily log to record student and team progress, selection of rewards for reaching goal.
Prep Time:	15 minutes.
Activity Time:	Varies based on grade and material. Approximately 20 minutes.
Preparation:	1. Design the peer tutoring lesson to reinforce a skill that has already been taught.
	2. Identify a specific learning objective, for example, student will be able to complete 20 subtraction with regrouping problems in 3 minutes with 85% accuracy.

Activity

1. Teach students how to be tutors. Introduce the script of prompts and the list of skills to cover. In the case of the subtraction with regrouping, provide a written example of how to do it and give the tutor systematic prompts based on the answers of the tutee.
2. Pair students who are close in skill level.
3. Have students work in pairs on the chosen material—in this example, a subtraction worksheet. The tutor will help the tutee as needed.
4. After 10 minutes, change roles and repeat the activity.
5. At completion of 20-minute peer tutoring session, give all students a 20-item quiz on subtraction with regrouping.
6. Record scores in a daily log and use individual scores and/or pair scores to determine whether a goal has been reached. Provide rewards as needed.

References

Adams, M. J. (1990). *Beginning to read: Thinking and learning about print.* Champaign–Urbana: University of Illinois.

Ardoin, S. P., Witt, J. C., Connell, J. E., & Koenig, J. L. (2005). Application of a three-tiered response to intervention model for instructional planning, decision making, and the identification of children in need of services. *Journal of Psychoeducational Assessment, 23*(4), 362–380.

Baker, S., Gerston, R., & Lee, D. S. (2002). A synthesis of empirical research on teaching mathematics to low-achieving students. *Elementary School Journal, 103,* 51–73.

Barrish, H. H., Saunders, M., & Wold, M. M. (1969). Good behavior game: Effects of individual contingencies for group consequences on disruptive behavior in a classroom. *Journal of Applied Behavior Analysis, 2,* 119–124.

Beck, I. L. (2005). *Making sense of phonics: The hows and whys.* New York: Guilford Press.

Beck, I. L., McKeown, M. G., & Kucan, L. (2002). *Bringing words to life: Robust vocabulary instruction.* New York: Guilford Press.

Beck, I. L., McKeown, M. G., & Omanson, R. C. (1987). The effects and uses of diverse vocabulary instruction techniques. In M. G. McKeown & M. E. Curtis (Eds.), *The nature of vocabulary acquisition* (pp. 147–163). Hillsdale, NJ: Erlbaum.

Bock, G., Stebbins, L., & Proper, E. (1977). *Education as experimentation: A planned variation model (Vol. IV A & B). Effects of follow-through models.* Washington, DC: ABT Associates.

Brown-Chidsey, R., & Steege, M. W. (2005). *Response to intervention: Principles and strategies for effective practice.* New York: Guilford Press.

Carnine, D. W. (1976). Effects of two teacher presentation rates on off-task behavior, answering correctly, and participation. *Journal of Applied Behavioral Analysis, 9*(2), 199–206.

Carnine, D. W. (1997). Instructional design in mathematics for students with learning disabilities. *Journal of Learning Disabilities, 30,* 130–141.

Cates, G. L. (2005). Effects of peer versus computer-assisted drill on mathematics response rates. *Psychology in the Schools, 42,* 637–646.

Chall, J. S. (1967). *Learning to read: The great debate: An inquiry into the science, art, and ideology of old and new methods of teaching children to read, 1910–1965.* New York: McGraw-Hill.

217

Chall, J. S. (2000). *The academic achievement challenge: What really works in the classroom.* New York: Guilford Press.

Chard, D. J., & Dickson, S. V. (1999). Phonological awareness: Instructional and assessment guidelines. *Intervention in School and Clinic, 34*(5), 261–271.

Cohen, P. A., Kulik, J. A., & Kulik, C. C. (1982). Educational outcomes of tutoring: A meta-analysis of findings. *American Educational Research Journal, 19*(2), 237–248.

Coyne, M. D., Kame'enui, E. J., & Carnine, D. W. (2007). *Effective teaching strategies that accommodate diverse learners* (3rd ed.). Upper Saddle River, NJ: Prentice Hall.

Coyne, M. D., Kame'enui, E. J., & Simmons, D. C. (2001). Prevention and intervention in reading: Two complex systems. *Learning Disabilities Research and Practice, 16*(2), 62–73.

Coyne, M. D, Kame'enui, E. J., & Simmons, D. C. (2004). Improving beginning reading instruction and intervention for students with LD: Reconciling "all" with "each." *Journal of Learning Disabilities, 37,* 231–239.

Crone, D. A., Hawken, L. S., & Horner, R. H. (2004). *Responding to problem behavior in schools: The behavioral education program.* New York: Guilford Press.

Cummins, J. (1981). Empirical and theoretical underpinnings of bilingual education. *Journal of Education, 163*(1), 16–30.

Darch, C., & Gersten, R. (1985). The effects of teacher presentation rate and praise on LD students' oral reading performance. *British Journal of Educational Psychology, 55,* 295–303.

Deno, S. L. (1986). Formative evaluation of individual student programs: A new role for school psychologists. *School Psychology Review, 15*(3), 358–374.

Doyle, W. (1986). Classroom organization and management. In M. Wittrock (Ed.), *Handbook of research on teaching* (3rd ed., pp. 392–431). New York: Macmillan.

Englert, C. S., Raphaet, T. E., Anderson, L. M., Anthony, H. M., & Stevens, D. D. (1991). Making strategies and self-talk visible: Writing instruction in regular and special education classrooms. *American Education Research Journal, 28,* 337–372.

Epstein, M., Atkins, M., Cullinan, D., Kutash, K., & Weaver, R. (2008). *Reducing behavior problems in the elementary school classroom: A practice guide* (NCEE #2008-012). Washington, DC: National Center for Education Evaluation and Regional Assistance, Institute of Education Sciences. U.S. Department of Education. Retrieved from *ies.ed.gov/ncee/wwc/pdf/practiceguides/behavior_gp_092308.pdf*

Florida Center for Reading Research. (2006). *Student center activities for teachers.* Retrieved July 1, 2008, from *fcrr.org*

Florida Center for Reading Research. (2008). *Frequently asked questions about reading instruction.* Retrieved August 2, 2008, from *www.fcrr.org/Curriculum/curriculumInstructionFaq1.htm#4*

Gardill, M. C., & Jitendra, A. K. (1999). Advanced story map instruction: Effects on the reading comprehension of students with learning disabilities. *Journal of Special Education, 33*(1), 2–18.

Gersten, R., Baker, S. K., Shanahan, T., Linan-Thompson, S., Collins, P., & Scarcella, R. (2001). *Effective literacy and English language instruction for English learners in the elementary grades: A practice guide* (NCEE 2007-4011). Washington, DC: National Center for Education Evaluation and Regional Assistance, Institute of Education Sciences, U.S. Department of Education. Retrieved from *ies.ed.gov/ncee*

Gersten, R., Carnine, D., & Williams, P. (1982). Measuring implementation of a structured educational model in an urban setting: An observational approach. *Educational Evaluation and Policy Analysis, 4,* 67–79.

Good, R. H., & Kaminski, R. A. (Eds.). (2001). *Dynamic Indicators of Basic Early Literacy Skills* (6th ed.). Eugene, OR: Institute for the Development of Educational Achievement. Retrieved from: *dibels.uoregon.edu*

Graham, L., & Wong, B. Y. L. (1993). Comparing two modes of teaching a question-answering strategy for enhancing reading comprehension: Didactic and self-instructional training. *Journal of Learning Disabilities, 26*(4), 270–279.

Graham, S., Harris, K. R., & Larsen, L. (2001). Prevention and intervention of writing difficulties for students with learning disabilities. *Learning Disabilities Research and Practice, 12*(2), 74–84.

Graham, S., Schwartz, S., & MacArthur, C. A. (1993). Knowledge of writing and the composing process, attitude toward writing, and self-efficacy for students with and without learning disabilities. *Journal of Learning Disabilities, 26*(4), 237–249.

Haager, D. (2007). Promises and cautions regarding using response to intervention with English language learners. *Learning Disability Quarterly, 30*, 213–218.

Haager, D., Klingner, J., & Vaughn, S. (2007). *Evidence-based reading practices for response to intervention.* Baltimore: Brookes.

Harcourt Assessment, Inc. (2008). *AIMSweb* [curriculum-based measurement system]. Retrieved from: *www.aimsweb.com/index.php*

Harris, V. W., & Sherman, J. A. (1973). Use and analysis of the "Good Behavior Game" to reduce disruptive classroom behavior. *Journal of Applied Behavioral Analysis, 6*, 405–417.

Hawken, L. S., Adolphson, S. L., MacLeod, K. S., & Schumann, J. (2008). Secondary tier interventions and supports. In W. Sailor, G. Dunlap, G. Sugai, & R. Horner (Eds.), *Handbook of positive behavior support* (pp. 395–420). New York: Springer.

Hawken, L. S., & Horner, R. H. (2003). Evaluation of a targeted intervention within a schoolwide system of behavior support. *Journal of Behavioral Education, 12*, 225–240.

Hawken, L. S., Vincent, C. G., & Schumann, J. (2008). Response to intervention for social behavior: Challenges and opportunities. *Journal of Emotional and Behavioral Disorders, 16*(4), 213–225.

Hosp, M. K., Hosp, J. L., & Howell, K. W. (2007). *The ABCs of CBM: A practical guide to curriculum-based measurement.* New York: Guilford Press.

Howell, K. W., & Nolet, V. (2000). *Curriculum-based evaluation: Teaching and decision making* (3rd ed.). Belmont, CA: Wadsworth Learning.

Hudson, R. F., Lane, H. B., & Pullen, P. C. (2005). Reading fluency assessment and instruction: What, why, how? *Reading Teacher, 58*(8), 702–714.

Huey, E. B. (1913). *The psychology and pedagogy of reading: With a review of the history of reading and writing and of methods, texts, and hygiene in reading.* New York: Macmillan.

Intervention Central. (2008). *Math worksheet generator.* Retrieved August 4, 2008, from *www.interventioncentral.org/htmdocs/tools/mathprobe/addsing.php*

Isaacson, S. (1989). Role of secretary vs. author: Resolving the conflict in writing instruction. *Learning Disability Quarterly, 12*(3), 209–217.

Isaacson, S. (2004). Instruction that helps students meet state standards in writing. *Exceptionality, 2*(1), 39–54.

Johnson, E., Mellard, D. F., Fuchs, D., & McKnight, M. A. (2006). *Responsiveness to intervention (RTI): How to do it.* Lawrence, KS: National Research Center on Learning Disabilities.

Kern, L., & Clemens, N. (2007). Antecedent strategies to promote appropriate classroom behavior. *Psychology in the Schools, 44*(1), 65–75.

Kilpatrick, J., Swafford, J., & Findell, B. (Eds.). (2001). *Adding it up: Helping children learn mathematics*. Washington, DC: National Research Council.

Kuergeleis, B., Deutchman, L., & Paine, S. (1980). *Effects of explicit timings on students' transitions*. Eugene, OR: Direct Instruction Follow Through Project, University of Oregon.

LaBerge, D., & Samuels, S. (1974). Toward a theory of automatic information processing in reading. *Cognitive Psychology, 6,* 293–323.

MacArthur, C., & Graham, S. (1993). Integrating strategy instruction and word processing into a process approach to writing instruction. *School Psychology Review, 22*(4), 671–682.

McDonald, E., & Ardoin, S. (2007). Interspersing easy math problems among challenging problems: Detection of interspersal effects in whole-class applications. *Journal of Behavioral Education, 16,* 342–354.

Medland, M. B., & Stachnik, T. J. (1972). Good-Behavior Game: A replication and systematic analysis. *Journal of Applied Behavior Analysis, 5,* 45–51.

Merriam-Webster Online Dictionary. (2008). Retrieved April 15, 2008, from *http://www.merriam-webster.com/dictionary/principle*

Moats, L. (2000). *Speech to print: Language essentials for teachers*. Baltimore: Brookes.

Moats, L. (2005). *Language essentials for teachers of reading and spelling (LETRS)* [modules 1–3]. Longmont, CO: Sopris West.

National Center on Student Progress Monitoring. (2008). *Review of progress monitoring tools*. Retrieved August 2, 2008, from *www.studentprogress.org/chart/chart.asp*

National Institute of Child Health and Human Development (NICHD). (2000). *Teaching children to read: An evidence-based assessment of the scientific research literature on reading and its implications for reading instruction*. Washington, DC: Author.

National Mathematics Advisory Panel. (2008). *Foundations for success* [final report]. Washington, DC: U.S. Department of Education.

Osborn, J., Lehr, F., & Hiebert, E. H. (2003). *A focus on fluency* (Product #ES0303). Honolulu, HI: Pacific Resources for Education and Learning.

O'Shea, L. J. (1984). Error correction in oral reading: Evaluating the effectiveness of three procedures. *Education and Treatment of Children, 7*(3), 203–214.

Peer Assisted Learning Strategies [website]. (2008). Retrieved August 4, 2008, from *kc.vanderbilt.edu/pals*

Piersel, W. C. (1985). Self-observation and completion of school assignments: The influence of a physical recording device and expectancy characteristics. *Psychology in the Schools, 22,* 331–336.

Powell-Smith, K. A., & Ball, P. L. (2008). Best practices in reintegration and special education exit decisions. In A. Thomas & J. Grimes (Eds.), *Best practices in school psychology,* V (pp. 263–280). Bethesda, MD: National Association of School Psychologists.

Rashotte, C. A., & Torgesen, J. K. (1985). Repeated reading and reading fluency in learning disabled children. *Reading Research Quarterly, 20,* 180–188.

Rathvon, N. (2008). *Effective school interventions: Evidence-based strategies for improving student outcomes* (2nd ed.). New York: Guilford Press.

Rohrbeck, C.A., Ginsburg-Block, M. D., Fantuzzo, J. W., & Miller, T. R. (2003). Peer-assisted learning interventions with elementary school students: A meta-analytic review. *Journal of Educational Psychology, 95*(2), 240–257.

Safer, N., & Fleischman, S. (2005). How student progress monitoring improves instruction. *Educational Leadership, 62*(5), 81–83.

Shapiro, E. S. (2004). *Academic skills problems: Direct assessment and intervention* (3rd ed.). New York: Guilford Press.

Sheridan, S. M., & McCurdy, M. (2005). Ecological variables in school-based assessment and intervention planning. In R. Brown-Chidsey (Ed.), *Assessment for intervention: A problem-solving approach* (pp. 43–64). New York: Guilford Press.

Simon, R., & Hanrahan, J. (2004). An evaluation of the Touch Math method for teaching addition to students with learning disabilities in mathematics. *European Journal of Special Needs Education, 19*, 191–209.

Sprague, J. R., & Walker, H. M. (2004). *Safe and healthy schools: Practical prevention strategies.* New York: Guilford Press.

Spring, J. (2007). *American education* (13th ed.). Belmont, CA: McGraw-Hill.

Stein, M., Kinder, D., Silbert, J., & Carnine, D. W. (2006). *Designing effective mathematics instruction: A direct instruction approach* (4th ed.). Upper Saddle River, NJ: Pearson–Prentice Hall.

Sugai, G., & Horner, R. (2002). The evolution of discipline practices: Schoolwide positive behavior supports. *Child and Family Behavior Therapy, 24*, 23–50.

Todd, A. W., Campbell, A. L., Meyer, G. G., & Horner, R. H. (2008). The effects of a targeted intervention to reduce problem behaviors. *Journal of Positive Behavior Interventions, 10*(1), 46–55.

Torgeson, J. K. (2000). Individual differences in response to early intervention in reading: The lingering problem of treatment resisters. *Learning Disabilities Research and Practice, 15*, 55–64.

Walker, H. M., Horner, R. H., Sugai, G., Bullis, M., Sprague, J. R., Bricker, D., et al. (1996). Integrated approaches to preventing antisocial behavior patterns among school-age children and youth. *Journal of Emotional and Behavioral Disorders, 4*(4), 194–209.

Walker, H. M, & Severson, H. H. (1992). *Systemic screening for behavior disorders kit.* Frederick, CO: Sopris West.

Walker, H. M., Stiller, B., Golly, A., Kavanagh, K., Severson, H. H., & Feil, E. G. (1997). *First step to success* (starter kit and resupply kit). Frederick, CO: Sopris West.

Watkins, C. (1997). *Project follow-through: A case study of contingencies influencing instructional practices of the educational establishment.* Cambridge, MA: Cambridge Center for Behavioral Studies.

Index

"f" following a page number indicates a figure; "t" following a page number indicates a table.